T0294087

THE
SCOTTISH
LEAGUE CUP

THE
SCOTTISH
LEAGUE CUP

75 YEARS
1946-2021

DAVID POTTER

First published by Pitch Publishing, 2022

Pitch Publishing
A2 Yeoman Gate
Yeoman Way
Worthing
Sussex
BN13 3QZ
www.pitchpublishing.co.uk
info@pitchpublishing.co.uk

A CIP catalogue record is available for this book
from the British Library.

ISBN 978 1 80150 056 2

Typesetting and origination by Pitch Publishing
Printed and bound in Great Britain by TJ Books, Padstow

Contents

INTRODUCTION

THE SCOTTISH League Cup is grossly undervalued. It suffers from being the third tournament in Scotland in terms of seniority and has never enjoyed the status of the Scottish Cup, for example. It has also suffered from sponsorship. Sponsorship earns money but seldom enhances the status of the competition. A competition called after a soft drink, an alcoholic drink or betting firm must lose *dignitas*, the impression given that we are talking about a Mickey Mouse pre-season tournament. We are not. We are talking about a national competition, and the competition should always be referred to as the Scottish League Cup.

It is a handsome trophy, certainly unusual and possibly unique in world football history in that it has three handles. It has been played for 76 times, with Rangers having by far the best record in the competition with 27 wins, a touch over a third of the years played. Celtic did not start well in this competition but have been successful 20 times. Aberdeen have won the trophy six times, Hearts (with a purple eight years in the late 1950s and early 1960s) have carried off the trophy four times, Hibs, Dundee and East Fife (whose glory years were the early ones) three times, Dundee United won it two years in succession around 1980, while supporters of Motherwell, Partick Thistle, Raith Rovers, Livingston, Kilmarnock, St Mirren, Ross County and St Johnstone have had one moment of triumph in this tournament.

Some years winning the trophy would confer entry to Europe. This did not always mean a great deal, since the winners of the Scottish League Cup usually won something else as well. In any case, the phrase 'entry to Europe' seems better than it actually is in the context of Scottish teams. Scottish teams seldom last long! At the moment, winning the trophy does not confer entry to Europe. This is no loss. It saves a club from the embarrassment of a dismissal before July is out. Not always, however. Raith Rovers got the opportunity to play Bayern Munich in 1995/96 because they won the Scottish League Cup in 1994/95. It would be hard to imagine it happening otherwise.

The Scottish League Cup was born in season 1946/47, the first 'proper' official season after World War II. The League Cup, however, had been in existence since 1940/41. This may seem to be a paradox and contradiction, but what is meant by this is that the actual trophy was in existence during the dark years of the Second World War and was known as the Southern League Cup. More difficult to explain, and even more contradictory, is the fact that the winners of the *Southern* League Cup in 1946 (its final year in that existence) were, in fact, Aberdeen! Aberdeen is by no stretch of anyone's imagination in the south of Scotland but, then again, funny things happen in wartime.

In 1939, when war was declared, the Scottish League and the Scottish Cup were put on hold and all competitions became unofficial. In the Glasgow area a Southern League was formed and, further north, a North-Eastern League. With the Scottish Cup having been put into abeyance for the duration, the Southern League decided that a cup competition would help to spice things up, and the Southern League Cup came into existence. Where the actual trophy came from, no one seems to know, but it was a success, certainly as far as Rangers were concerned. They won the trophy in four years out of six – 1941, 1942, 1943 and 1945 – while Hibs won it in 1944 and Aberdeen in 1946. Rangers would maintain their love affair with the Scottish League Cup, off and on, for the next 75 years.

Aberdeen's triumph in 1946 was significant, nevertheless, for the new trophy was now seen as a Scottish rather than a Southern one, and for the first official season, 1946/47, it was decided to incorporate this new tournament into the calendar and call it the Scottish League Cup. The other two national competitions, the Scottish League and the Scottish Cup, had been going from 1890 and 1873 respectively. There was a long way to go to catch up.

It is often assumed, sometimes even by those who should know better, that the Scottish Football Association and the Scottish League are the same thing. In fact, they are not and, although phrases like 'bitter rivalry' are not entirely appropriate, they have always been quite keen to assert their individuality. The Scottish League were very keen to keep their own Scottish League XI internationals (until they went out of fashion) and, in 1946, there appeared a chance to have their own trophy, which might even compete with the SFA's Scottish Cup.

More mundanely and cogently, the Scottish Cup had been more or less a licence to make money before the war with everyone still remembering the 1937 final between Celtic and

Aberdeen which yielded a crowd within a kick in the pants of 150,000. The Scottish League wanted a piece of that. No one should ever underestimate the love for the game that the Scottish public has. And it certainly loved football in the immediate post-war era of the late 1940s. Football had not gone out of fashion during the war and now the game went from strength to strength. People came back from the war desperate for football, and football did not make the mistake of pricing itself out of the market. (Arguably, it has done so since in certain areas.) Facilities were shocking, but no one seemed to mind too much. It was only later when prosperity and increased expectations kicked in that football began to struggle to attract supporters. There was no such problem in 1946. Business was about to boom. Atom bombs, fuel shortages and the beginnings of the National Health Service gave way to football.

Since then, the tournament has brought its fair share of triumph, disaster, ecstasy and despair to all clubs in Scotland. It is not unheard of for clubs, when they receive their marching orders from the tournament (as of course happens to every club bar one every year), to put a brave face on it and to say that it is 'just' the League Cup. Often there follows a cliché to the effect that 'We can now concentrate on the League.' This is, of course, specious, even dangerous, rubbish and phrases like 'sour grapes' spring to mind. The tournament, much mucked about with and altered by flavour-of-the-month legislators and wicked self-seeking sponsors, has survived and flourished and remains an integral part of the Scottish season. Just talk to a supporter of a team involved in the League Cup Final just five minutes before kick-off and ask him/her if it is 'just' the League Cup! Similarly, five minutes after his captain has lifted the three-handled trophy draped in his team's colours, 'Is that "just" the League Cup?'

It is also a tournament that has been neglected by the football historian. This book is an attempt to redress that omission.

CHAPTER ONE

THE NEWCOMER
ON THE BLOCK
1946–1949

SEASON 1946/47 was a remarkable one, as was always likely
to be the case after the end of the major global conflict. The
map of Europe had been redrawn and there was no permanent
guarantee of peace. Our erstwhile Allies in the Soviet Union
were proving no easier to deal with in certain matters than the
late regime in Germany. But at least there was some temporary
peace, although various parts of the world like Germany itself,
the Middle East and India (funnily enough, not Ireland this
time) were threatening trouble.

Worse still, according to some newspapers, was the
fact that there was now a Labour Government with a huge
majority, and a vigorous, determined one at that. The middle
classes, we were led to believe, were throwing their arms up
in despair and wondering whether the war had been worth
it since the working classes voted for a Labour Government,
and the middle classes were paying the price. Newspapers

and Churchill himself predicted, even suggested, wholescale emigration! It was laughable.

What was really happening was that, for the first time ever, the Government cared about its people. Improvements, revolutionary ones, in health, housing, education and all the important things in life would soon be on their way. It would be true to say that there was by 1946 no immediate sign of any such changes, but a revolution was indeed happening, a revolution all the more powerful and potent because it happened without any violence or bloodshed, and a revolution that was tacitly accepted by its opponents. When Winston Churchill returned to power in 1951, he emphatically did not dismantle the National Health Service. Indeed, the old warlord showed his kinder, more pragmatic side (he had, of course, at one time been a Liberal) by saying things like 'I can think of no better investment for the future than putting milk into babies.' However, conditions were still hard for most people in 1946, not least those whose principal breadwinner had failed to return from the war. Failure to return from the war was not always due to being a military casualty. That, at least, was easier dealt with than the many cases of those who had found themselves a new lady in Italy, Austria or even England. But everyone had a job now, and such was the need for industrial recovery that overtime was frequently offered and everyone's standard of living began to rise slowly but steadily. Dole queues were a thing of the past. Rationing remained for a few years, but gradually reduced in its intensity as more and more commodities became available.

There was also, as had happened in the early 1920s, a certain feeling that it was great to be alive and that life was for the living. Theatre and cinema, both of which flourished during the war, now began to enjoy even more of a boost and so did football to a very large extent, particularly now that unofficial football was over and 1946/47 was to be a real season with the return of full international games, the Scottish League, the Scottish Cup and the newcomer on the block, the Scottish League Cup.

In 1946, there were only 30 teams in the top two divisions of the Scottish League: 16 in Division A and only 14 in Division B. Why they did not make it 16 in both is one of those mysterious decisions that the historian cannot understand. The newspapers at the time cannot understand it either, wondering why respectable teams like Forfar Athletic and East Stirlingshire, for example, were denied admission to Division B when there seemed to be places available and had to play against reserve teams in Division C.

'There are things that a feller just can't understand,' says a well-known character in *The Pickwick Papers*, but it meant that for the new Scottish League Cup, there were to be eight sections. Now 32 would have neatly divided everyone into eight sections of four, but as it was, there were two sections of three each. Sensibly, the Division A teams had their sections and Division B had theirs. The winners would then join the quarter-finals and from then on it would be a straight knockout.

The first-ever games in the Scottish League Cup were played on Saturday, 21 September 1946, and then sectional games were played on the next five Saturdays. No one had floodlights in those days and midweek football would only really have been possible in the month of August, but even then there was a certain discouragement from the Government who feared that a midweek fixture might encourage absenteeism from the factories and the mines where production was so necessary for the country's recovery. Changed days indeed from when there were large groups of men hanging around street corners with nothing to do!

The new tournament proved an instant success with large crowds at all games, over 40,000, for example, at Easter Road to see Hibs beat Celtic 4-2. The Scottish League Cup could be a psychological good; perhaps a team who had started the League programme badly might have a chance in a whole new tournament, but the *Glasgow Herald* is distressed to have to report that all the Glasgow teams other than Rangers (who beat St Mirren 4-0) were off to a bad start in the new competition.

The sectional format proved to be a great success with most of the groups going to the last day. Rangers were an exception, winning all their games against St Mirren, Morton and Queen's Park, as indeed were Dundee who comfortably beat Raith Rovers and Stenhousemuir in their three-team section. They were joined in the quarter-finals by Hibs, Hearts, Aberdeen, Dundee United, East Fife and Airdrie. Interestingly, patterns were set very early in this competition. East Fife, who were to make their name in this competition in future years, duly qualified whereas Celtic, who would not win the tournament in its first decade, lost out to Hibs and failed to qualify.

The tournament now went into hibernation as it were until early March. No games could have been played in February in any case; February 1947 sent a shiver down the spine of all those who lived through it for many years afterwards, as it probably was the worst winter of them all. Interestingly, only a few crackpots wrote letters to newspapers blaming it all on the bombs dropped on Japan; nowadays it would have been the fault of man and his cynical indifference to the welfare of the planet. Carbon footprints and fossil fuels would have been execrated. In 1947, more thought it was because God was unhappy about a Labour Government!

By 1 March, when the first legs of the quarter-finals were scheduled, the ferocity of the weather had abated slightly – or, more accurately, Scotland learned how to cope with it – but even so, Herculean efforts were needed to prepare pitches at Broomfield, Ibrox, Tynecastle and Dens Park with German prisoners of war on occasion drafted in to clear the snow. This strikes the modern eye as not being a million miles away from slave labour, but the end result was successful and the four games went ahead with the Germans allowed to watch the games for nothing! Most of them would, in any case, be repatriated by the summer, we are glad to report.

It had been decreed that a Division A team would play a Division B side. The second legs were played on Wednesday, 5 March with a 4pm kick-off in most cases. Although the Division B sides had all done well in the first legs, the Division A sides all won through in the end. Rangers did the business against a plucky Dundee United at Dens Park (Tannadice being deemed unsuitable for a large crowd); Hearts, who had lost to East Fife on Saturday, came good at Methil to win 5-3 on aggregate; Aberdeen got the better of Dundee at Pittodrie, and the game at Easter Road eventually saw a goal scored by Hibs against Airdrie.

This last game is a veritable collector's item in Scottish football history. These two teams had drawn 4-4 at Broomfield on Saturday, but this game had to invoke the rule which stated that if the teams finished level on aggregate, another 20 minutes extra time had to be played. If still no decision was reached, they played on, ten minutes each way, until someone could score what would now be called a golden goal. It must have been dark before Willie Finnigan scored the decisive goal for Hibs on a heavily sanded pitch after a total of 35 minutes of extra time! It was Scottish football's longest-ever match, before 22,000 spectators who had a clear view of the moon as a frost began to come down. No one had, as yet, thought up the idea of a penalty shoot-out!

Those who might have wished to see an Edinburgh derby in the first-ever Scottish League Cup Final were to be bitterly disappointed on 22 March when the semi-finals were played. Jack Harkness in the *Sunday Post* makes an odd reference to Rangers enjoying 'real grass under their feet' (the snow and ice having departed) as they beat Hibs 3-1 in front of an astonishing crowd of 125,154 at Hampden. The *Glasgow Herald*, never a Rangers supporting newspaper, is less than totally impressed with a bad foul committed by Torry Gillick on Sammy Kean which led to loads of retaliatory fouls by Hibs and spoiled the game. Hibs had already put Rangers out of the Scottish Cup and there was not a little 'previous' here.

A 125,154 crowd was probably the largest that either side had played before in their history and showed what an instant success the Scottish League Cup had become. It also showed the sheer appetite for football that consumed Scotland in those days. A considerably smaller but still substantial crowd (36,210) was at Easter Road to see Aberdeen beat Hearts by the remarkable score of 6-2. It was 2-2 at half-time, but then George Hamilton inspired Aberdeen to a further four goals.

The first-ever Scottish League Cup Final was thus between Rangers and Aberdeen, the two teams who had contested the previous year's unofficial Southern League Cup trophy. A huge crowd was expected for the final on 5 April. Aberdeen had more or less emptied itself for the Scottish Cup Final of 1937, their first-ever cup final, and a similar phenomenon was expected here. Aberdeen would actually make it to the Scottish Cup Final in 1947 too, meaning that the traditionally parsimonious Aberdonians would have to make two trips to Glasgow to see their favourites in cup finals!

Aberdeen travelled down on the Friday and stayed at Largs. In an interesting comment on social habits of the late 1940s, they spent the night in the premises of a local junior football team at a whist drive! This was after they had had a light training session in the afternoon on a public park. Life was a great deal more couthy and simple in those days, was it not?

Easter weekend was 5 April 1947 and although Easter was not a holiday in Scotland, people thought that this game might see Hampden's record attendance given the crowd that turned up for the semi-final between Rangers and Hibs and the ability of Aberdeen (sadly maintained in future years) to persuade more supporters to attend a cup final at Hampden in Glasgow than they could entice to Pittodrie for a league game. That a world record was not established that day was due to nothing other than the weather, for the rain was torrential and there was a cruel wind blowing from the Mount Florida end to the King's Park end of the ground. Many supporters, even those who had bought tickets and even some of those who had travelled from Aberdeen, opted to spend the afternoon in one of Glasgow's department stores or even a café. Others stayed at home and listened to the game on the radio but, even given the foul conditions, a remarkable 83,684 turned up to watch the game on the uncovered terraces.

The pitch might not have survived an inspection today, with puddles clearly seen in several areas of the playing field. Referee Bobby Calder of Rutherglen (in later years, ironically, to become a scout for Aberdeen) may have been under pressure from above to get the game played, but whether he was or not, the game went ahead and no one criticised him for his decision. Aberdeen fans, however, had cause to blame captain Frank Dunlop.

Dunlop won the toss and opted to play against the wind and the rain in the first half. The thinking was that if Aberdeen could hold them until half-time, they would then have the advantage of the conditions in the second half when Rangers were tiring. All this depended on Aberdeen having a good first half which, frankly, they didn't. Aberdeen's nervous left-winger Willie McCall fluffed a couple of early chances, but Rangers were far more clinical and scored through Torry Gillick and Billy Williamson. Even then, at 0-2 down, the Dons did not feel entirely out of it until just before half-time Jimmy Duncanson scored what proved to be the killer. The same player then scored early in the second half against the wind and rain, and Rangers' defence (not yet called the 'Iron Curtain', for Churchill had yet to make his famous speech about the Soviet Union's occupation of half of Europe) was unyielding, and the game finished Rangers 4 Aberdeen 0.

The teams were:

Rangers: Brown, Young and Shaw, McColl, Woodburn and Rae, Rutherford, Gillick, Williamson, Thornton and Duncanson

Aberdeen: Johnstone, Cooper and McKenna, McLaughlin, Dunlop and Taylor, Harris, Hamilton, Williams, Baird and McCall

It was a good win for Willie Struth's Rangers who also won the Scottish League that year, but Aberdeen would have more than ample compensation a fortnight later when they returned to Hampden to beat Hibs in the Scottish Cup Final. But the big winner was the Scottish League Cup itself. Looked upon with a little suspicion by the conservative elements of Scottish football at the start of the season, it had now clearly established itself on the Scottish scene and would be, from now, an integral part of the Scottish season.

If one had had to choose a winner of the second Scottish League Cup, one would have taken a long time before coming up with East Fife. East Fife were in Division B, but then again their greatest successes had been when they were in the lower tier. In 1927, in the aftermath of the General Strike which devastated the community of Methil and Buckhaven, East Fife reached the final of the Scottish Cup; then in 1938 when the war clouds were gathering ominously, they went one better and won the trophy. Now in the best era of their existence, they would win the Scottish League Cup three times in seven years, winning the trophy long before Celtic, Hibs, Hearts or Aberdeen did. The old Bayview stadium is now built over and the club plays closer to the Firth of Forth, where the waves seem to threaten on a wild day. The area, one would have to say, is run-down with more than its fair share of social problems. But that is now. In the late 1940s and 1950s the area was vibrant, active and bustling, with the area living up to its motto of Carbone Carbasoque (by coal and canvas), the twin sources of local wealth, namely coal and shipping.

The country needed coal and was now prepared to pay miners a decent wage to get it. The mines had been nationalised so the Fife miners were now working for the National Coal Board rather than the Wemyss family, whom they heartily and with cause detested. Accidents were still distressingly frequent, as were the lung and other diseases associated with coal mining, but there was now the feeling that things were getting better and that miners were now valued as much-needed workers rather than in their pre-war condition, something that was little better than wage slavery.

And their team had appointed a good manager in James Scotland Symon, commonly known as Scot. He had already made his mark on Scottish society by having played for Scotland at both football and cricket, and his football career had included spells with Dundee, Portsmouth and Rangers. Intelligent, thoughtful and articulate, occasionally considered aloof and snobby, Symon would produce a good collection of players for the Fifers and develop a winning mentality.

For season 1947/48, the Scottish League Cup showed at least two improvements from the previous year. One was that, as there were now 32 teams in the Scottish League Divisions A and B, there were now eight groups of four teams; the other was that it was decided that the tournament would be over and done with by the end of October when the weather was still reasonably good.

Midweek football was still not really encouraged all that much and the six matches in each section were played on the first six Saturdays of the season beginning on 9 August. The draw put Rangers and Celtic in the same section, Hearts and Hibs in another. Celtic beat Rangers once, but Rangers won through, whereas in Edinburgh, Hearts beat Hibs twice, something that was surprising in the context of the season in which Hibs would win the League. Aberdeen also qualified by the expedient beating of Queen of the South 9-0 on the final Saturday whereas their rivals Motherwell could only put three past St Mirren. They were joined in the quarter-finals by Falkirk, Hamilton Academical, East Fife, Stenhousemuir and Leith Athletic, the last named two earning some welcome cash by doing so.

Unlike 1946/47, the quarter-finals were not two-legged affairs and thus 27 September saw the four ties being played. Aberdeen duly beat Leith Athletic and Rangers won through 2-0 against Stenhousemuir, although the newspapers are united in giving praise to the Warriors for their brave performance. The other two games went to extra time with Falkirk eventually getting the better of Hamilton Accies, but the performance of the round was East Fife's 4-3 win over Hearts after extra time. Jack Harkness of the *Sunday Post*, himself an ex-goalkeeper of Hearts, was full of praise for East Fife, particularly the half-back line of Philp, Finlay and Aitken (Aitken had been a doubtful starter) which controlled the game throughout.

A crowd of 27,000 saw this thrilling game in which Hearts went ahead, but then East Fife scored twice and looked to be on the edge of glory until Hearts equalised at the death to take the game to extra time. Hearts then went ahead and that looked as if it were the end of the matter, but Tommy Adams scored direct from a corner kick and then rounded a couple of defenders to prod home the winner. Jack Harkness was very impressed by Scot Symon who, while everyone else was standing on their feet cheering at the end, simply slipped away as if to say, 'Well, that's that!'

The *Aberdeen Press and Journal* was happy with their team's draw in the semi-final when they came out of the bag against East Fife. The writer pointed to the fact that the final could be the third consecutive year (counting the unofficial Southern League Cup Final of May 1946) that Aberdeen played Rangers in the final, assuming that Aberdeen would beat East Fife at Dens Park and Rangers would do likewise over Falkirk at Hampden. But 11 October 1947 was to confound them all.

The bookmakers offered odds of 29/1 against an East Fife v Falkirk final, but that is precisely what happened. Rangers were probably guilty of complacency against Falkirk and their fans were similarly over-confident, for only 44,000 turned up at Hampden to see Archie Aikman score the only goal of the game for Falkirk, while the 33,000 at Dens Park looked on in amazement as Aberdeen spurned chance after chance to score and Henry Morris, himself a Dundonian, scored the only goal of the game for East Fife. The writer of the *Dundee Courier* was very impressed when the whole East Fife party (wives and even mothers as well) went out for tea afterwards to the Val d'Or restaurant: 'It was a real family party and there was great rejoicing.'

The *Falkirk Herald* was similarly upbeat about the performance of their team. Both teams in the final had won the Scottish Cup once each, although Falkirk's triumph was as far back as 1913, and for the next two weeks the conversation in both Methil and Falkirk centred on little other than the prospects of their respective teams. Although the second half was to be on the radio with Peter Thomson doing the commentating, the national newspapers encouraged as many people as possible to go along to Hampden to see the game, 'even, if necessary, forsaking your own team for one Saturday, at least.'

Special trains brought spectators from both towns to Hampden. In the event, a creditable 53,000 turned up, but they were very disappointed to see a goalless draw in which both goalkeepers, John Niven and Jerry Dawson, excelled. The other players were all 'too nervy' according to the *Dundee Courier* and play only reached a high standard in the latter stages. East Fife, who would have won on corners if they had been counted, made an effort to have the replayed final played at Tynecastle. It was a sensible suggestion and would have been equidistant for both teams, but it would have meant an all-ticket final and, as the game was scheduled for next Saturday, 1 November, there would have been little time to print and distribute the briefs. So Hampden Park it was once again.

This time the attendance had fallen to 31,000 (still not bad for two provincial teams) but the East Fife fans saw a great performance by their team who won the second Scottish League Cup with a marvellous 4-1 victory.

The teams were:

East Fife: Niven, Laird and Stewart, Philip, Finlay and Aitken, Adams, D Davidson, Morris, J Davidson and Duncan

Falkirk: J Dawson, Whyte and McPhie, Bolt, Henderson and Gallacher, Fiddes, Alison, Aikman, Henderson and K Dawson

Referee: Mr P Craigmyle, Aberdeen

Falkirk lost an early goal thanks to a bad goalkeeping error by Jerry Dawson, a man who had excelled for Rangers in the past but whose best days were clearly behind him. He was also partly to blame for at least one of the others, as Tommy Adams scored one and Davie Duncan three with only one goal in reply from Archie Aikman. It was a well-taken goal by the Falkirk centre-forward but there was little else for the Bairns to cheer about.

The *Dundee Courier* singles out four Fifers for fine performances and being responsible for bringing the League Cup back to Methil. In the first place there was Davie Duncan for his three well-taken goals and his throw-ins (!) which usually split the defence, Sammy Stewart at left-back was good enough to be chosen for Scotland, *The Courier* thought, and even more worthy of a cap was left-half George 'Dod' Aitken, while the best man on the park was the wing wizard Tommy Adams, whose wife was even quoted as saying how delighted she was that he now had a medal to show for his efforts.

Another story carried in *The Courier* says a great deal about the professionalism of Scot Symon, even at the greatest moment of his career so far. The players had been presented with the now-famous three-handled trophy on the field of play. They then disappeared into the dressing-room along with manager Scot Symon. Symon then locked the door, even excluding a couple of East Fife directors who had a bottle of champagne to celebrate! It was his own way of stating that the dressing room, even in this most euphoric of moments, belonged to the manager and players. Once they had been showered and dressed, Symon would then allow them to meet their adoring public.

The adoring public was also well out in strength at Bayview that evening even in spite of the heavy rain as the League Cup was shown to all who assembled, some of whom were unashamedly in tears at what had come to pass. It was a fine day for the brave little team from one of the most heavily industrial parts of the Kingdom of Fife. It meant also that part of the world could enjoy its Christmas and New Year, safe in the knowledge they had, once again, lifted a Scottish trophy from the second tier of the Scottish League. Not that they were going to be in the second tier for long, because they used this triumph as a springboard for winning Division B at the end of the 1947/48 season.

It was an important stage in the career of Scot Symon. He was far from the conventional idea of a football manager – the foul-mouthed, aggressive, prickly stereotype that was common even in the 1940s. No, he was always well dressed, sophisticated, dignified, suave almost and a man who was polite but never ever too friendly to anyone. His career had a long way to run yet, but for the moment, he was the man who was building East Fife to be a major force in Scottish football.

The other honours would be won by Hibs and Rangers that year, Hibs winning the Scottish League for the first time since 1903 and Rangers beating Morton in the final of the Scottish Cup, but the Scottish League Cup had clearly established itself as a credible trophy. The one downside of the tournament (and this became more pronounced as the league expanded to include more teams) was the effect that it had on regional tournaments like the Glasgow Cup, the Stirlingshire Cup and the Forfarshire Cup, for example. Such tournaments now began slowly to decline in importance as the Scottish League Cup continued its inexorable rise.

As is often the case, success is infectious, and 1948/49 was a great year for East Fife's local rivals Raith Rovers. Raith had been a great side in the early 1920s but had disappeared from prominence almost as quickly as they had risen and the 1930s had been a poor decade. But now under a crusty character called Bert Herdman (who had never played the game at a professional level but had arisen from the Supporters' Association of Raith Rovers), a man with a dreadful stammer but a grim determination, a foul tongue and a fine sense of humour, they had picked up a few good players like Andy Young, Willie McNaught and Willie Penman. Inspired by the success of their neighbours along the coast, Raith Rovers made an impact on the Scottish scene in 1949.

They would win Division B at the end of the season and they would also have a very good run in the Scottish League Cup, but without the triumph at the end that East Fife had enjoyed the previous season. The League Cup started in September this year, which meant that the final could not really be played until the spring. (Unlike 1972, 1973, 1982, 2018 and 2019 for example, they did not make the questionable decision to play the final in December!) Once again, the tournament proved a winner in terms of exciting games and good attendances.

The group which caused the greatest interest was the one in which Rangers, Celtic and Hibs were all involved. For a while Celtic had the upper hand but, once again in this competition, the Parkhead side pressed the self-destruct button to lose to Rangers on the last Saturday at Ibrox in a game watched by, of all people, Eamon de Valera, the Irish patriot and politician. He had been (incredibly) invited by Rangers! Rangers were joined by Dundee, East Fife, Hamilton, Airdrie, Alloa, St Mirren and Raith Rovers. The section involving St Mirren, Hearts, Third Lanark and Morton was a fascinating one, for each of the four teams won two, drew two and lost two! They all had six points, and goal average had to be deployed to settle the winner with St Mirren just edging it over Aberdeen by ·33 of a goal.

All exciting stuff, and the tournament organisers did everyone a favour by deciding against a two-legged format for the quarter-finals. The ties were set for 30 October and included a mouth-watering Fife derby at Stark's Park between Raith Rovers and East Fife. An all-ticket crowd of 24,000 crammed into Stark's Park to see a thrilling, high-scoring derby in which Raith led 3-0 at half-time, Henry Morris then scored a hat-trick for East Fife, but in the middle of it Willie Penman had scored for Raith – 4-3 – and then in a lung-bursting climax which brought the whole stand on its feet, Francis Joyner scored a spectacular goal to make it 5-3 for the home side.

It was by some distance the best tie of the round, and *The Courier* does not go too far overboard when it says that it was 'the best game in Raith Rovers history'. Elsewhere, only Rangers qualified for the semi-finals with a lacklustre 1-0 win over St Mirren, while Dundee needed a replay to beat Alloa after a shocking first game at Dens Park. Hamilton Accies needed three bites of the cherry to get the better of their Lanarkshire rivals Airdrie, the three games not doing any harm at all to the coffers of both clubs, as the cynics were not slow to point out.

The Scottish League was rightly castigated for playing the semi-finals of a major tournament on the date of 20 November, a day of ferocious wind and rain. Attendances were poor: 50,996 at Hampden to see Rangers v Dundee and a mere 16,751 at Celtic Park to see Raith Rovers take on Hamilton. By the standards of the time these were poor and, on a better day a month or so earlier perhaps, one might have expected to have seen both these attendances doubled.

The day was not without its comic touches, nevertheless. A bus load of Dundee fans who had never been to Hampden before arrived uncomfortably close to kick-off time, parked on some waste ground and dashed to the ground. They had paid their money and were in the ground before they realised that they had gone to nearby Cathkin and were watching Third Lanark v Celtic! Even more bizarre was what happened at the kick-off at Hampden. Rangers won the toss, sensibly chose to play with the wind, and then took the kick-off. Neither Jock Shaw, the Rangers captain, nor Bobby Ancell, the Dundee captain, nor the referee, Mr Livingstone, noticed the error until some journalist at half-time asked the question why Dundee, who had apparently won the toss, chose to play against the wind. By then, it was too late to do anything about it, and it was certainly too late for Dundee to rescue the game.

Eddie Rutherford, Ian McColl and Jimmy Duncanson had all scored within the first ten minutes and Willie Thornton scored before the half-hour mark. 'Job done' seemed to be the feeling of the Rangers team and for the rest of the first half, and all the second half, the Iron Curtain descended with a vengeance. Dundee, always a good ball-playing team, managed to string together a few passes and even earned a penalty late in the game to make the score 4-1, but by that time the crowd, even the Rangers crowd, had decided that enough was enough and that it was time to go home and get out of the incessant rain which drenched the open terraces of Hampden.

Over at Parkhead, the rain was just as bad and most of the 16,000 crowd sheltered under the somewhat porous roof of what a Celtic supporter who had served in the Far East in the war had now christened 'the Jungle'. The fare on offer there was generally admitted, even in Raith Rovers sources, to have been poor but goals from Jimmy Ellis before half-time and Willie Penman soon after were enough to see the Kirkcaldy side through to the second national cup final in their history.

It's a long time from 20 November until 12 March, and it may be that a great deal of interest in the tournament had gone over the winter. Or it may be that Rangers and their supporters, going strongly in the other tournaments as well, thought that there would be no contest against the Division B side, but for whatever reason, the authorities were disappointed to see a crowd of only 57,450 there on a fine, sunny spring day.

Certainly, there does not seem to have been any lack of interest from Kirkcaldy with four special trains laid on and some enthusiasts even planning to cycle to Glasgow. The town was agog with excitement for days before, with one local businessman offering to commission a replica of the Scottish League Cup for each player if they won. Not only that, but the supporters' club had presented the Rovers with a special set of red jerseys for the game so as not to clash with Rangers. This was more of a gift than it sounds, for clothes were still rationed in 1949.

The reason for the disappointing crowd may have, one suspects, more to do with some kind of protest from the Rangers supporters themselves at the Iron Curtain defensive tactics. It was certainly efficient and won games for the Ibrox side, but those who had seen Alan Morton and Tommy Cairns in years gone by expected more entertainment. Almost two years previously, Winston Churchill had said, 'From Stettin in the Baltic to Trieste in the Adriatic, an Iron Curtain has descended across the continent.' He was of course referring to the Soviet Union, but the phrase was now freely used to describe prickly dance-hall attendants, less than totally co-operative ladies on a night out, and now the niggardly Rangers defence of Young, Shaw, Woodburn and Cox.

The teams were:

Rangers: Brown, Young and Shaw, McColl, Woodburn and Cox, Gillick, Paton, Thornton, Duncanson and Rutherford

Raith Rovers: Westland, McLure and McNaught, Young, Colville and Leigh, Maule, Collins, Penman, Brady and Joyner

Referee: Mr WG Livingstone, Glasgow

Both teams were without key men. Rangers lacked Willie Waddell (the Deedle, as he was called) and Torry Gillick was brought back, whereas for Raith Rovers, young Andy Leigh, who had only played a few games for Raith Rovers, discovered only on the morning of the game at the Kenilworth Hotel that Ernie Till had called off injured and that he was playing. To calm his nerves, he and his father went for a walk round Glasgow and got back to the hotel to discover that the bus had gone. He and his father then had to commission a taxi (an astonishingly extravagant and expensive experience in 1949) to get him to Hampden in time for kick-off.

Rangers won 2-0, but that was not anything like the full story. The first half was all Raith Rovers with only Bobby Brown in the Rangers goal keeping them out. Near the end of the first half, with the scores still level, came the moment which some veteran Raith Rovers supporters recall to this very day and which Willie Penman himself would regale admirers with for years. He seemed to take about three steps forward to pick up a Collins cross-field pass and to hammer home a brilliant goal, only to find that a linesman's flag was up and that Mr Livingstone was disallowing the goal. The press, with surprising unanimity and belying the common perception that they always support Rangers, declared the goal was legitimate and it remains a pity that this was 1949, not the 21st century, where we could have seen for certain with the benefit of TV. Storms of boos rang round the ground, but that made no difference.

The League Cup was won and lost in the early part of the second half when Willie Thornton made two goals, one for the indolent and moody Torry Gillick to score and the other for Willie Paton. And yet, as Rangers retreated into their shell yet again, the gallant Division B Raith Rovers kept at them with Penman and Collins both coming close on several occasions. *The Courier* felt that Raith Rovers should have had at least two penalties; one when the ubiquitous and hard-working Andy Young was held when about to shoot, the other was when Penman was pushed off the ball. Later on he was downed by goalkeeper Brown (normally a very gentlemanly and sporting character) as well in a tackle which might nowadays have earned the goalkeeper a red card. The game finished with Raith Rovers still on top but Rangers 2-0 winners!

It was difficult for many years afterwards to persuade Kirkcaldy people that the 'All referees favour Rangers' mantra is not true and even some Rangers supporters were embarrassed enough to stay silent during the presentation of the trophy. It was presented on the field by Mr Scott, the President of Queen's Park. Some cries of 'Shame!' were heard coming from the Raith Rovers fans and the sizeable neutral support. The writer of *The Sunday Post* sympathises while the *Glasgow Herald* damns Rangers with faint praise and singles out Torry Gillick for a 'disinclination to exert himself'.

But 'facts are chiels that winnae ding' says Robert Burns. Rangers had won the League Cup for the second time in three years. They would win the first-ever treble that year, but they never came closer to losing it than they did that day against Raith Rovers. Raith Rovers would be compensated with the Division B championship, but it would be a long time before they ever saw another League Cup Final. Funnily enough, Rangers too would now go through a barren period in this competition for the next decade or so.

The 1949/50 Scottish League Cup was dominated by the Kingdom of Fife, and yet it was a strange one as well, for Raith Rovers, the heroes of last year's competition, were the only Fife team who did not make it to the quarter-finals. They had had the misfortune to be drawn in the same section as East Fife and Hearts. This section certainly yielded much excitement and generated high income with the large crowds but it was East Fife who won through, dropping only one point, and that was to Hearts at Tynecastle.

As far as the administration of the League Cup was concerned, a large penny had dropped when they realised that if you began the season with the League Cup in August, there was still enough daylight to play Wednesday night games (possibly with an earlyish kick-off) and the group sections could be finished by the first Saturday in September. Wednesday nights could also be deployed for one of the legs of the quarter-finals and the whole competition could be comfortably completed by the end of October before the start of the winter. This sensible format made the competition a compact and self-contained one and would be a great success over the next 20 years until the authorities in the early 1970s, disobeying the truest of all aphorisms 'If it ain't broke, don't fix it!', began to plaster about with the competition – to its severe detriment.

Celtic and Rangers were drawn together for the third year in a row. Eyebrows were raised and knowing glances exchanged, but Aberdeen and St Mirren did not complain. There was a lot of money involved in that section! For the third year in a row, Rangers qualified at the expense of Celtic, but this was the year of the infamous occasion at Ibrox when Sammy Cox turned around and deliberately kicked Charlie Tully in the pit of the stomach in full view of the Celtic end of Ibrox. Bottles flew (throwing beer bottles was the preferred method of causing trouble for the football hooligans in those days) and Celtic generally took their eye off the ball and lost the game. Neutral observers like the respected Jack Harkness in the *Sunday Post* were appalled. That appropriate action was not taken against Cox by referee Gebbie was a major factor in the Celtic paranoia complex which continues in some areas of their support to this day.

Rangers and East Fife were joined in the quarter-finals by Hibs and Partick Thistle from the Division A sections and by Airdrie, Forfar, Dunfermline and Cowdenbeath from the Division B sections. The first legs were played on Saturday, 17 September, and the second legs in the following midweek. East Fife had little bother beating Forfar Athletic but the other ties were exciting ones. Rangers had a surprising amount of bother in beating Cowdenbeath, while Dunfermline beat Airdrie 4-3 in the first leg at Broomfield and had to struggle to hold them to a 0-0 draw at East End Park, but the most impressive performance of them all was Hibs. They were 2-4 down to Partick Thistle from the first leg at Firhill but rallied to defeat Thistle 4-0 at Easter Road in a performance which had *The Scotsman* (not the most football-orientated of newspapers and, in so far as it did take an interest in the game, widely believed to be pro-Hearts) purring with pleasure at 'their [Hibs] individual and collective skill' and singling out Lawrie Reilly as a match winner.

The semi-final draw paired the two former winners together, Rangers and East Fife at Hampden, while Hibs and Dunfermline met each other at Tynecastle. The games were to be played on Saturday, 8 October and hardly anyone expected anything other than a final between the two best teams in the country: Rangers and Hibs. How wrong they were! In what was arguably Fife's best footballing day, the establishment was confounded, as in 1947, and an all-Fife League Cup Final emerged.

The game at Hampden attracted a crowd of 74,000 and boiled down, according to the *Glasgow Herald*, to a duel between Rangers right-winger Willie Waddell and East Fife left-back Sammy Stewart. This duel was won marginally by Stewart and it was so important because, according to the writer, Waddell was the only forward worthy of being associated with Rangers. Little wonder that the Rangers fans sang, 'The right foot, the left foot, the noddle. When you can buy all these wonderful things, then you can buy Willie Waddell!' But it was East Fife, 'the best team I have seen this season' (the *Glasgow Herald* reporter states), that won through in extra time after Rangers, down after 45 minutes, had rallied in the second half. Still singing the praises of East Fife, the writer singles out the winning goal by Charlie Fleming (sometimes called 'Cannonball', other times 'Legs') as one of the best that Hampden has ever seen. One gets the impression that 'our football correspondent' was delighted at this turn of events for the game turned nasty for a spell and Willie Woodburn was singled out more than once for being the culprit. There was a tragic end to the game, however, when John McArthur, the chairman of East Fife, collapsed and died on the final whistle. He had had a heart condition and was attending the game against medical advice.

Across the country at Tynecastle, Hibs, the odds-on favourites, were turned over by Dunfermline Athletic, who were strangers to this level of football. It was one of these games which the League Cup would throw up many times in the future where, for no apparent or rational reason, the favourites lost to a vastly inferior team who simply all seemed capable of raising their game on that day. Managed by Webber Lees, Dunfermline refused to accept defeat even when Lawrie Reilly put Hibs ahead. Gerry Mays (sometimes written 'Mayes') equalised with a header, then scored with a hook shot with quarter of an hour to go. Then Dunfermline, their defence well marshalled by a giant of a man called Jimmy Clarkson, held out against a Hibs forward line which contained three of their Famous Five, namely Lawrie Reilly, Eddie Turnbull and Willie Ormond. It was an unlikely but nevertheless thoroughly deserved victory for Dunfermline Athletic, whose first big occasion this was.

It is often assumed that Dunfermline Athletic have always been a strong team in Scottish football. Not so. Until the arrival of Jock Stein in 1960, their history had been one of woeful underachievement at a run-down little ground with an old, creaky wooden stand (affectionately called the Hen House) from which one could easily get splinters in one's rear quarters. They had had the occasional good player – a man called Bobby Skinner, for example, in the 1920s – but never a good team, and their nickname the Pars (for paralytics, perhaps, but there are at least six other theories!) goes back to the 1920s and possibly earlier. They were poorly supported and generally regarded as the weakest team in Fife. Their achievement on 8 October 1949 was the best result of their history, and everyone from the Provost, the Burgh Council and Ministers of the Kirk downwards were impressed by this mighty feat.

An interesting note on the status of the competition was struck when a move was made by some folk in the press to take the game away from Hampden. The argument was that there was going to be a poor crowd at Hampden and some place closer might have sufficed. Stark's Park, Kirkcaldy, ideal for the travelling support of both clubs, was not nearly big enough. Either of the Edinburgh grounds was mooted as a possibility, or even Dens Park, Dundee, but the Scottish League refused on the grounds that as the Scottish League Cup was now a recognised national trophy the recognised national ground of the country should be deployed. Hampden on 29 October it was.

In the event, 39,744 turned up, a good attendance for two out-of-town teams, although considerably fewer than the 45,000 about a mile away at Celtic Park, for example, to see Celtic play Hibs (two well-supported teams) in a league match. A great deal of support was expressed for Division B Dunfermline by the neutrals, but there were still quite a few empty spaces around the vast bowl of Hampden as the following teams ran out:

East Fife: McGarrity, Laird and Stewart, Philp, Finlay and Aitken, Black, Fleming, Morris, Brown and Duncan

Dunfermline Athletic: Johnstone, Kirk and McLean, McCall, Clarkson and Whyte, Mays, Cannon, Henderson, McGairy and Smith

Referee: W Webb, Glasgow

East Fife were wearing a new strip of old gold and black collars and cuffs, Dunfermline wore black and white hoops. Both teams looked nice but the game was a massive disappointment in that East Fife scored three goals in the first 20 minutes and then settled down to play some good football and await the final whistle. Long before the end, the Pars were a beaten team. The goals were scored by Charlie Fleming pushing home a Davie Duncan cross, Davie Duncan himself hammering home another cross from right-winger Bobby Black, then with the game less than a quarter over, Henry Morris scoring a third after a good through ball from the same Bobby Black. The Pars tried hard but getting back into this game was simply beyond them, although at one point Clarkson hit the post. In modern terminology, they simply had not turned up. So it was another triumph from the men from Methil. *The Courier* reports rather improbably that 'hosts' of representatives from English clubs like Manchester City, Newcastle United and Burnley were there, chequebook in hand, to persuade Scot Symon to part with his men. It was unlikely to be quite so dramatic, but it was certainly true that East Fife contained quite a few players who would fit in rather well at a richer team than East Fife. In time, some of them would succumb to the temptation of going down south.

So, after four years, the League Cup had only two winners and, of the eight finalists, three had been Division B teams. Larger teams like Celtic, Hearts and Hibs had yet to show face in a final as the decade of the 1940s came to an end. There was something rather symbolic about all this, as if the 1940s with all the horrors and triumphs that it had brought to the world were now heroically moving aside as it were to allow the entry of the 1950s, that peace-loving, prosperous new decade. The 20th century was now, as it were, at half-time. The second half would indeed prove to be different.

CHAPTER TWO

THE EARLY 1950s
1950–1953

WAR RETURNED to the world in 1950. It was frightening and devastating, as all wars are, but the saving grace about this one was that it was far away in distant Korea. It would involve British troops and it would lead to many pointless casualties, however, and would carry on until 1953, when the West would be able to claim some sort of Pyrrhic victory. The problem has not exactly been solved and continues well into the 21st century, although it is sometimes hard to resist the conclusion that if the USA had left them alone in the first place, all Koreans might get on a little better now.

At home, the recovery was continuing slowly and things were gradually getting better with more and more commodities and food coming off the ration. The Labour Government, weakened by so much energetic and vigorous action, staggered in 1950 and finally fell in 1951, but its triumph surely lay in the fact that it was able to persuade the incoming Conservatives that what they had done was good.

The Conservatives did not dismantle the National Health Service nor the Welfare State. The reforms, so necessary and welcome, were here to stay. Babies were now healthier and there were more of them. One of them has written this book.

Football continued to thrive with large attendances and great excitement. The first Scottish League Cup of the new and vibrant decade began on 12 August 1950. A major talking point emerged very early when it became apparent that neither of the two previous winners, Rangers nor East Fife, had qualified. Rangers lost to Aberdeen on two Wednesday nights at both Pittodrie and Ibrox, the game at Ibrox revealing alarming holes in the Iron Curtain, exploited by Jackie Hather and Archie Baird. East Fife lost on the opening day to Celtic at Parkhead and never really recovered after that. Celtic, on the other hand, were now beginning to show some of the form that their vast support expected and duly qualified.

Celtic were joined in the last eight by Motherwell, Hibs, Aberdeen, Dundee United, Queen of the South, Ayr United and Alloa. Once again the ties were played home and home with the first game on Saturday, 16 September and then the following Wednesday, 20 September. The first-leg results showed two remarkable 4-1 victories. One was by Motherwell over Celtic at Parkhead, and the other was at Pittodrie where Aberdeen beat Hibs 4-1. There was no way back for Celtic at Fir Park on the Wednesday but, remarkably, Hibs reversed the 4-1 scoreline at Easter Road on the Wednesday night. Motherwell thus joined Ayr United and Queen of the South in the semi-finals, but the business between Aberdeen and Hibs was far from settled.

The game at Easter Road before a huge and barely credible crowd of 60,000 had seen Hibs at their best and at 90 minutes they had levelled the score by leading 3-0. The crowd is all the more remarkable when we hear that there was a downpour at the start of the game and there was no shelter on the Easter Road terracing. No away goals rule in these days, so extra time was played. Hibs scored again and looked to have won the tie until, in the gathering gloom, 'a figure which appeared to be that of Yorston' (in the words of the *Glasgow Herald*) scored an equaliser to make it peels, as they would say in bowls. No one had ever thought of a penalty shoot-out (and wouldn't do so for another 20 years) and so a replay had to be played at Ibrox on Monday, 3 October with a 4pm kick-off to allow supporters from Edinburgh and Aberdeen to get there.

As luck would have it, the two teams also played each other in a League game on Saturday, 30 September at Pittodrie – Aberdeen won 2-1 – so they really knew each other by the time Monday came round. Once again, there was a crowd of 60,000. It was a bank holiday Monday which helped swell the crowd, but there were also a large smattering of Glaswegians who simply loved football and they saw plenty of it that evening. The score was 1-1 after extra time and the *Glasgow Herald* reported at the end, 'a remarkable burst of applause from the crowd, the like of which has not been exceeded even when Rangers gained a triumph on their own ground.' Eddie Turnbull and Archie Baird had been the scorers, there had been many misses, and the decision was taken to play tomorrow night, this time at Hampden.

Aberdeen presumably didn't go home, staying in a Glasgow hotel, but their supporters had no such luxury and had to go back to their work on the Tuesday. Edinburgh supporters would have found it easier to attend and British Railways were not slow off their mark in putting on football specials. As a result of the extreme difficulties of Aberdeen supporters to get there, 'only' 30,000 were at Hampden to see the third attempt, something that tells us a great deal about neutral Glasgow football supporters. This time, in the traditional Hampden swirl, Hibs made no mistake, and it was generally regarded as the night that the Famous Five of Smith, Johnstone, Reilly, Turnbull and Ormond won their spurs as a unit, if they had not done so before that. Generally speaking, Hibs were a younger side than Aberdeen and had been less worn out by the heavy pitch at Ibrox the night before. Hibs won 5-1 with every forward bar Willie Ormond scoring (Bobby Johnstone scored twice) while exhausted Aberdeen were also given loads of praise for their sporting demeanour throughout the contest, which had now lasted seven hours!

Following all this, the semi-finals on the Saturday immediately after might have been an anti-climax. That was possibly the case at Tynecastle where Hibs disposed of Queen of the South 3-1 as Eddie Turnbull notched a hat-trick, but the other semi at Ibrox threw up another thriller. Motherwell were going well and were confidently expected to get the better of Division B Ayr United. But the Somerset Park men played a good, sensible game even when handicapped by an injury to left-back Nesbit and more than held their own against the much-vaunted Motherwell side. With time running out, Ayr United were 3-2 ahead, but then John Aitkenhead, Motherwell's left-winger, used the element of surprise and wandered into the centre, scoring with his right foot to everyone's amazement including, one suspects, his own. Then, with everyone expecting extra time and/or a replay, Willie Kilmarnock crossed for Jimmy Watson to finish things off. It was a scarcely deserved win for Motherwell, and desperately unlucky for Ayr United who won all the plaudits from the press.

Thus we had Motherwell v Hibs in the final on 28 October 1950 at Hampden. It was generally agreed that these two were the best teams in Scotland at the time. Hibs were looked upon as favourites, but anyone who had seen Motherwell on their day had been very impressed by them. The trouble with both of these teams was that they did not generally win very much in the way of trophies.

True, Hibs had been League Champions in 1948, but they had had no great success in the Scottish Cup, their last success having been as far away as 1902 (and their lack of love with that competition had a long time to run yet). Motherwell had won only one trophy in their history, the Scottish League in 1932. Most people agreed that they had suffered bad luck in their two Scottish Cup finals against Celtic in 1931 and 1933. Their manager was now George Stevenson, one of the famous left wing of Stevenson and Ferrier of that era, and the manager of their 1930s side John 'Sailor' Hunter was still working for the Fir Park side as a secretary. Hibs' manager was Hugh Shaw, following the sudden death a few years previously of Willie McCartney.

On the morning of the game, the *Glasgow Herald* was concerned about darkness. The clock had been changed the previous week and, with the possibility of extra time, the game might not finish until after 5.15pm, rather late if it were a cloudy day. Bizarrely, the Scottish League had thought of this and had brought the kick-off time forward by a whole *five* minutes! The game would start at 2.55pm rather than 3pm. Moments like this make one realise that the ridicule and contempt in which football authorities were held by the fans was not entirely unjustified. The press, however, were fairly unanimous that Hibs were the favourites. Even if the rumours of injuries to some of the Hibs forwards were true, the rest of the forward line was still good, and although Motherwell had shown some fine form of late, their defence would never cope with Hibs. Such thoughts were probably echoed as 64,074 fans made their way to Hampden that dull, but dry day.

Hibs' heavy programme to get to the final had taken its toll, and although most players were fit enough to start, poor Eddie Turnbull had to miss out. Willie Ormond was moved to inside-left and young Jimmy Bradley started on the left wing.

The teams were:

Motherwell: Johnston, Kilmarnock and Shaw, McLeod, Paton and Redpath, Watters, Forrest, Kelly, Watson and Aitkenhead

Hibs: Younger, Govan and Ogilvie, Buchanan, Paterson and Coombe, Smith, Johnstone, Reilly, Ormond and Bradley

Referee: Mr JA Mowat, Rutherglen

It was an odd cup final. Hibs started off attacking the Mount Florida end and for a while looked as if they were going to play Motherwell off the park. But no goal came before half-time and for a long time after that, even though there were times when, such was the pressure, it looked as if they simply had to score. It is, however, a truism in football that if you fail to score when you are on top, you will live to regret it. That is what happened here. Turnbull's cannonball shooting was badly missed, and both Reilly and Smith had off days.

Seventy-five minutes had gone of what had become a rather tedious final when, in a rare Motherwell attack, Archie

Kelly shot straight at goalkeeper Tommy Younger, but the goalkeeper could only parry the ball back and Kelly headed home the rebound. The *Sunday Post* uses the word 'hypnotised' to describe Hibs because when, a couple of minutes later, Willie Watters sent over an anodyne-looking cross, no Hibs defender got near it and James Forrest had the simplest of jobs to head home. Hibs were now shattered and Tommy Younger's day of misery was completed when he miskicked a clearance and Willie Watters simply turned the ball into an empty net.

Poor Tommy Younger! The final whistle went soon afterwards and the dejected Tommy was so upset at his awful last 15 minutes that pictures appeared of him in the press the following day with the vicious caption of 'the greetin' goalie' and other such things. Only Jack Harkness of the *Sunday Post*, who himself had been a goalkeeper, sympathised. Younger recovered and duly went on, as Harkness had done, to play for Scotland – and with distinction.

Not for the last time would Hibs and their supporters discover that Hampden can be a cruel, cruel place and their reputation as a trophy-shy team grew. They would, however, have more than ample compensation when they won the Scottish League this season by some distance. Motherwell, on the other hand, were so taken by surprise that they had no celebration dinner laid on. They tried at short notice to find a place in Glasgow but eventually returned to their own Fir Park as the winners of the fifth Scottish League Cup. History does not record whether they sent out for fish suppers or not. They would soon be back at Hampden next April for the Scottish Cup Final, but this time they would be less successful, losing 0-1 to Celtic.

For the next two years, Dundee came to prominence. The city of Dundee, that strange place where in 1922 all the drunkards voted for a prohibitionist rather than Winston Churchill, with a fanatically right-wing press which failed to dissuade its readers from voting Labour, and which had been built on the three 'j's of jute, jam and journalism, extended its paradoxical behaviour into football. The city was football mad but had only one success to show for itself, when John 'Sailor' Hunter had led them to success in the Scottish Cup of 1910. It was a long time ago for Dundee. They had had the occasional great player like Alec Troup or Scot Symon (now manager of East Fife) but seldom a great team.

They also had a disturbing tendency to self-destruct spectacularly, never more obviously than two years before when they had taken Rangers to the very last day of the league campaign and would have won the title had they been more able to handle the emotional demands of the situation. As it happened they blew up and lost 1-4 to Falkirk at Brockville for no obvious reason, and Rangers won the league.

But success came their way in the League Cup of 1951/52. The tournament was once again a thrilling one and the final was one of the best games ever seen at Hampden Park. The qualifying sections needed goal average (goals for divided by goals against) to decide in two cases, Celtic getting the edge over Morton, and Dundee needing to win 3-1 on the last day of the section at Raith Rovers to get the better of Hearts. They were joined in the quarter-finals by Motherwell, Rangers, Forfar Athletic, Falkirk, Dunfermline and St Johnstone.

As was the wont in those days, the two-legged quarter-finals were played on a Saturday and Wednesday in mid-September. Celtic had few problems in beating Forfar at Celtic Park, although Forfar did well to hold them to a draw at Station Park on the Wednesday night, a game in which, mysteriously, the ball disappeared when it went into the crowd and was never found! Last year's winners Motherwell had little bother in disposing of St Johnstone 4-0 and 3-0, but the closest quarter-final of them all was between those old rivals, Dundee and Falkirk.

The game at Brockville on the Saturday had been a tough-fought but not really very interesting 0-0 draw. Twenty-thousand were at Dens Park on the Wednesday night to see a truly great game in which Dundee, not for the first or the last time, were indebted to their talismanic forward Billy Steel. Falkirk had scored first but then, after Dundee equalised, Steel and Christie combined to score a remarkable goal as Steel more or less ran through two Falkirk defenders and crashed home a great goal. Falkirk fought well in the second half but could make no impression on a Dundee defence in which Doug Cowie was outstanding.

It was at Ibrox where there was most drama and controversy, though. Dunfermline Athletic, 1-0 up from the game at East End Park, were by some distance the better team against Rangers yet lost 1-3. Dunfermline managed to miss a penalty kick, then Rangers' aggregate winner was (in the opinion of Jack Harkness in *The Courier*) not a goal in that it never crossed the line. The 50,000 Rangers fans tried to say that it did, while most other sources agree with the judgement of Mr Harkness. However, all that they could offer was sympathy for the Pars who had 'won a few friends in the West of Scotland'.

The semi-final draw paired Rangers with Celtic and Dundee with Motherwell in games to be played on 13 October at Hampden and Ibrox respectively. Both games, much built up as 'knife edges' and 'thrillers', nevertheless finished one-sidedly, Rangers winning 3-0 and Dundee 5-1. Glasgow was a busy place that crisp autumnal Saturday. The general election campaign of 1951 was in full swing with loads of meetings and rallies, and a total of 108,000 watched the games, 83,000 at Hampden and 25,000 at Ibrox – a healthy pay day for all clubs, for the gates were pooled so that every club received a quarter of the total.

The larger crowd saw a very one-sided Old Firm game, a tremendous disappointment to the Celtic fans who felt that, after their Scottish Cup win last April, some sort of revival might have been in progress. As it was, Willie Thornton scored for Rangers, then just before half-time Celtic felt that they should have had a penalty when Woodburn fouled McPhail, Boden was then badly injured and Rangers scored again through Johnson. Only one more goal was added, but the victory was a comprehensive one for Rangers.

The other game, in which the journalist of the *Evening Times* claimed improbably that he could have counted the amount of people in the Main Stand at Ibrox as kick-off approached, ended up similarly one-sided. Dundee went into a 2-0 lead but then Motherwell pulled one back as half-time approached to make it a good contest. But Dundee had Billy Steel and a very strong half-back line in Gallacher, Cowie and Boyd. Johnny Pattillo suffered from multiple injuries in a brief spell just after half-time, but he was still able to avoid the attentions of Motherwell goalkeeper Johnston to score the crucial third goal. Then Bobby Flavell scored another two to give Dundee a commanding victory and to dump last year's winners out of the Cup. These two teams, Motherwell and Dundee, would meet again in the Scottish Cup Final next April, and the result would be completely different.

And so the League Cup Final was now set up for Rangers v Dundee. Rangers, it would have to be said, had had a few dodgy games this year so far – they would lose out in the Scottish League yet again to Hibs – but they were still considered to be the favourites against a Dundee team which had some brilliant individualists, notably Billy Steel whom Dundee fans of that era rate the best of them all. Steel, however, was not always a team player. Nevertheless, Dundee on song were a good team to watch, and it was predicted that the League Cup Final would be a great contest.

Rarely has *The Courier* had such a good few days as it did in October 1951. Thursday, 25 October had seen the general election which returned the Conservatives under Winston Churchill. This may not have gone down well among the jute workers of Dundee who obstinately refused to do what the DC Thomson press told them, but *The Courier* went into overdrive about 'return to greatness' and 'clearing up the mess that the Socialists had left', and then Pelion was piled on top of Ossa for DC Thomson when Dundee won the Scottish League Cup. The hyperbole continued when it was said 'There Was Never A Final Like This.' It certainly was a good game, and I suppose for a long-suffering Dundee supporter, it was about as good as it was likely to get.

Rangers, as previously said, were the favourites. Provincial teams going to Glasgow to take on Rangers often have a huge problem in convincing themselves that there is no law which states that Rangers have to win in front of their own support. Rangers also had their Iron Curtain defence and, up front, they had the man who was generally reckoned to be the best player around in Scotland at the moment, Willie Waddell. They were still managed by the legendary Bill Struth, a man who insisted on everything from his players being well dressed to them attending church on a Sunday (and it had to be the Church of Scotland, for religious diversity had not yet reached Ibrox).

Dundee's manager was a man called George Anderson, an interesting character, not always well beloved of his players. His attitude to dress was no less strict, but he himself was not unknown to wear bowler hats and even spats. He was more flamboyant than Struth and, in some ways, this came across in the play of the two teams – Dundee more adventurous and composed of flair players like Billy Steel, Rangers more solid, dour and grimly Presbyterian in defence. Rangers had not lost a national Cup final since 1929 and had twice won the Scottish League Cup to add to their 13 Scottish Cup victories, whereas Dundee had only twice contested a Scottish Cup Final – winners in 1910, gallant losers in 1925.

The weather was once again crisp and autumnal on 27 October 1951, but an earlier start at 2.30pm was necessary in case of extra time. The *Evening Times* tells of Dundonians arriving with 'rattles, bells and weird sounding trumpets', but clearly loads of people did not realise there was to be an early kick-off and only about 70,000 were there at the start. After about half an hour the crowd had swollen to 90,000. A new set of steps had been built in the stand to allow the players to go up and collect the trophy. Before then, the cup had been presented at the pitch side.

Both teams were at full strength, Billy Steel having decided that his cold was not bad enough to stop him playing. Dundee were in white while Rangers were in their normal blue but with a red and white band. By an odd quirk, both goalkeepers were called Brown – Bobby of Rangers and

Bill of Dundee – and both were Scotland internationals. It was Rangers who opened the scoring through Willie Findlay after a fine move which he himself had started and which involved Willie Waddell and Willie Thornton. Half-time came with Rangers comfortably one up and looking likely winners.

Soon after half-time, however, Bobby Flavell got Dundee back on level terms with a goal which the newspapers rightly describe as funny. A miskicked clearance came to Flavell who shot for goal and Bobby Brown got his hand to it but was unable to prevent it from crossing the line. About halfway through the second half Johnny Pattillo put Dundee ahead with a fierce drive from just inside the box, and Dundee supporters could be forgiven for thinking that the League Cup was coming to Dens Park, for the Dundee half-back line of Gallacher, Cowie and Boyd now took a grip of the game until Rangers equalised through a very unlikely source, a long free kick from George Young which deceived everyone and went in. Dundee protested that their goalkeeper Bill Brown had been pushed out of the way by Willie Thornton, but referee Mr Mowat would not hear of it. Only two minutes remained, Dundee were heartbroken.

But Dundee would triumph yet. They were awarded a free kick halfway inside the Rangers half. Alf Boyd ran past Billy Steel as he was about to take it. He told Steel that he was going to the right of the goal and that he wanted a high one for a header. Steel then proved just why he was considered the best player in the world by some of his fans when he put the ball exactly on Boyd's head. All Boyd had to do was head the ball straight. This he did without any bother, and Rangers, euphoric a second ago, were now shattered.

The teams were:

Dundee: Brown, Fallon and Cowan, Gallacher, Cowie and Boyd, Toner, Pattillo, Flavell, Steel and Christie

Rangers: Brown, Young and Little, McColl, Woodburn and Cox, Waddell, Findlay, Thornton, Johnson and Rutherford

Referee: JA Mowat, Rutherglen

The next few hours were like a dream for Dundee as they travelled home to a great welcome. By sheer chance the railway policeman who was guarding the gate at Dundee West Station had also been there on duty 41 years ago in 1910 when they came back home with the Scottish Cup after their win over Clyde. It was a great night for the city and the monotonous jute mills on the Monday would be a little less boring.

King George VI died in February 1952. It was a cause of sadness, even for those with no great love of the royal family, for he was a kind, shy man who had overcome immense personal problems to do a good job. His daughter now came to the throne. She had an upper-class accent which was difficult to identify with, but her young children (who had not yet disgraced her as one in particular would do in future years) did seem to symbolise that this was the decade of the young. Prosperity was in the air, the NHS was now kicking in, slums were being demolished and working-class society now seemed to be saying 'We want a piece of this!' No more wars or unemployment!

But there was still loads of football. Dundee might have added the Scottish Cup to their haul in 1952 but, having reached the final and having held Motherwell to 0-0 in the first half, collapsed piteously and inexplicably in the second to go down 0-4. They did, however, defend their League

Cup come the autumn and became the first team to win the trophy in successive years. They came close, once or twice, to failing to do so, but once again 'The Bonnets o' Bonnie Dundee' were sung to the skirl of the bagpipes in the city centre. 'Bonnie' was, incidentally, a most inappropriate description of the city with all its many jute mills all belching out smoke. (And yes, the pedants will tell me that the song is not about the city of Dundee at all, but more to do with Lord Graham of Claverhouse, Viscount Dundee who did not like William of Orange in 1689.) One of the prices that one has to pay for full employment and bustling industrial production is that the environment suffers. Dundee did not smell good.

Dundee had little bother in qualifying from their comparatively easy section of Clyde, Raith Rovers and Airdrie. Clyde drew with them twice but did not do so well against the other teams in the section. Rangers and Third Lanark also qualified (both rescuing themselves from previous poor displays by good wins on the last day) but the best performance of the last day of the section was surely that of Hibs. Celtic approached Easter Road knowing that a draw would be sufficient to see them qualify, but Hibs (last year's league champions) were virtually unbeatable that day with the Famous Five in full flow and they beat Celtic 3-0. The other four teams who qualified were Morton, Stirling Albion, Kilmarnock and St Johnstone.

The major sensation of the quarter-final first-leg games on 13 September came at Annfield, the home of Division B Stirling Albion where the home side, taking advantage of an injury to Tommy Gallacher, beat Dundee 3-1. *The Courier* runs out of excuses for its favourites and takes refuge in the obvious 'It will be quite a day on Wednesday' when the return leg was due to be played. Fortunately for Dundee, Billy Steel turned it on against the gallant Stirling Albion, and the 24,000 crowd saw a 5-0 victory for Dundee. Elsewhere, Rangers edged through against Third Lanark, Hibs had little bother in seeing off Morton and, in the battle of Division B, Kilmarnock got the better of St Johnstone.

The semi-finals were played on 4 October 1952. The better game appeared to be Hibs v Dundee at Tynecastle which looked like a close encounter between last year's Scottish champions and last year's winners of the Scottish League Cup, whereas not very many people gave Kilmarnock (admittedly, going well in Division B) much chance against Rangers, even though a few holes were beginning to appear in the Iron Curtain defence. More or less everyone, however, believed that we were heading for a final between Scotland's two best teams of the era – Rangers and Hibs.

But that was not the way it turned out. Both games attracted crowds of about 45,000 and late goals decided both games. Rangers v Kilmarnock was actually a good, well-contested game, but Rangers supporters did not see it that way. Rangers, for all their pressure (with Derek Grierson in particular having bad luck), could not score against Kilmarnock, and the usual symptoms of a poor Rangers performance began to appear – players arguing with each other on the field, their support first turning silent, then beginning to grumble and finally abusing their own players. By an odd coincidence, both goalkeepers were called Niven (George of Rangers and John of Kilmarnock) and both had good games until a couple of minutes from time when Rangers' Johnny Little tried to clear a Matt Murray cross and the ball bounced off Willie Jack to give Kilmarnock a fortuitous but not entirely undeserved 1-0 win.

This was technically a giant-killing in the definition of a Division A team being beaten by a Division B side. It was one of the few times that this had happened to Rangers in their 80-year history and it would be Kilmarnock's first-ever League Cup Final. They were not, by any means, the first team from Division B to make it to the final, but it was nevertheless a great achievement by Malky MacDonald's men. Malky had been a member of Celtic's 1938 Empire Exhibition side and would be a successful manager for the Ayrshire men.

At Tynecastle, 44,200 saw managerless Dundee get the better of Hibs. Dundee boss George Anderson was ill with a severe dose of pleurisy in an Aberdeen nursing home and was compelled to rely on phone calls from trainer Reggie Smith in the first half for progress of the game before he was able to listen to the radio commentary in the second half. The second half must have been a real tonic to him for Dundee, after being 1-0 down through a Lawrie Reilly strike, suddenly turned it all round with two goals from Billy Steel and Bobby Flavell. For Dundee, the best men were the two Hendersons; Bobby Henderson, the goalkeeper, who had some wonderful saves, one from Bobby Johnstone; and Albert Henderson, a youngster who had recently broken into the team to the inside-right position.

Hibs manager Hugh Shaw, whose side had now won the league championship three times since the war but who always seemed to come up a little short in Scottish Cup and Scottish League Cup games, was gracious in defeat, admitting that Dundee were the better side. It was a happy bunch of Dundee supporters who made their way out of the ground to

Haymarket Station, and they were even happier when they heard that their opponents in the final were not going to be Rangers, but Division B and part-time Kilmarnock.

The attendance at the Scottish League Cup Final on 25 October 1952 would have to be described as a little disappointing at 51,830 in contrast to the Scottish Cup Final six months previously when Dundee and Motherwell drew 136,274 and the gates had to be closed with thousands outside unable to get in. This can be put down to several factors. One was that Motherwell were possibly a better-supported team than Kilmarnock, and there may also have been a certain amount of turnstile fatigue among the Dundee support for whom a trip to Hampden had now lost a little of its novelty effect, but the other thing was that the Scottish League Cup, unless Rangers were involved, now seemed to lack the ability to draw neutral fans. Yet it was disappointing that day when the final had Glasgow to itself (Celtic were in Edinburgh, Rangers had no game and the only other attraction was Clyde v Hibs at Shawfield) to see empty spaces on the terracing.

After this game, a look at the evening papers would show that Kilmarnock were fourth from the bottom of Division B with only Forfar, Cowdenbeath and Albion Rovers below them, but anyone who had been at Hampden that day would have said that the Ayrshire part-timers were at least the equals of Dundee for long stretches of the game. The *Evening Times*, knowing that the clock was due to go back that weekend, made a pun in its headline when it said 'the 'nock put back', for Kilmarnock (the 'nock) frankly deserved to win the trophy with only the brilliance of Bobby Henderson in the Dundee goal denying them, particularly in the first half.

But full-time training eventually told, and in the second half with the wind behind them Dundee eventually began to come more into the game. Yet Tommy Gallacher was not playing and Billy Steel, although on the field, was out of touch (suffering from toothache, it was said, although many Dundee fans thought that what he really suffered from was 'temperamental hypochondria') and, as the last ten minutes were entered, it looked as if extra time might be needed. But then Dundee struck. A long pass from Jimmy Toner found Bobby Flavell in some space and he ran on and scored. That was in the 83rd minute, then with the stuffing now knocked out of the gallant Kilmarnock, Flavell scored a similar goal, this time from a goalkeeper's clearance. Full time came soon after that and Dundee had won the Scottish League Cup for the second year in a row, but all the glory that day went to Kilmarnock, a point admitted by Dundee's gracious Doug Cowie who had played so well that day. 'I admit we were a wee bit lucky,' he said.

But lucky or not, Dundee returned again to a heroes' welcome as the League Cup was shown that night from an open-topped bus and Dundonians cheered themselves hoarse. *The Courier* had a picture of manager George Anderson, still not recovered from his pleurisy, listening to the game on the radio but also admitted that it was Dundee's defence which 'stole the pictures', an indirect way of saying that Killie were the better team. Killie would have some compensation when they gained promotion to Division A at the end of the season.

The teams were:

Dundee: Henderson, Fallon and Frew, Ziesling, Boyd and Cowie, Toner, Henderson, Flavell, Steel and Christie

Kilmarnock: Niven, Collins and Hood, Russell, Thyne and Middlemass, Henaughan, Harvey, Mayes, Jack and Murray

Referee: Mr JA Mowat, Rutherglen

The year 1953 is generally regarded as a 'good year'. The coronation of Queen Elizabeth II was well celebrated on the infant medium called television by those lucky enough to have one, while every child in the land was given a cup and a bar of chocolate (a rare treat for 1953), but there was more than that. The Korean War came to an end, a British party conquered Everest, Stanley Matthews (everyone's favourite football player) won an English FA Cup medal and Gordon Richards (everyone's favourite jockey) won the derby. Celtic struck a blow for Scottish football by winning the all-British Coronation Cup. But how embarrassing! It was meant to be a final between the two establishment, royalist teams of Rangers and Arsenal, but everyone at Hampden at the final between Celtic and Hibs were singing republican songs and waving Irish flags! Apart from the coronation, everything was now a lot better than previously. Prime Minister Winston Churchill, getting old, ill and forgetful, was nevertheless benign and well disposed to Labour's National Health Service and Welfare State, houses were being built, children were becoming healthier and rationing had almost disappeared. It was indeed a new, healthy, prosperous age.

The topic of conversation in Dundee was whether the team could win a hat-trick of Scottish League Cups. Dundee, East Fife and Rangers had all won the trophy twice and Motherwell once, and there could now be no doubt whatsoever that the trophy was a great success, with big crowds normally and usually good weather at the start of the season in August.

Dundee came to spectacular grief, however, in their last game of the sectional stage on 29 August 1953. They went to Firhill to take on Partick Thistle knowing that a draw or a moderate defeat would qualify them for the quarter-finals. Thistle, managed by ex-Ranger Davie Meiklejohn, had been mediocre up till then but always had the reputation of being unpredictable. It was a fine day, the crowd was 25,000 and Thistle turned it on to win 4-0 and qualify on goal average. One goal might have saved Dundee, but *The Courier* was quite scathing about them saying that 'it was the worst Dundee in years', refusing to invoke excuses about injuries and allowing their cartoonist to show two Dundee United supporters laughing at the discomfiture of Dundee. The *Glasgow Herald* said that Dundee were 'astonishingly disappointing' but praised Thistle whose four goals were scored by Bobby Howitt, Joe McInnes, Willie Sharp and Alec Wright.

It was not the only dramatic act on the final sectional day, for East Fife defeated Aberdeen at Pittodrie 4-3 to guarantee their qualification and a Fife derby against Dunfermline in the quarter-finals, while Third Lanark and Kilmarnock were also indebted to goal average for their qualification. On the other hand, Hibs and Rangers qualified easily while Celtic realised that their Coronation Cup success was illusory and that they were, in fact, still a rather mediocre side.

The quarter-finals were not without their excitement, for although Hibs and East Fife qualified with a degree of ease over Third Lanark and Dunfermline Athletic, Rangers were pushed all the way by a gallant Ayr United who beat them 3-2 in the second leg at Somerset Park after losing 2-4 at Ibrox. Partick Thistle and Kilmarnock's first game was a thriller won 4-3 by Killie at Rugby Park, but in the second leg, Thistle once again advanced in this tournament by scoring four goals to make the aggregate 7-4 and thrilling their fans in the process.

One of Partick Thistle's best days in their history came on 10 October 1953 when, against all the odds, they beat Rangers 2-0 at Hampden in the semi-final. The day was dominated by a very strong wind and Partick Thistle won the toss and decided to play with the breeze. They took full advantage, and their first goal was very much wind-assisted when a fierce drive from Johnny McKenzie from about 30 yards crashed against the woodwork and rebounded to Alec Wright, who hammered home from about the penalty spot. Then, just about half-time, another distance shot was played by Rangers goalkeeper George Niven against the bar. He may have been fouled as he tried to regain the ball but referee Phillips thought otherwise as Bobby Howitt prodded it home.

Thistle then had a long struggle against the wind in the second half but they were organised and well marshalled (as befitted a team with Davie Meiklejohn as their manager) with goalkeeper Tommy Ledgerwood outstanding and the rest of the defence wising up about how to deal with the wind: keep the ball on the ground. Rangers had a few chances, but Thistle held out to win 2-0 and put themselves into their first Hampden final for well over 20 years.

Across in the east at Tynecastle, the wind was no less severe as Hibs, the strong favourites even without the injured Eddie Turnbull, took on East Fife, but it was East Fife who took the lead against the wind before half-time through Jimmy Bonthrone. Hibs then equalised through a controversial shoulder-charge goal by Laurie Reilly, and a far better goal – a header from the same player – put them ahead. Hibs now looked likely to win until Howie gave away two penalty kicks, one a handball and the other a silly tackle, and both were duly sunk by Don Emery, although the second one was a rebound.

Once again, Hibs showed their inability to win the League Cup, for all their undeniable talent, and East Fife, now managed by Jerry Dawson rather than Scot Symon who had now moved to Preston North End, had reached the final of the Scottish League Cup for the third time in eight years. Rangers too, although twice winners, were now beginning to fall out of love with the League Cup (they would suffer a spectacular hammering in a few years) and the final, although interesting for the neutral, would suffer from a poor attendance as Partick Thistle were a comparatively poorly supported Glasgow side, and East Fife, for all their pedigree in the League Cup, were a team from a small mining town.

A total of 38,529 turned up on a fine, dry October day at Hampden on 24 October to see what was, in playing terms, one of the better League Cup finals with a good fightback and a twist at the end. East Fife wore white shirts with gold collars and black pants while Partick Thistle were in a most unusual blue with white sleeves. There was not much of a wind and four of the five goals were scored at the Mount Florida end of the ground.

The teams were:

East Fife: Curran, Emery and S Stewart, Christie, Finlay and McLennan, J Stewart, Fleming, Bonthrone, Gardiner and Matthew

Partick Thistle: Ledgerwood, McGowan and Gibb, Crawford, Davidson and Kerr, McKenzie, Howitt, Sharp, Wright and Walker

Referee: Mr J Cox, Rutherglen

East Fife were 2-0 up at half-time with an early freak goal from Jimmy Gardiner which looked more like a cross, then a better one from Charlie 'Legs' Fleming (a man who was already attracting the attention of English clubs like Sunderland) even though he got the benefit of a deflection. These were early goals, but that was still the score at half-time. But Partick then mounted a great fightback with goals from Jimmy Walker and the excellent Johnny McKenzie. From then on, Thistle looked the better team but, as often happen in such circumstances, it was the other team who got the winner, as Frank Christie (a man who had spent some time with Liverpool) lashed home from the edge of the box after Thistle had failed to deal with a cross. This was three minutes from the end and not enough time for Thistle to mount another fightback. So, for the third time in eight years, the Scottish League Cup was presented to the captain of East Fife (in this case, Sammy Stewart) and the small mining community celebrated with a gusto.

It was a great triumph for manager Jerry Dawson, who had played in goal for Rangers and Falkirk and had played for Falkirk in the 1947/48 Scottish League Cup when they had lost to East Fife.

CHAPTER THREE

HEARTS AND SEVEN
1954–1959

THERE IS no more enigmatic club in Scotland than the Heart of Midlothian. They are also the greatest underachievers of the lot. Set in the capital of Scotland, they really should be the 'establishment' club but, sadly, their dismal record has prevented this from happening.

Never was this dismal record of gross underachievement so exemplified as during the 48 years of trophy hunger which came to an end when they won the Scottish League Cup of 1954/55.

They had last won the Scottish League in 1897 and the Scottish Cup in 1906. They had reached the final of the Scottish Cup in the following year but, since then, their record had been poor and they had not been back to a Hampden final, nor had they come vaguely close to lifting the Scottish League apart from the first season of the First World War. Their record in the new Scottish League Cup had been not so much dismal as disastrous.

And yet, during all these lean years between the wars, they always had a large support, often averaging a larger home crowd than Celtic and even, now and again, defeating Rangers in that particular attendance league. They also consistently finished a great deal higher than their rivals from the east of Edinburgh, Hibs. They had produced many fine players for Scotland, men like Bobby Walker of the Edwardian era, commonly known as Houdini for his ability to wriggle past defenders, and the fine right-half Alex Massie, generally regarded as the best of his day and earning the nicknames Ace of Hearts and Classy Massie. Tommy Walker, now their manager, had been a great forward, famous for the scoring of the penalty at Wembley in 1936 for Scotland when the wind blew the ball off the spot and he calmly replaced it several times before hammering it past the goalkeeper, Ted Sagar of Everton.

There had been no lack of ability and no lack of support, but disappointment had been the order of the day. They had every reason to be proud of their men who in late 1914 had enlisted in the colours virtually en masse in a brave, if perhaps misguided, act of solidarity and commitment. Things might have been different if Hearts had embarked on the course which seemed to be obvious to outsiders, namely to share a ground with the Scottish Rugby Union at Murrayfield across the railway from Tynecastle, thus providing more funds and preventing them from being hemmed in at Tynecastle by schools, houses and the railway. An agreement with the SRU would have allowed expansion, but it never happened.

The years since the Second World War sat very ill with Hearts and their fans. It had been the great era of Hibs and their Famous Five forwards, and the Hibees had won three league championships, in 1948, 1951 and 1952. Admittedly, Hibs had not won either cup, but they had come close in 1950/51 and their record was markedly better than that of Hearts. Hearts had occasionally beaten Hibs in the Scottish League and in the various local Edinburgh tournaments but, in 1954, if someone had asked who the better Edinburgh team was (there were now only two – St Bernard's, Edinburgh City and Leith Athletic having all fallen by the wayside), the answer would undeniably have had to be Hibs.

The Scottish League Cup of 1954 changed that and ushered in a golden era for Hearts in which they won the Scottish Cup in 1956, the Scottish League in 1958 and 1960 (with a heartbreaking second in 1959) and no fewer than four Scottish League Cups and another narrow miss. By 1962, Hearts and Rangers were the top Scottish League Cup winners with four each.

Managed by Tommy Walker, Hearts had built themselves up. If Hibs had their Famous Five, then Hearts had their Terrible Trio of Alfie Conn, Willie Bauld and Jimmy Wardhaugh. Now they began to strike a rich vein of form, impressing everyone by their play. Their supporters now began to attend away games in large numbers and (in pleasing contrast to later years) behave themselves.

The summer of 1954, in which Celtic had won the league and cup double for the first time since before the Great War, saw a major cultural shock delivered to Scotland on the international front. They reluctantly decided to go to the World Cup in Switzerland (presumably being of the belief that such things were beneath them) and lost 0-1 to Austria (that was bad enough), but then appalled their supporters who were able to get themselves in front of a small, flickering black and white television by going down 0-7 to Uruguay, a country that hardly anyone had heard of. This was tragic, but it was also comic as well for stories were told of Scotland playing in blistering heat in heavy traditional Scotland shirts that would have served well in November. In addition, the manager having resigned before the game was played (you couldn't have made that up, could you?), the encouragement and tactics from the bench were along the lines of 'Come on Scotland, get stuck in!'

That was a shocker, but it was quickly forgotten about when the 'real' football started in August with the Scottish League Cup. The football was good and qualification was in doubt in most of the groups until the very last day. When Hearts beat Celtic at Tynecastle on that fateful day of 4 September, it was only the third time that they had reached the last eight. They had done so in the first two years of the competition but never since, and their qualification was received with a fair amount of joy in Edinburgh. They were joined by Motherwell, East Fife and Rangers who had all qualified after a bit of a struggle from their respective groups, but the team who really attracted attention were the men from Airdrie who were going to have a good season in 1954/55. Morton, Ayr United and St Johnstone were also there, Morton having required goal average to beat the other teams in their section. Those who enjoy statistical peculiarities pointed out that they all started with the letter 'A': Alloa, Albion Rovers and Arbroath.

The quarter-finals saw a slight change this year with the first legs being played on a Wednesday night and the second legs played the following Saturday. Hearts progressed with very little bother against St Johnstone, whom they beat with an aggregate score of 7-0 having defeated the Perth men at Muirton Park 5-0 in the first leg, but a major surprise was sprung when Motherwell beat Rangers. Motherwell won 2-1 at Fir Park and by sheer hard work earned a 1-1 draw at Ibrox to see them through against a Rangers side staggered by the recent *sine die* suspension of Willie Woodburn after years of misconduct. Airdrie thrashed Ayr United 6-1 in the second leg to win through and East Fife, these inveterate lovers of the Scottish League Cup, beat Morton 2-0 at Bayview after being lucky to get off with a draw at Cappielow.

Thus 9 October saw Hearts v Airdrie and Motherwell v East Fife in the semi-finals. The *Glasgow Herald* was dismayed at the attendance at Hampden to see Motherwell v East Fife – a mere 18,833 – but the weather was not good with constant drizzle and Hampden in 1954 was notorious for having no shelter whatsoever unless you were a member of the Queen's Park bourgeoisie and could pay big money to go to either of the stands. The result was that the game, though keenly fought, lacked atmosphere, and it would surely have made more sense to allocate the game to Tynecastle or perhaps Dens Park where the crowd could still have been accommodated and, in addition, the atmosphere would have been a great deal better.

East Fife's love affair with the Scottish League Cup came to an end that day, or at least a serious spoke was put in the wheel of the carriage, when Motherwell won 2-1 in a poor game. East Fife, as was their wont, scored early through Ian Gardiner, but Motherwell, a strong team, fought back and their right-back (with the confusing name of Willie Kilmarnock) equalised with a fierce drive before half-time.

In the second half, Alec Bain, who was in rich form that season, scored the equaliser and Motherwell finished well on top, although Charlie 'Legs' Fleming might have equalised at the death.

The *Evening Times* made a name for itself in corny headlines when it led with 'Well, All Very Hearty' because Hearts had won the other semi-final against Airdrie at Easter Road. The weather was no better in Edinburgh but it attracted a good crowd of 34,127 and they saw a far better game in which Hearts, in spite of the loss of a goal in the first minute, scored four to beat an Airdrie side which perhaps deserved more out of the game than it got. Hearts' goals were scored by Jimmy Wardhaugh (twice), Johnny Urquhart and Willie Bauld, and this was enough to put Hearts into their first-ever Scottish League Cup Final. The opponents were Motherwell. It looked like a very attractive game between two good football sides, but once again fears were expressed about the size of the crowd at Hampden as there were no Glasgow teams involved.

They need not have worried, for a huge Hearts support and a sizeable Motherwell presence ensured that a crowd of 55,640 appeared even though the weather was far from pleasant. It was cold with persistent drizzle. A new phenomenon appeared that day, however: an invasion of the park. This occurred at the end of the game and the idea seemed to be simply to get a better view of the League Cup being presented to the winning Hearts side.

There was no malice or harm intended and the point was well made in the press that, as 48 years had elapsed since Hearts last won any national trophy, it was sheer unfamiliarity and novelty that caused it all. The police and authorities were similarly unaware that it could happen because it, quite simply, was not an age when crowds did this sort of thing. Nevertheless, harmless although it was, it could not be tolerated for the crowd might contain some unruly or hostile elements and the pitch was liable to be damaged.

The game was a great triumph for the Edinburgh side and centred almost entirely on Willie Bauld. He scored twice in the first 15 minutes, then after Willie Redpath had pulled one back from the penalty spot, Jimmy Wardhaugh restored Hearts' two-goal lead just before half-time. Motherwell tried hard to reduce the leeway in the second half, but there was no further scoring until the very end of the game when Willie Bauld got his hat-trick and Alex Bain got a late consolation goal.

The teams were:

Hearts: Duff, Parker and McKenzie, Mackay, Glidden and Cumming, Souness, Conn, Bauld, Wardhaugh and Urquhart

Motherwell: Weir, Kilmarnock and McSeveney, Cox, Paton and Redpath, Hunter, Aitken, Bain, Humphries and Williams

Referee: J Mowat, Rutherglen

Thus began a glorious era in Hearts history. As the open-top bus came along Princes Street that night to the cheers of the fans, very few dared to hope what might be in store for them, although one Hearts fan with a sense of humour said he was glad Hearts had won the League Cup because he was fed up hearing Hibs fans boasting about the last time that they had won a national cup – the Scottish Cup of 1902! Trophy processions, open-top buses and Edinburgh football triumphs were far from a common occurrence. There were even jokes that the last time an Edinburgh team won a trophy, Mary, Queen of Scots, granted everyone a half-holiday!

The League Cup having been introduced to Hearts in October 1954, it was now time to introduce her to another grand old gentleman of Scottish football: Aberdeen. There are those who argue – and one has a certain amount of sympathy – that Aberdeen had already won the trophy in 1946. Technically, however, they are wrong, for 1945/46 was still a wartime unofficial season and the trophy was still called the Southern League Cup. Aberdeen had reached the final of the first official Scottish League Cup and been defeated 4-0 by Rangers but, since then, they had failed to distinguish themselves in the competition, unable to qualify for the quarter-finals rather too often for the liking of their vast potential support.

But things had changed for Aberdeen in recent years. They had reached the final of the Scottish Cup in 1953 and 1954 and had been unlucky to lose on both occasions, and in 1955, for the first time ever, they had won the Scottish League. Davie Halliday's fine side absolutely sparkled with talent, with wingers Graham Leggat and Jackie Hather in particular showing the benefits of what is now called wide play, and their triumph was generally welcomed in Scotland.

For the 1955/56 Scottish League Cup, a change was enforced. The Scottish League had been expanded in summer 1955 so that it now contained 18 in the First Division (no longer to be called Division A) and 19 in the Second Division. Not everyone was necessarily in favour of all this, for the odd number in the Second Division meant that on any given Saturday one team would have a day off and more midweek games would be required in the spring.

It had a knock-on effect in the Scottish League Cup, for instead of eight sections of four teams each, there would now have to be nine with the last five teams in the previous year's Second Division playing in section nine. They played each other only the once, then the winners would have to play a supplementary round of a home and away leg against the winners of another section for qualification into the quarter-finals. It was clumsy and unsatisfactory, but that system would now prevail for some time.

Dumbarton won section nine in 1955/56 and then beat Morton, the winners of section eight, in the supplementary round to reach the quarter-finals. They were joined by Aberdeen, Rangers, Hearts, Hamilton, St Johnstone, St Mirren and Motherwell. Once Aberdeen had beaten Hibs on the opening day of the season they had little bother in qualifying, Motherwell (now in the Second Division) won every game they played, Hearts, last year's winners, qualified comfortably enough but the tightest section was that involving the Old Firm.

The arrangements of fixtures in that section was an odd one. It involved Celtic playing Rangers in back-to-back fixtures on Saturday, 27 August and Wednesday, 31 August. Both games resulted in convincing victories for the away side. Celtic were well on top at Ibrox, whereas Rangers won well at Parkhead, although Celtic did at least have the excuse that their centre-half and captain, Jock Stein, was badly injured – an injury, in fact, which, to all intents and purposes, finished his career and compelled him to turn to coaching and management. On the final Saturday, it was just a question of who scored the most goals. It was Rangers who won 6-0 against Queen of the South while

Celtic could only draw 1-1 at Brockville against Falkirk in a game badly marred by crowd disturbances. On the same day, although St Mirren lost 0-3 to Dundee at Dens Park, this was still enough for them to qualify on goal average over Kilmarnock.

In the quarter-finals, Hamilton Accies did well to hold Rangers to a 1-2 defeat at Douglas Park but were then well and truly annihilated 8-0 on the Saturday at Ibrox. No one had ever thought of the away goals rule in 1955, nor the penalty shoot-out, so when Motherwell won 2-1 at Muirton over St Johnstone, and St Johnstone won 1-0 at Fir Park, and extra time failed to separate the teams, a replay had to be held the following Wednesday. It was duly won 2-0 by Motherwell in what the *Glasgow Herald* describes as a 'drab' game at Ibrox before a miserable crowd of 5,000, the choice of venue upsetting St Johnstone's manager Johnny Pattillo. St Mirren's first-leg performance was good enough to see them home against Dumbarton, but the game that really caught the attention of everyone was the high-scoring clash between Aberdeen and Hearts.

It was Wednesday, 14 September when a Graham Leggat hat-trick saw Aberdeen beat holders Hearts 5-3, but this was a significant night in footballing history, for Hibs beat a team called Rot-Weiss Essen in a new tournament called the European Cup and it was played in Germany under floodlights. Many people thought that neither the European Cup nor floodlight football would last, but Saturday's game at Tynecastle saw another large crowd to see another high-scoring game, this time won 4-2 by Aberdeen, now generally agreed to be the form team of Scotland and favourites to win their first Scottish League Cup.

This impression was confirmed in the semi-final on 1 October. A crowd of about 80,000 turned up at Hampden on an overcast day to see Aberdeen outplay a poor Rangers team and, but for a shoulder injury to Graham Leggat, the score would have been a great deal more than 2-1. It was Leggat himself who scored the first goal before sustaining his injury, then Bobby Wishart added another. Johnny Hubbard scored for Rangers after half-time, but Aberdeen's passing of the ball to each other, even with only ten men, was a sight to behold. Rangers' lack of current success in the League Cup since their victories in 1946/47 and 1948/49 was once again apparent.

The other semi-final at Ibrox between St Mirren and Motherwell before a smaller crowd of 19,000 ended in a draw, although there was a bizarre incident which led to Motherwell's first and hotly disputed goal. It was a free kick to St Mirren just outside their own penalty area and Willie Telfer passed it back to his goalkeeper only for Willie McSeveney of Motherwell to nip in and score. Telfer claimed that the ball was not yet in play and that he was merely passing the ball back for the goalkeeper to take the free kick, but referee Willie Brittle disagreed; 2-2 at full time, and each side scored again in extra time to make it 3-3. The replay at Celtic Park a week later saw St Mirren score twice to beat Motherwell, and to put them into their first-ever League Cup Final.

The Buddies were always regarded as good cup fighters and certainly had a tradition of winning against the odds. Their older supporters enjoyed telling the story of the Scottish Cup Final of almost 30 years ago when they were up against league champions Celtic and not given much of a chance. They scored early, however, and went on to lift the trophy for their one and only time. Nevertheless, just about everyone fancied Aberdeen to win the League Cup at Hampden on 22 October.

So it transpired. The weather was fine, crisp and autumnal that afternoon for the 44,106 crowd that turned up. The attendance was slightly disappointing but Aberdeen is a long way away and the final did not even have Glasgow to itself, for Celtic were playing at Clyde about a mile away at Shawfield. The kick-off was 2.30pm to allow for the possibility of extra time, and, as had happened in previous League Cup finals, many of the crowd were quite clearly under the misapprehension that the game started at 3pm for there were less than 20,000 in the ground at the appointed time. A less charitable interpretation of this phenomenon, however, lay in the fact that pubs closed at 2.30pm!

Both teams were at full strength and neither side was able to gain an advantage in the first half. It was Aberdeen who took the lead early in the second half when a cross from Jackie Hather missed the diving head of Graham Leggat but instead hit the chest of defender Jimmy Mallan and the ball went in for a very fortunate own goal. Mallan, who had spent most of his career at Celtic, was distraught, but the Buddies were not behind for long, and this time it was a beautiful goal scored by a diving header from Bobby Holmes to reach a Davie Lapsley free kick.

Gradually, Aberdeen regained control of the game and with 12 minutes left scored what turned out to be the winner with a drive from Graham Leggat well outside the box which caught goalkeeper Jim Lornie off his line. St Mirren battled hard but the full-time whistle came with Aberdeen beginning to play their excellent passing game at which they had excelled last season when they won the league championship. It was generally agreed that Aberdeen had played below their potential and that St Mirren were possibly worth a draw and extra time, but there could be little doubt that Aberdeen from their earlier performances were worthy of the trophy, their second of the calendar year. It was a great day out for their much-travelled fans.

The teams were:

Aberdeen: Martin, Mitchell and Caldwell, Wilson, Clunie and Glen, Leggat, Yorston, Buckley, Wishart and Hather

St Mirren: Lornie, Lapsley and Mallan, Neilson, Telfer and Holmes, Rodger, Laird, Brown, Gemmell and Callan

Referee: H Phillips, Wishaw

The tournament had reached its tenth birthday, if we ignore its years as the Southern League Cup in the war. East Fife had won it three times, Rangers and Dundee twice each, and now Aberdeen joined Hearts and Motherwell as having won it once. There was one famous Scottish team which had so far failed to reach the final, yet they had the deserved reputation of being the best cup fighters of them all.

Celtic had never come close in this tournament. Only in recent years was there beginning to be any sign of the 'Celts of old' that their fans kept talking about. They had a dreadful Second World War and, give or take the odd spectacular moment, had failed to recover until 1954 when they won a league and cup double. But they had, as yet, failed to land the Scottish League Cup. They had good-enough players (Charlie Tully, Willie Fernie, Bobby Evans, Bobby Collins, Bertie Peacock) but mystified their fans with awful team selection and a curiously insipid performance in last year's Scottish Cup Final to Hearts. Their fans were far from happy.

But a new season is a new start. Celtic found themselves in a section containing Rangers, East Fife and holders Aberdeen. Playing with a new confidence and assurance, Celtic won through by playing competent football. Games were won narrowly, albeit without the flair that the Scottish public associated with Celtic teams of old. Any chance that Rangers had was dissipated at Ibrox on 29 August on a wet, blustery Wednesday night. The sun disappeared quickly and darkness fell rapidly but Celtic's defence held out for a 0-0 draw before an astonishing crowd of 84,000. Celtic then won at East Fife to finish the job and to qualify for the quarter-finals for only the third time in 11 years.

Elsewhere. Dundee qualified comfortably along with Partick Thistle (whose section included both Edinburgh teams and who had to fight to earn the necessary draw in the last game at Easter Road) and Dunfermline Athletic from the First Division sections. But the tightest section of them all was section seven where Dundee United, Ayr United and Stenhousemuir all gained seven points, but Dundee United won through on goal average by 0·38 of a goal. They did this by beating Third Lanark 2-1 at Tannadice on the last day while Ayr United beat Stenhousemuir 3-1. In the days before calculators or computers, it was slide rules that were required to work that one out.

The nine qualifiers had an odd look about them. There were three from Glasgow in Celtic, Clyde and Partick Thistle, two from the city of Dundee, two from Fife in Cowdenbeath and Dunfermline, and two from the county of Angus in Brechin City and Arbroath. Of these nine, only Dundee had won the trophy before and only another two had appeared in a final – Partick Thistle and Dunfermline. Dundee United beat Arbroath in the supplementary round to set up a Dundee derby, Celtic took on Dunfermline, Partick faced Cowdenbeath and Clyde were paired with Brechin City.

A Dundee derby was a rarity in 1956, for Dundee United were anchored in the Second Division and Dundee in the First. There was even an element of social snobbery involved, for Tannadice was a dreadful stadium with an awful stand which creaked as you sat down in it, whereas Dundee, with a reasonable amount of success in recent years (not least in the Scottish League Cup), were looked upon as the establishment club of the city.

The first leg on Wednesday, 12 September was much talked up in the local press, but it was a heavy defeat for the Tannadice side, although the 7-3 scoreline in the drizzling rain did give their fans in the 20,000 crowd something to be happy about. Similarly, at Parkhead, a 6-0 scoreline seemed to make Celtic's second leg at Dunfermline a formality. Both Dundee United and Dunfermline would win their second-leg games, but not by enough to put the winners of the tie in any doubt.

The closest games were the ones involving Partick Thistle and Clyde. Thistle beat Cowdenbeath 2-1 on both occasions but without being any too convincing. The real heroes of the round were Brechin City who managed to beat Clyde 2-1 at Glebe Park and then, after going 0-3 down at Shawfield, pulled one back and were distinctly unlucky not to get at least extra time. Brechin would do better next year.

The provincials having departed, the League Cup semi-finals boiled down to three Glasgow teams and Dundee. On form, Dundee were probably marginally the favourites, but Celtic seemed to have the easier draw against Second Division Clyde, a team who, having won the Scottish Cup in 1955, were relegated in 1956. No one knew it at the time, but they would be promoted in 1957 and win the Scottish Cup in 1958. The unusual came at no extra cost with the Shawfield men.

By this time, however, a general fear of unease, mingled with dangerous excitement, was beginning to take over the country concerning Egypt and the Suez Canal. History is now able to see that it was all a piece of vainglorious bullying and jingoism on the part of the British Prime Minister Anthony Eden, but that was not the way in which it was portrayed in the newspapers of the time. Nasser, the Egyptian leader, was compared to Hitler and much was the talk about 'standing up to aggression' as Britain and France joined forces with Israel to square up to Egypt. The United Nations, the USA and the British Labour Party were a great deal less impressed. In the meantime, in a far more tragic situation, the Russians were muscling in on Hungary who not only had a great football team but had shown subversive signs of not wanting to do what the Russians said.

The crises would not go away and were still there by 6 October when the semi-finals were played. The game at Ibrox between Dundee and Partick Thistle is candidly described as 'boredom' by the normally restrained *Glasgow Herald* and agreed with in *The Courier*, whereas the only winners of the day were Celtic at Hampden who turned on a great display to beat Clyde 2-0 with Willie Fernie on song, Bobby Evans back from a recent injury, and both goals coming from ex-Clyde man Billy McPhail. Newspapers were puzzled about the attendances though; only 36,697 at Hampden and a great deal fewer than that at Ibrox. On a reasonably dry day, more might have been expected.

The replay of the Dundee v Partick Thistle game was scheduled for Ibrox on Tuesday, 9 October. History was made. It was the first Scottish League Cup game to be played under floodlights (a couple of Scottish Cup games had been played earlier that year) but the crowd was a disappointing 18,000 when there was the incentive to see the Ibrox lights, much vaunted and boasted about and opening up all sorts of possibilities for night games. Some clubs looked upon them with suspicion, Aberdeen in particular, but Rangers and Hibs saw the possibilities and would eventually win their point. The game itself was a great deal better than Saturday, although a trifle on the rough side with three players finishing the game limping. But Partick scored twice early on, then after allowing Dundee back in the game, scored the decisive goal in the second half and held on for a 3-2 win.

The final between Celtic and Partick Thistle was disappointing for two reasons. One was the attendance of 58,794 when one might have expected more from a support like that of Celtic – but then again they were still bitter about last year's Scottish Cup Final and their recent form had been none too great – and the other disappointment was that it was really a dreadful game finishing 0-0 after extra time in the gathering gloom, even though it had been a 2.15pm kick-off. Celtic were particularly subject to the scorn of their own support and the press, for Thistle sustained two injuries and finished the game with only nine fit men – and even then, they were the better team!

By the time that the replay kicked off at 2.15pm on Halloween, Wednesday, 31 October, the international situation had deteriorated badly. Israel had attacked Egypt on 29 October, and it was only a matter of time before Britain got involved. Indeed, the *Evening Times* of 31 October carried the headline that the British and French had invaded Egypt at dawn with the avowed intention of protecting the Suez Canal. Reservists had been called up, and serious action was expected soon, as well as the rationing of petrol. Better to enjoy the football while we could, then. The crowd was a paltry 31,156, leaving loads of elbow room in the vast bowl of Hampden, and this time they did at least see a better game, particularly from the chastened Celtic who had seen the light and brought back Neil Mochan.

All the action happened in the first quarter of an hour of the second half, by which time the crowd had swollen considerably with the influx of schoolboys, and it was Celtic, inspired by Charlie Tully, who won the day. Billy McPhail scored twice and Bobby Collins once and there was no way back for Thistle from this 0-3 setback. Celtic retained command and skipper Bobby Evans lifted the League Cup half an hour later as the crowd departed to an uncertain future. Fortunately, the Egyptian adventure didn't come to much other than the resignation of the Prime Minister after a global humiliation for Great Britain. The Hungarian situation, however, got a lot worse, as the world saw just what sort of a country the Soviet Union was.

The teams were:

Celtic: Beattie, Haughney and Fallon, Evans, Jack and Peacock, Mochan, Collins, McPhail, Tully and Fernie

Partick Thistle: Ledgerwood, Kerr and Gibb, Collins, Crawford and Mathers, McKenzie, McParland, Hogan, Wright and Ewing

Referee: J Mowat, Rutherglen

Thus Celtic joined the ranks of the winners of the Scottish League Cup. For a trophy that they had striven to win for so long without success, the actual way they won it was a huge anti-climax in front of a small crowd on a dull Wednesday afternoon, but their small support that day celebrated in style. Next year they would win it again, but the circumstances would be remarkably different. Indeed, it would be hard to imagine a bigger contrast.

The 1957/58 Scottish League Cup ended spectacularly, but the team that surprised everyone in the early stages was Brechin City. They had enjoyed a good couple of years in the Second Division since being admitted in 1955 and Brechin was always an interesting place to go to. The term 'City' was much reviled and mocked by supporters of other clubs, but it was technically correct in that there was a cathedral in this small Angus town. The football ground, with a hedge running up one side, was quaint.

Brechin's qualification could hardly have been any tighter. Three teams, Brechin, Dunfermline and Ayr United, all finished on seven points and Brechin qualified by 0.10 of a goal on the goal average system, but even that does not tell all the tale, for they actually lost 1-3 to Dunfermline Athletic on the last day and were really indebted to their 7-1 thumping of Cowdenbeath on the previous Wednesday.

If another goal for Dunfermline would have knocked out Brechin City, the same was true of Rangers who lost 3-4 to Raith Rovers on the last day at Stark's Park when another goal for the Rovers would have knocked Rangers out. Perhaps with the benefit of hindsight, that might have been no bad thing for Rangers whose fans were already far from happy with their defence since George Young retired.

Celtic qualified from their group of Hibs, East Fife and Airdrie but needed a win over Hibs at Parkhead on the last day to do so, but this was a Hibs team whose glory days had long gone and whose Famous Five were now reduced to three. Aberdeen showed a welcome return to League Cup form by winning their section with maximum points and the other First Division section was won by the fast-developing Kilmarnock who had unluckily lost last season's Scottish Cup Final but would now be a force to reckon with in Scottish football for some time. Their victims included Hearts, generally reckoned also to be one of the best teams around, although no one at this stage would have predicted that Hearts were to be the league champions.

Clyde also won their section with maximum points. The other qualifiers were Hamilton Accies, Third Lanark and Montrose. Hamilton beat Montrose in the supplementary round and lined up against the other Angus team Brechin City, while Celtic took on Third Lanark and Clyde faced Aberdeen. But the tie of the round looked like Kilmarnock v Rangers.

Things were happening in the outside world as prosperity continued in Great Britain. On 31 August, the last day of the qualifying sections, Scottish Television was launched, financed by commercials. It operated mainly from the Theatre Royal in Glasgow and, soon after, the football programme *Scotsport* first appeared. Meanwhile, the Russians had plans for outer space and in October would launch their Sputnik to travel round the earth. It was as yet unmanned but clearly they had started something. In the meantime, in Scotland, a mysterious flu virus was spreading in spite of the efforts of the National Health Service.

The quarter-final first legs on Wednesday, 11 September threw up a real surprise when Clyde went to Pittodrie and won 2-1; Brechin City also shocked Hamilton Accies by winning 4-2 at Douglas Park, but this was no more of a shock than Hamilton's strip of all black which made them look like a team of undertakers or referees and obliged the real referee to wear khaki. Less surprising was Celtic's 6-1 defeat of Third Lanark at Parkhead whereas Rangers, although going down 1-2 at Rugby Park, were the better team and really should have won.

Bright sunshine greeted the return legs and the sun shone on the Glasgow teams. Celtic finished off Third Lanark at Cathkin, Clyde confirmed their superiority over Aberdeen with a 4-2 win at Shawfield while Rangers in a thrilling finish delighted their fans with a 3-1 win over Kilmarnock. It was an unhappy return to Ibrox for old favourite Willie Waddell who had recently taken over as manager at Rugby Park. At distant Glebe Park, Brechin City joined the three Glasgow sides with a 1-0 win over Hamilton, something which provoked a great deal of excitement locally, for it meant that Brechin City were travelling to Hampden to play Rangers in the League Cup semi-final on 28 September.

It was a Rangers side weakened by the flu virus (they were short of four regulars) but they were still far too good for the plucky Brechin City and won 4-0 with two goals scored by a young reserve called Harry Melrose who would in future make his mark on Scottish football with Dunfermline Athletic and Aberdeen. Across the city at Ibrox, Clyde were also weakened by the flu virus but they put up a great performance to go down 4-2. Celtic were 2-0 up but then the Bully Wee scored on either side of half-time to level the score before Celtic, with

Bobby Collins on song and scoring a particularly good goal in the second half, made it 4-2.

These results threw up the first Old Firm Scottish League Cup Final and the first national final between the two of them since the Scottish Cup Final of 1928. Excitement was high, but the attendance was poor with a crowd of 82,293; something that was put down to continuing effects of the flu bug which had indeed caused several minor games to be postponed and was causing serious problems for those in Glasgow and surrounding districts who already had breathing problems caused by the dreadful pollution hanging permanently over the huge, busy industrial city.

All the players seemed to be healthy, however. The consensus of opinion did seem to favour Celtic (they had beaten Rangers in a League game a month previously) but it was an Old Firm game and they were notoriously unpredictable. No one quite got it right, however.

A couple of days before the game, there was a dressing-room spat between two of Celtic's stars, Bobby Evans and Charlie Tully. Both were prodigiously talented players but they were not close friends and their relationship had taken a dip when Tully had written a piece for a newspaper in which he had seemed to criticise Evans' performance in a recent game for Scotland. Words were exchanged and fisticuffs only narrowly avoided by the intervention of other players and the calm words of captain Bertie Peacock. It was kept out of the newspapers, but Glasgow being Glasgow, word got out and rumours spread. The way they played, however, would have given no one any encouragement to think that they had fallen out.

Celtic had long had great players. Willie Fernie, Bertie Peacock, Bobby Collins, Bobby Evans, Charlie Tully and

Neil Mochan were as good as anyone, but they didn't always gel and produce the football of which they were capable. They did so on 19 October 1957, however, and Rangers were simply swept aside. By half-time Sammy Wilson and Neil Mochan had scored, in the second half Billy McPhail scored a hat-trick, Neil Mochan got another and, just in time, Willie Fernie sunk a penalty awarded by the relentlessly fair referee Jack Mowat. In between all that, Rangers had pulled one back through Billy Simpson, but the astonishing score of 7-1 was one which would haunt Rangers for many years.

It was the biggest score between the two clubs and remains the record for a major cup final in Great Britain. There was serious trouble at the Rangers end as the League Cup was being presented to Bertie Peacock. Rangers supporters went around in a profound state of shock for some time after. They never recovered that season, for Hearts won the league and Clyde the Scottish Cup.

The teams were:

Celtic: Beattie, Donnelly and Fallon, Fernie, Evans and Peacock, Tully, Collins, McPhail, Wilson and Mochan

Rangers: Niven, Shearer and Caldow, McColl, Valentine and Davis, Scott, Simpson, Murray, Baird and Hubbard

Referee: Mr J Mowat, Rutherglen

Celtic's great triumph is deservedly commemorated to this day in song and story by their supporters, but it remains a mystery why they didn't do this more often, and indeed what happened to their fine team after that. Within a matter of weeks, the squad began to disintegrate. Some like Sean Fallon

THE SCOTTISH LEAGUE CUP

and Charlie Tully got old, but Fernie, Collins and Evans were allowed to depart with disastrous results for the club who now entered upon a dark period of their history. They had won the Scottish League Cup two years in a row, but it would be a long time before they were successful again. The League Cup now went east.

The year 1958 was a time when football was always in the news. In February, there was the tragedy of the Manchester United plane crash in Munich. In the summer, Scotland took part in the Sweden World Cup, now more accessible than previously as more and more households were able to afford a television. Scotland were predictably dreadful but there were hints that it was going to happen when television also showed them going down 0-4 to England at Hampden in April and the laughable (if it had not been tragic) spectacle of the SFA failing to appoint a manager and hoping that things would turn out okay. Four years ago the manager had resigned halfway through the World Cup; this year they didn't even have one! It was scarcely believable, but it was the way the football was run in Scotland at that time.

Hearts won the Scottish League in 1958 and the Tynecastle men now treated themselves to their second League Cup as well. It did not look that way, however, when Rangers beat them 3-0 at Ibrox in the opening fixture, treating them with the contempt that almost seemed to say, 'How dare you win the league last year?' But Hearts fought back to beat them narrowly 2-1 at Tynecastle and dealt with Third Lanark and Raith Rovers a great deal better than Rangers did. Celtic also qualified by beating Clyde at Shawfield comprehensively on opening day and maintaining their form in the other sectional matches.

Partick Thistle qualified by fending off a challenge from Motherwell on the last day but there was real drama in the other section when Kilmarnock just got the better of Hibs. Hibs came to Rugby Park two points ahead of Kilmarnock but such was their goal average that any win by Kilmarnock would qualify the home side. Kilmarnock scored twice in a couple of minutes in the first half and looked secure until McLeod pulled one back for Hibs with only eight minutes remaining. The last minutes were great entertainment for the fans and the home fans were mightily relieved to hear the final whistle.

The other qualifiers were Dunfermline Athletic, who had a 100per cent record; Arbroath, who had to beat Stranraer in the supplementary round; and Cowdenbeath and Ayr United who needed a draw in their last fixture at Forfar Athletic to make it. For the first time, the quarter-finals were to be played in successive midweeks on 10 and 17 September (the Scottish League now feeling that they would rather keep Saturdays for league fixtures) and the draw paired all the First Division teams with the Second Division teams.Perhaps it was because of the nature of the draw or perhaps it was because of the games being played in two midweeks, but the quarter-finals lacked their usual interest. Celtic, for example, beat Cowdenbeath easily over the two legs and Hearts beat Ayr United 8-2. Dunfermline put up a good fight against Kilmarnock, at least in the second leg, but still lost 4-7, and the only really close tie was between Arbroath and Partick Thistle. Arbroath, who would earn promotion at the end of the season, lost 1-2 at Firhill, and at Gayfield failed by only a whisker to beat Partick on aggregate after a 1-1 draw.

A new factor had entered the equation as well. Several clubs now had floodlights. There had been a certain resistance to this by the authorities in the Scottish League and the SFA, but the floodlights were now tried and tested and there was the undeniable new phenomenon of the European Cup, played in midweek and attracting large crowds under floodlights. The semi-finals on Wednesday, 1 October did not involve Hampden because it did not yet have floodlights (Queen's Park were ultra-conservative, as always) so the Celtic v Partick Thistle game was scheduled for Ibrox and Hearts took on Kilmarnock at Easter Road. The games kicked off at night, and such forward-looking thinking was awarded by reasonably large crowds of 41,000 at Easter Road and approximately the same at Ibrox, in spite of it being a rainy night.

Partick Thistle beat Celtic 2-1 at Ibrox. This game could be seen as the start of the decline of Celtic until the arrival of Jock Stein in 1965, for it meant that they had failed to defend the Scottish League Cup which they had won for the past two years. Their 7-1 team was now much changed. Evans was injured but Bobby Collins had been transferred to Everton, apparently because he had been seen as a troublemaker, and there was a conscious effort to introduce new young players. Some, like Billy McNeill and Bertie Auld, came good; others less so. But Partick Thistle, despite an injury to their goalkeeper Tommy Ledgerwood which feckless Celtic finishing failed to capitalise on, scored through Davie McParland and Johnny McKenzie. Celtic's consolation goal was too late to make any material difference. Thistle were now through to their third League Cup Final of the decade.

A packed Easter Road saw a fine performance from Hearts which showed why they were the League champions.

John Cumming and Dave Mackay kept a tight rein on the Kilmarnock forwards, and Hearts scored three goals without reply, one from full-back George Thomson in the first half – a lucky affair when the Kilmarnock goalkeeper was baulked from diving by one of his own men – and then two goals within a minute of each other in the second half from regular goalscorers Ian Crawford and Willie Bauld.

It was Hearts and Partick Thistle for the final at Hampden on 25 October 1958. Once again, the issue of the lack of floodlights at Hampden became an important one since, to allow for the possibility of extra time, the Scottish League was obliged to bring the kick-off forward to 2.30pm when the other games kicked off at 3pm. An investment in floodlights might have obviated this necessity. Hearts were certainly the favourites for this game, but Gair Henderson stated in his preview in the *Evening Times* that it was 'far from a foregone conclusion'.

There was no need for extra time because, sadly for the fans of Partick Thistle in the 59,960 crowd, the game turned out to be very one-sided. After Willie Bauld opened the scoring in the fifth minute, the result was indeed a foregone conclusion. Hearts had somewhat controversially dropped their prodigiously talented Alec Young in favour of Jimmy Murray and it was Murray who added the second goal. Before half-time, both Bauld and Murray had scored again to make it 4-0. There was then a flicker of a Thistle revival when George Smith scored soon after half-time but Johnny Hamilton then scored a sublime goal to make the final score 5-1. Hearts finished well on top and long before the final whistle; although Thistle kept fighting, the crowd and the radio commentators knew the identity of the League Cup winners. The final was as one-sided as last year's Celtic v

Rangers one had been. Partick Thistle, the old unpredictables, had failed to turn up.

The teams were:

Hearts: Marshall, Kirk and Thomson, Mackay, Glidden and Cumming, Hamilton, Murray, Baird, Wardhaugh and Crawford

Partick Thistle: Ledgerwood, Hogan and Donlevy, Mathers, Davidson and Wright, McKenzie, Thomson, Smith, McParland and Ewing

Referee: RH Davidson, Airdrie

Poor Thistle had now lost three League Cup finals in six years. It would be Davie Meiklejohn's last big Hampden occasion as well, for he was fated to die suddenly at a game at Airdrie at the start of the following season. Hearts had now won the League Cup twice and were seemingly going from strength to strength. However, they narrowly lost out to Rangers in the Scottish Cup in an early round and they would lose the league championship next April in scarcely believable circumstances. On 19 April, Rangers lost on the last day. So too did Hearts, unable to beat a mediocre Celtic side at Parkhead who thus achieved the unlikely feat of winning the Scottish League for Rangers! St Mirren won the Scottish Cup, but Hearts were far from finished with the Scottish League Cup.

By summer of 1959, television had not so much arrived as was beginning to take over. Some objected to it on bogus religious grounds, others thought it would hinder children's educational progress, but the financial problem of getting a TV was alleviated by the number of firms who were encouraging renting to make it something that most households could afford. In the meantime, prosperity increased – some working-class families even aspired to a car, let alone a TV – and the Conservative Prime Minister Harold Macmillan felt able to call a general election in October on the slogan 'You've never had it so good'. He won handsomely.

The Scottish League Cup opened in early August as usual but very few people could have predicted the four qualifiers from the First Division sections. Hearts were there certainly, but no Rangers, no Celtic, no Hibs, no Aberdeen and no Dundee. They were joined by Raith Rovers, Third Lanark and Motherwell. Motherwell were by some distance the most impressive of the qualifiers, winning all their games, including Rangers twice. As the other teams in the section were Dundee and Hibs, this was no mean feat for the steel men. Raith Rovers had beaten Celtic at Stark's Park on opening day and never really looked back apart from a narrow 0-1 defeat in the return fixture at Parkhead, while Third Lanark, now managed by ex-Rangers George Young and playing very impressively, had few problems in beating Dunfermline, Clyde and Scottish Cup holders St Mirren.

From the Second Division sections came Arbroath, Falkirk, East Fife, Cowdenbeath and Dundee United. Falkirk duly got the better of Dundee United in the supplementary round while Arbroath (who were in the First Division having been promoted last year) were possibly rather fortunate to end up above Albion Rovers. East Fife, keen to keep up their great League Cup traditions, were undefeated in their section.

We thus had three Fife teams in the last eight. East Fife were paired with Cowdenbeath, a pairing from which Cowdenbeath emerged, while Raith Rovers lost narrowly to Arbroath. Third Lanark beat Falkirk and the tie of the round (which would have made a very good final) was Hearts v Motherwell. The first leg between the two of them at Fir Park was a 1-1 thriller with the tie in such balance that 40,000, in circumstances which were highly dangerous, were persuaded to cram into Tynecastle for the return leg. Two men who would later make their names on Merseyside – Alec Young and Ian St John – scored for their respective teams, but then the decisive moment came in the head injury to Motherwell's influential centre-half John Martis. In pre-substitute days, this tipped the balance very much in favour of the Edinburgh side and Hearts scored two quick goals while Martis was off being treated. Motherwell never recovered.

Of the other ties, Arbroath needed extra time to beat Raith Rovers at Arbroath but the other two ties were more clear cut. Cowdenbeath reached one of the few peaks of their history by disposing of East Fife with a degree of ease, while the press were all impressed by the way that Third Lanark, another club on whom the sun seldom shone these days, dealt with Falkirk, goals coming from Bobby Craig and the Hilley brothers, Dave and Ian.

The semi-finals were held on Wednesday, 7 October 1959, the very eve of the 1959 General Election. Third Lanark took on Arbroath at Ibrox in a game that failed to attract more than 10,000. Arbroath brought a few busloads but Third Lanark's support was rapidly dwindling. Arbroath put up a brave fight but an impressive spell at the start of the second half by Third Lanark gave them a 3-0 victory and saw them into their first-ever Scottish League Cup Final, their first big Hampden occasion since 1936. There were more spectators at Easter Road for the other semi-final between Hearts and Cowdenbeath and a great deal more goals – 12 in all. Second

Division Cowdenbeath clearly decided to give it a go and scored three goals, but in the process conceded nine! They were given a great round of applause from the Hearts support at the end, a crowd that had now recovered from their shock of seeing ex-Hibee Gordon Smith (once of the Famous Five) in their team.

The smart money on 24 October was on Hearts, so far undefeated this season, but there was a tremendous amount of sympathy for Third Lanark, generally regarded as the poorest team in Glasgow and beginning to struggle with the financial problems that were to kill them eight years later in 1967. At the moment, though, they were well organised with George Young as their manager and, although a part-time team, they had some fine players in the Hilley brothers, Matt Gray and Joe McInnes.

Founded as the Third Lanark Rifle Volunteers, they were founder members of the SFA, winning the Scottish Cup in 1889 and 1905, and the Scottish League in 1904. Since losing in the final of the Scottish Cup to Hearts in 1906, they had played good football but had won nothing. They had loads of nicknames: the Hi Hi His, Thirds, the Warriors, the Sodgers and the Redcoats to name a few, but success had been elusive. They were no strangers to Second Division football and, although no one knew it, the Scottish League Cup Final of 1959/60 would prove to be their last big occasion. Physically very close to Hampden (their ground had been one of the precursors to the modern Hampden Park and had staged cup finals and international games), they would have the support of all Glasgow on this occasion.

In total, 57,994 assembled for the 2.30pm kick-off on a dullish day at Hampden in which the sun occasionally poked through the clouds but more often disappeared. There was also a capricious breeze and this was at least partly responsible for Third's early goal. A high ball seemed to hold up in the wind and it duly deceived Gordon Marshall in the Hearts goal to allow Matt Gray to finish the job and put the Thirds into the lead. This incident further confirmed the impression that the King's Park goal was a goalkeeper's nightmare.

The Cathkin men held the lead for a good hour but were indebted to some fine goalkeeping from little Jocky Robertson, the legendary goalkeeper of Thirds. Hopes were beginning to grow among the Cathkin faithful that this might just be the day that would end the trophy famine which had lasted since the Russo-Japanese War of 1905, but it was not to be. After the turnaround, Hearts' prolonged battering of the Third Lanark goal eventually took effect and it was Johnny Hamilton from a good 30 yards who broke the deadlock. Their attempts to walk the ball into the net had not succeeded, but this was a great goal. It broke the resistance, for a few minutes after that Alec Young ran through the defence and put Hearts on top.

From then on, Hearts took command and, although Thirds had a few half-chances near the end, Hearts deserved their win. They were clearly an accomplished side and would deservedly win the Scottish League as well in 1960. They had now won the trophy three times in six years and joined East Fife on the top of the tree with three victories. Everyone, however, was sorry for Third Lanark. Life might have been different for them, if they had won.

The teams were:

Hearts: Marshall, Kirk and Thomson, Bowman, Cumming and Higgins, Smith, Crawford, Young, Blackwood and Hamilton

Third Lanark: Robertson, Lewis and Brown, Reilly, McCallum and Cunningham, McInnes, Craig, D Hilley, Gray and I Hilley

Referee: RH Davidson, Airdrie

CHAPTER FOUR

THE RANGERS RETURN
1960–1964

THE EARLY 60s were the time when Rangers took control of Scottish football, and the League Cup in particular, with four wins out of five. They had a good side, very efficient and competent if perhaps lacking the flair of Hibs in the early 1950s or Celtic in the late 1960s, and they were good enough to beat most teams who faced them. Dundee and Kilmarnock had their moments but, being provincial teams, they failed to maintain a challenge. Hibs and Hearts had possibly peaked, Celtic were cursed with dreadful management and Aberdeen consistently failed to rise above the mediocre.

Rangers had, incredibly, failed to win the League Cup throughout the 1950s. They were still haunted by the 7-1 defeat by Celtic in 1957, something that hurt every bit as much as Celtic's 1967 European Cup success would do in the future. But in 1960, they had won the Scottish Cup for the first time since 1953 and their supporters felt that a success in the League Cup was also overdue. The realisation that

Scottish football was no longer the best in the world (if they hadn't realised it before) came home to Rangers when they conceded 12 goals on aggregate to Eintracht Frankfurt in the European Cup semi-final of 1960, and then the same Eintracht conceded seven to Real Madrid in that never-to-be forgotten final at Hampden in May 1960.

The 1960 League Cup sectional stages were remarkable for several things. One was the necessity for a play-off in one section and the other was that there was an all-Glasgow section of Celtic, Rangers, Partick Thistle and Third Lanark. Celtic drew first blood by winning 3-2 at Ibrox and with two games left seemed certain to qualify, but then chose to obey the self-destruction complex which prevailed at Parkhead and lost to Partick Thistle 1-2 in the second-to-last game. They lost then to Rangers, also 1-2, on a torrentially wet Saturday. Thus Rangers found themselves in the quarter-finals. Kilmarnock and Dundee joined them, but last year's winners, Hearts, didn't.

The circumstances were odd and unprecedented. Hearts' 2-1 win over Motherwell on the last day coupled with Clyde's 0-0 draw with St Mirren meant that both Hearts and Clyde finished level on points and goal average, and a play-off was necessary to determine who was to go through. It was in this game at neutral Celtic Park that Hearts fell temporarily out of love with the Scottish League Cup as they went down 1-2 to Clyde. Clyde failed to capitalise and went on to lose to Kilmarnock both home and away in the quarter-finals – although it was hardly surprising that they lost the first leg, for they were compelled to play two days after the play-off for the sectional stages. Meanwhile, Hamilton beat Stenhousemuir and, in a couple of close games, Queen of the South got the better of Dumbarton. The tie of the round, however, was the clash of the titans between Dundee and Rangers.

Dundee, a side hinting at future greatness, qualified very impressively in their section and did well to restrict Rangers to 1-0 at Ibrox. They felt that they could win through at Dens Park and might well have done so if their centre-half Billy Smith had not injured himself and been compelled to play on the wing while Alan Gilzean played at left-half alongside Ian Ure. Rangers were three up on aggregate at half-time but then Dundee fought back magnificently to level the scores before Rangers scored two late goals to win the tie 5-3, but in a way which singularly failed to impress the writer of the traditionally anti-Rangers *Glasgow Herald*; 30,000 were crammed into Dens Park to see this game.

The semi-finals were an anti-climax after all that. On 12 October at Ibrox, Kilmarnock beat Hamilton Accies 5-1. In the other one (delayed a week because Rangers were playing in the European Cup Winners' Cup), Rangers went to Celtic Park and beat Queen of the South 7-0 with a young man called Baxter, who had recently joined them from Raith Rovers, orchestrating the show to set up a League Cup Final between Rangers and Kilmarnock. By coincidence these two teams had contested the Scottish Cup Final in April and the score had been 2-0 to Rangers. By a further coincidence, this was the score on this occasion as well, although the circumstances were quite different.

The teams were:

Rangers: Niven, Shearer and Caldow, Davis, Paterson and Baxter, Scott, McMillan, Millar, Brand and Wilson

Kilmarnock: J Brown, Richmond and Watson, Beattie, Toner and Kennedy, H Brown, McInally, Kerr, Black and Muir

Referee: T Wharton, Clarkston

Rangers' supporters, aware that 11 years had passed since they won the Scottish League Cup, were beginning to wonder if there was a hoodoo on this cup in the same way as there had been over the Scottish Cup between 1903 and 1928. Their team was, however, playing well and with confidence. Kilmarnock, on the other hand, were also a good side and aware that they had let themselves down badly in the Scottish Cup Final of April of that year. But they had a good manager in ex-Ranger Willie Waddell and an enthusiastic bunch of players. Most newspapers on the morning of the game predicted a good fight from the Ayrshire men but an almost inevitable win for Rangers.

So it turned out. The crowd was a good 82,063 and they saw a good first half in which Rangers led by 1-0 thanks to a goal created by Jimmy Millar for Ralph Brand who scored brilliantly. In the second half Kilmarnock came out fighting, but Cyril Horne of the *Glasgow Herald* summed Kilmarnock up well when he said they had 'abundant spirit but no great forward ability'. The same writer also castigated them for allowing no fewer than four corner kicks to go out of play. The professional Rangers soaked up the pressure and then killed the game with quarter of an hour to go. Alec Scott on the right wing sent over what seemed to be a cross but the Hampden swirl once again played tricks and Kilmarnock's goalkeeper and captain Jimmy Brown (an interesting, colourful character who always wore a jockey cap) missed the ball altogether and the ball went in off the post.

Rangers then simply played the game out and had now recorded their third Scottish League Cup success. It was also the third League Cup for manager Scot Symon who had won it twice with East Fife. The trophy had now been played 15 times. Rangers, East Fife and Hearts had all won it three times, Celtic and Dundee twice each while Motherwell and Aberdeen had been once winners. It was now well established as an integral part of the Scottish season – some had doubted its ability to do that – and the idea of the trophy being over and done with by the end of October was a good one. The final was usually played on the same Saturday as the clocks changed from British Summer Time to Greenwich Mean Time and there was a clear symbolism that autumn was passing, and that winter with early kick-offs, muddy pitches and seemingly inevitable Scottish rain was now here.

One bad aspect of the Scottish League Cup was the adverse effect that it had on regional competitions like the Glasgow Cup, for example. The Glasgow Cup used to be played every October but now was struggling to find a spot, sometimes being played at the end of the season and inevitably edging out the Glasgow Charity Cup which would disappear after 1960. Yet the Scottish League Cup was itself under threat from Europe. Already a game had been postponed, to allow Rangers to play a European fixture, now a new competition – the European Cup Winners' Cup – had appeared on the scene. Floodlights were now sprouting up all over the country, with even the conservative Hampden having reluctant plans for their construction. As Prime Minister Harold Macmillan would say, in a different context, 'the winds of change' were blowing.

But the Scottish League Cup returned to Ibrox in season 1961/62, a season which was quite remarkable in some ways. It saw a prolonged but ultimately unsuccessful attempt by the national team to reach the World Cup in Chile and, on the domestic scene, the rise of Dundee to win the Scottish League championship playing football often described by the late Bob Crampsey as the best he had seen in Scotland.

As the season opened with the League Cup sections (as normal) there was no indication of how good Dundee would be. They were well beaten at Ibrox on the first Wednesday night of the season, although they did earn a draw on the return at Dens Park as Rangers qualified with a degree of ease. Celtic, last year's beaten finalists in the Scottish Cup, could not get past St Johnstone, losing both home and away, with the game at Muirton Park, Perth showing one of the worst displays of hooliganism ever seen in the Fair City. Celtic had a nasty and frustrated support in those days. The team's performance had been profoundly disappointing but that could provide no possible excuse for what occurred.

There had also been crowd trouble, albeit of a different sort, on the opening day at Cathkin Park for the Third Lanark v Rangers game, but there was nothing really malicious about it. The gates had had to be closed but the walls were not particularly high or difficult to climb over and many fit, young men duly did so. In addition, an exit gate had earlier been broken down by frustrated fans trying to get in to see the game through the decidedly slow and primitive turnstiles. As a result, the ground was distinctly overcrowded. Fortunately, there did not seem to be any serious injuries, but encroachment meant that the game had to be stopped on several occasions with the referee Mr Phillips threatening to abandon things altogether. All this had followed prolonged discussions about whether fans were going to come back to football matches or not as 'they' (the football authorities) had raised the admission price to three shillings!

The toughest group was the one involving Hearts, Kilmarnock, Raith Rovers and St Mirren. Although all teams took points off each other, crucially Hearts won both the head-to-heads against Kilmarnock and that was enough to see them through. Kilmarnock, last year's finalists, put up some good performances – 6-1 v St Mirren and 7-1 v Raith Rovers (at Stark's Park) – but, ultimately, Hearts, still playing some good football, were too good for them.

A great deal of interest centred on Dunfermline Athletic, very much the *nouveaux riches arrivistes* of Scottish football. They had won the Scottish Cup last season for the first time and, now managed by Jock Stein, radiated ambition and desire to go places. Unfortunately, they lost to Aberdeen in the opening game at East End Park and never really recovered enough, even though they beat qualifiers Motherwell on the last day.

The other sections were won by Stirling Albion, Hamilton Accies and the team whose glory days in this competition might have passed but still made a mark, East Fife. They all won with a degree of ease, but in another section, Ayr United won through following a thrilling last-day game at Brockville when Falkirk almost beat them, the game ending in a 4-4 draw on a day when parts of Scotland were bedevilled by flash floods and thunderstorms. Albion Rovers won the five-team section nine, but East Fife were too good for them in the supplementary round and won themselves a tie against Rangers in the quarter-finals.

It was perhaps unfortunate that East Fife had to play their first leg at Ibrox, for although they played well there and impressed the press and the Ibrox support, the 3-1 win for Rangers meant more or less that the tie was over. The scoreline was duly replicated at Bayview the following week. Hearts had more than a little trouble in beating Hamilton Accies, and Ayr United continued their tradition of exciting League Cup ties, although this time they were on the wrong side of a narrow extra-time defeat as Stirling Albion (previously undistinguished competitors in the Scottish League Cup) came from behind to pip them in extra time at Annfield.

But the most exciting tie of the round was between Motherwell and St Johnstone. Both teams paid great attention to good scientific football with the emphasis on passing and running, and both games were much appreciated by their fans. St Johnstone, now managed by Bobby Brown, won 3-2 at Fir Park, then held Motherwell to a 1-1 draw at Muirton Park to qualify for the League Cup semi-finals for the first time and to introduce some footballing excitement to an area of Scotland where there had never been too much of it in the past.

When the draw paired Rangers with St Johnstone and Hearts with Stirling Albion in the semi-finals on Wednesday, 11 October, hardly anyone expected anything other than a Rangers v Hearts final. So it turned out, but not without some major scary moments for the two big sides, for both games went to extra time.

The crowd of 41,000 at Parkhead saw a thrilling contest in which Rangers were 0-2 down at half-time, pulled the game round to level it before 90 minutes and then scored the winner in extra time. Gardiner and Bell put the Saints ahead at half-time, but then Rangers crucially scored in the first minute of the second half and then with a penalty late on in the game before Davie Wilson headed the winner. Although the *Evening Times* the following night paid tribute to the tactical nous of Scot Symon, the Rangers manager, it was also quite happy to use words like 'luck' in the context of this performance.

In the other semi at Easter Road, 19,000 saw Hearts behind for a long period of the second half after Dyson had opened the scoring and Hearts indebted not for the first time to Willie Bauld for bringing them back into the game. In extra time, full-time training played its part. The exhausted Stirling Albion conceded a good goal to Willie Wallace and never really looked like getting back into it, even though they had squandered a good chance just before 90 minutes. Hearts too had needed more than a fair share of luck to join Rangers in the final on 28 October.

The build-up was characterised by a certain amount of criticism of Hearts' team formation. It was 4-2-4, considered almost to be treason by the press, the public and even the Tynecastle support who thought that the Scottish 2-3-5 was not only sacrosanct but the only way in which football could possibly be played; 4-2-4 was 'continental' (pronounced with a distinct sneer) and 'not real football'. Shame on Hearts! But other teams would soon follow and, undeniably, Hearts were playing the system with a degree of success. But they had no wingers!

Hampden could kick off its League Cup finals on the last Saturday of October with a 3pm kick-off since it now, a year or two behind most grounds, had floodlights. They were magnificent in the opinion of all who saw them, and had been hanselled on 17 October, some 11 days before the League Cup

Final, in a game between Rangers and Eintracht Frankfurt. Rangers lost, but the fact that they had been invited to play in the opening game of the Hampden floodlights did little to dispel the commonly held belief in those days that Rangers, for all their offensive and anxious sectarian recruitment policy, were more intimately involved in the Scottish football establishment than was desirable.

Both Rangers and Hearts were off to a good start in the league but the general impression was that Rangers were just a little better, certainly than they had been in recent years. A crowd of 88,635 attended the final, a huge crowd, some of whom were delayed by a huge fire at the Metropole Theatre which covered Glasgow in smoke, but they saw what was generally agreed to have been a poor final. Rangers scored in the first half with a 35-yard shot from Jimmy Millar which took everyone by surprise, including Hearts goalkeeper Gordon Marshall who made no effort to stop it.

After that, Rangers took command but were never totally convincing. Yet they looked likely winners until a clumsy tackle (but not a dirty one) by Harry Davis on Alan Gordon was punished by a penalty. Only ten minutes remained but John Cumming kept calm and equalised the tie. The penalty award (dispelling the widely held view that Rangers never got penalties awarded against them) was not universally agreed with and one Rangers fan ran on the field at full time in an attempt to punch the referee, Bobby Davidson.

Extra time took place under the floodlights. Rangers came close on one occasion but there was no further scoring and full time came with a feeling of anti-climax. The League Cup was forgotten about for a few weeks, simply because there was no available date to play the replay. It was scheduled for Monday,

4 December but was snowed off until the appallingly late night of Monday, 18 December. Scotland were embroiled in a prolonged World Cup campaign and there were other internationals as well as European games with Rangers involved in a barely believable saga against Vorwarts Berlin.

It would have made sense to postpone the replayed final until the spring but it went ahead on a night of freezing fog a week before Christmas. Not surprisingly the crowd was down to 47,500 with the Hearts support in particular hard hit by difficult driving conditions from Edinburgh. TV highlights programmes on BBC and STV were compelled to apologise for the poor quality of the pictures from foggy Hampden and the Hearts supporters who stayed away did themselves a favour, for Rangers were well on top throughout with goals from Jimmy Millar, Ralph Brand and Ian McMillan as distinct from one by Norrie Davidson. All the action came early on and the rest of the game was dull. It was not one of the Scottish League Cup's better nights, but no one could tell the Rangers supporters that as they cheered the presentation of the cup and the medals to their players. It was their fourth Scottish League Cup success.

The teams were:

Rangers: Ritchie, Shearer and Caldow, Davis, Baillie and Baxter, Scott, McMillan, Millar, Brand and Wilson

Hearts: Cruickshank, Kirk and Holt, Cumming, Polland and Higgins, Ferguson, Davidson, Bauld, Blackwood and Hamilton

Referee: RH Davidson, Airdrie

When the draw was made for the sectional stages of the 1962/63 Scottish League Cup, there was one section which stood out over all the others, and it was the one which contained Hearts, Celtic and the two Dundee teams. Dundee were on the crest of a wave having deservedly won the league championship last year, Celtic had promised for long and, we were told, were about to deliver, Hearts were last season's defeated finalists and then there was Dundee United, a genuine success story of a team who had come up from the Second Division after decades of underachievement and, with a new stand and a redeveloped stadium, had intentions to stay in the First.

The section lived up to its billing with the lead changing hands throughout, everyone beating one another with teams tending to win their home games. Celtic came to Tannadice Park on 1 September needing to beat Dundee United to win the section. In a game which had everything, including a ball that was clearly over the line and the goal not given by referee Hugh Phillips, Celtic just failed to score and were pipped at the post by Hearts who recovered from some substandard performances and beat Dundee at Tynecastle.

It would be wrong to think that this was the only exciting section, though. Rangers were taken to the last day as well, having had to fight off a challenge from a revivalist but still infuriatingly inconsistent Hibs, and, similarly, Aberdeen, who had virtually disappeared from the competition for several years, put up a bit of a fight before losing out to Partick Thistle. The only First Division section which did not go to the last day was the one won by Kilmarnock, whereas in the Second Division sections, things were equally close with all sections going to the last day and having to be decided on the tightest of goal average deciders.

On the last day both Clyde and St Johnstone won 4-1. This meant that St Johnstone had scored 18 goals and Clyde

17, and as both teams had conceded seven goals, this was enough to qualify St Johnstone by a minuscule percentage difference. They were joined by Queen of the South, Morton and Dumbarton after Dumbarton had disposed of Berwick Rangers in the supplementary round.

Around this time there was a certain amount of criticism around the goal average system for determining qualification in the event of a tie on points. Basically, goals scored were divided by goals conceded and this meant that there was rather too much emphasis on the loss of a goal. It could also lead to a ludicrous situation whereby on the last day a 0-0 draw would see one side qualify whereas a 1-1 draw would see another side in the quarter-finals! There was the additional point that while goal average might make sense over 34 games in the Scottish League, we were dealing here with only six games.

On the other hand, life was certainly exciting in the first part of the season, a point agreed with by the fans who turned out in large numbers, often when the weather was still good for watching the games. Non-qualification was always a disappointment but seldom a disaster because there was still the football to be played in the league campaign, which was just starting.

Perhaps a more valid criticism might have been made about the quarter-finals. The fact that they were two-legged ties often meant that the first leg was a cat-and-mouse affair with neither side willing to give much away; on the other hand, a decisive win for one team in the first leg would render the second leg of little value. Possibly it was better to have one tie and let the luck of the draw decide the venue, or even more revolutionary (and maybe less lucrative, hence the reason that no one seriously suggested it) would be the idea of seeding the eight qualifiers so that the Second Division team would always get a home tie. All these ideas were kicked around in the press, but 'if it ain't broke, don't fix it' is always a sensible maxim and the Scottish League Cup was clearly a success in terms of spectator interest and money-making.

The arguments about the quarter-finals were neither proved nor disproved in 1962. Rangers were booed off the field at Ibrox after a dreadful 1-1 draw against Dumbarton but they had won the first leg comfortably, so it didn't matter. Hearts won both legs against Morton with a degree of ease and the second leg saw a poor crowd at Tynecastle with many early departures. On the other hand, the remaining two quarter-finals were absolute thrillers. At Muirton Park, St Johnstone, 0-1 down from the first leg, fought back to take Queen of the South to extra time and then won comfortably in that period, while the Kilmarnock v Partick Thistle tie which ended 5-2 for Killie nevertheless was in doubt for a long time until Killie took command.

The two semi-finals were set for 10 October: Hearts v St Johnstone at Easter Road and Rangers v Kilmarnock at Hampden. Fears of fog disrupting both games proved unfounded and both games were thrillers. The 4-0 scoreline for Hearts over St Johnstone is rather deceptive, for St Johnstone played well throughout and it was only the sheer professionalism of Hearts and in particular their rising star Willie Wallace who won the day for them by scoring the goals when the opportunity presented itself.

The other tie drew a huge 77,000 to Hampden to see Rangers and Kilmarnock. They were currently the best two teams in Scotland but on this occasion it was Kilmarnock who won through. It was a game not without controversy, however. Kilmarnock scored first early on. Rangers scored twice through Ralph Brand and then seemed to score a third one from John Greig, but referee Bobby Davidson (never the darling of Ibrox following a brave handball decision in the Scottish Cup semi-final of 1958) ruled correctly that Brand had helped the ball in with his hand. Davidson's popularity in Govan dipped even further when Kilmarnock equalised not long after that to make the score 2-2, rather than the expected 3-1 at half-time.

It was then that Killie manager Willie Waddell spotted a weakness in Rangers' defence and that was in the air. His instructions were to send in high balls and this paid dividends within the last ten minutes when Bertie Black headed home a corner kick to put Killie into the final and to deny Rangers the chance of winning the Scottish League Cup for three years in a row.

The 1956/57 League Cup Final was played with the world under the shadow of potential war in Egypt. Fortunately, that one went away, but 27 October 1962 saw an even greater threat to world peace in the shape of the Cuban Missile Crisis, where the USA and the Soviet Union stood up to each other with nuclear war clearly threatened before common sense prevailed and an agreement was reached. The Soviets would take their nuclear weapons away from Cuba if the US did the same in Turkey. In retrospect, it was possibly not quite as scary as it was portrayed. Indeed, it could be described as a superpower version of 'nuclear handbags'. But, at the time, people were understandably frightened for the future of the planet.

No doubt the matter was discussed at length as the 51,280 made their way through the unpleasant wind and rain to

Hampden. It was a difficult game to call. Hearts had more flair with fair-haired Willie Hamilton singled out as a class act, but Kilmarnock were more compact, determined and ruthlessly professional.

The game was a poor one in the wet blustery conditions, but at half-time Hearts were 1-0 up. A brilliant piece of play saw Willie Hamilton make ground, beat a few men and then pass to Norrie Davidson to score an easy goal. In the second half, Kilmarnock came more into it with the benefit of the wind blowing towards the King's Park goal, but the grim defending and attention to duty of Hearts seemed to have won the day for them as the minutes ticked away. But then in injury time came the moment which defines this League Cup Final.

A free kick was foolishly conceded by the Hearts defence too far out for a direct shot. Jim Richmond took it and the ball found the head of Frank Beattie who headed down and into the net to score a goal. Or so everyone thought, but referee Tom Wharton was of the opinion that Beattie had used a hand and ruled the score out. Pressurised into consulting his linesman, he did so, but it was still no goal. Seconds later, with the crowd in an uproar, he blew for full time to indicate that Hearts had won the League Cup for the fourth time.

Boos and vitriol filled the air as the League Cup was presented and it was a long time before Mr Wharton was accepted with any degree of equanimity by the Kilmarnock support, but most writers agreed that Hearts had been the better team and were worthy of their win. They returned to Edinburgh in triumph and TV coverage that night featured the singer Andy Stewart, more famous for his 'Scottish Soldier', singing 'The Heart of Midlothian' instead. 'In the capital of Scotland by the great kirk of St Giles …' But those Kilmarnock fans who were jealous of Hearts that day would have no cause to be. History would wreak a bitter revenge on Hearts (Kilmarnock would do so by winning the league at Tynecastle in April 1965), and a long 35-and-a-bit years would pass before Hearts would have any further cause to celebrate. Someone, it was claimed, put a curse on Hearts that day. It certainly worked.

The teams were:

Hearts: Marshall, Polland and Holt, Cumming, Barry and Higgins, Wallace, Paton, Davidson, W Hamilton and J Hamilton

Kilmarnock: McLaughlin, Richmond and Watson, O'Connor, McGrory and Beattie, Brown, Black, Kerr, McInally and McIlroy

Referee: T Wharton, Clarkston

Sex was a major topic of conversation as the football season started in 1963. Nothing unusual about that, but this time it concerned the Minister of War John Profumo. He had had a dalliance with a lady called Christine Keeler. He was by no means the first or last Cabinet Minister to do that sort of thing, but Christine had simultaneously been having it away with an attaché at the Soviet Embassy. This represented a security risk and Profumo had to go, and so too, eventually, did Prime Minister Harold Macmillan who may have known all about it and tried to cover it up.

This kept British newspapers going all summer (and there was the added bonus for them of the Great Train Robbery as well) but the football season came round, opening in very heavy rain on 10 August. Rangers had won a league and cup double last season, beating Celtic 3-0 in the replayed cup final. As luck would have it, the season opened with an Old Firm clash at Parkhead. Celtic, who had not recovered from last year, were frankly beaten before they started and collapsed woefully to a Rangers side that they were simply afraid of. Rangers qualified with little bother while Celtic supporters showed every sign of not being able to take much more.

Motherwell, Hibs and Dundee also qualified, all with a degree of ease, holders Hearts never really recovering from a 0-3 defeat at Fir Park on the first Wednesday night. The team that really impressed in the Second Division sections was Greenock Morton who finished with a 100 per cent record. Things would happen in a big way in Greenock this year. They were joined by these inveterate qualifiers East Fife, Stirling Albion and Berwick Rangers who surprisingly beat St Johnstone in the supplementary round.

St Johnstone had qualified from section seven on goal average in what had been a two-horse race between them and East Stirlingshire, both teams finishing with ten points out of 12. They were then confidently expected to beat the Englishmen from Berwick, for the winners of section nine seldom made any further progress, but this year was different as Berwick drew 2-2 at Muirton Park, then won 4-2 at Shielfield Park two days later.

The quarter-finals were symmetrical in several respects this year. The first legs on 11 September were all draws, in the return leg the home team won in every case. The best game was a thriller at Dens Park when Dundee and Hibs shared six goals, while East Fife, with only 11 fit men available, surprised and delighted their fans by holding the seemingly all-powerful

Rangers 1-1. The best game, however, was at Motherwell where 'Well, who had yet to concede a goal in this year's competition, were lucky to preserve this record against a spirited Morton side who finished the game with only ten men.

The return legs on 18 September were all 2-0 with one exception, and that was at Berwick where the home side snatched a win in the very last minute over Stirling Albion in the tie that attracted the smallest crowd but nevertheless provided the best entertainment. Berwick's first appearance in the semi-final would be against the other Rangers, from Glasgow, who qualified with a 2-0 win and a degree of ease over East Fife. Hibs made a reappearance in the semi-finals for the first time in a decade when they beat Dundee at Easter Road and Morton showed the world that their runaway success in the Second Division was no fluke when they beat Motherwell 2-0 at Cappielow, scoring early in each half and holding on to the lead with little bother.

The semi-finals were arranged for separate dates. Rangers earned a great deal of criticism from the fans for their performance against Berwick, even though they won comfortably 3-1 at Hampden on Wednesday, 2 October, but it was the other semi between Morton and Hibs that raised more interest. The first game at Ibrox on Monday, 7 October saw a 1-1 draw, a highly creditable result for the Greenock men considering that Allan McGraw, their star scorer, was injured and only a passenger for the latter half of the game. The game was rescheduled for the following Monday, also at Ibrox, and Morton wrote their names in the history books with a narrow but deserved 1-0 win, the goal coming from a penalty kick halfway through the second half scored by Allan McGraw.

It was by no means unprecedented for a Second Division team to reach the final – East Fife had even won it from the Second Division – but it was unusual and there could be little doubt that the final attracted the imagination of the whole nation, not least because it involved the league leaders of the top two divisions. There seemed to be little that could stop Morton in the Second Division, but Rangers had a point to prove to their own fans. They had just been beaten 0-6 by Real Madrid in the European Cup – something that, added to their defeat by Tottenham Hotspur last year, perhaps indicated that they were not as good as they thought they were and would be susceptible to a challenge from within Scotland as well. Could this come from the totally unexpected quarter of Greenock?

The Scottish League Cup's first-ever six-figure attendance, 105,907, were at Hampden on 26 October to see the final. It was Morton's biggest day since the Scottish Cup Final of 1948 between the same two sides and there were still a few people around who could recall Morton's greatest ever day of 1922 when Jimmy Gourlay scored the goal over Rangers which gave the Greenock men their only moment of glory in the Scottish Cup. Very few people could have been left in Greenock that day, one felt, as Morton ran out to a louder cheer than that which greeted Rangers. It was a final which attracted more than the usual attention in England and abroad as well. The weather was dull but dry with hardly any wind at all (unusual for Hampden) and Morton did themselves proud in the first half, holding Rangers to a 0-0 draw although Rangers had clearly been the better team.

Those of the glass-half-full persuasion in the Morton support wondered whether a huge upset was on the cards.

More realistic assessments suggested that once Rangers scored, that would be that. Indeed, Jim Forrest scored early in the second half and then, Rangers having upped a gear, Forrest scored another three while his cousin Alec Willoughby scored the other to make it 5-0. Morton felt that they had not let themselves down, however, and were given a sporting cheer by the Rangers fans, some of whom looked just a little relieved.

The teams were:

Rangers: Ritchie, Shearer and Provan, Greig, McKinnon and Baxter, Henderson, Willoughby, Forrest, Brand and Watson

Morton: Brown, Boyd and Mallan, Reilly, Kiernan and Strachan, Adamson, Campbell, Stevenson, McGraw and Wilson

Referee: H Phillips, Wishaw

Morton would go on to earn promotion by a veritable country mile, and Rangers, profiting from the feckless management and lack of self-belief of Celtic, the money-grubbing selling of players by Dundee and the infuriating inconsistency of Kilmarnock, won a deserved domestic treble that year. They had now won the Scottish League Cup five times, and seemed unstoppable – in Scotland at least.

In 1964/65 Rangers again qualified from the sectional stage with a degree of ease, a 4-0 win on opening day over Aberdeen seeming to put them on the way to another great season, and certainly sentencing the Dons and their supporters to another season of doom and gloom. The Dundee teams were once again drawn together in the same section and on this occasion it was United who came out on top, defeating Dundee at both Dens Park and Tannadice. It was probably about this time that one could begin to say that United were taking over as the top team in the city. They would show initiative by bringing in Scandinavian footballers later in the season, while Dundee remained trapped in their parsimonious, penny-pinching, pusillanimous institutionalised habits of selling their best players.

Celtic showed a long overdue return to form. After an uncertain start, they beat Kilmarnock, Partick Thistle and Hearts with no little skill and qualified, but not before a vicious game at Rugby Park when Kilmarnock exacted a degree of revenge by crocking Billy McNeill and Bobby Murdoch. Dunfermline Athletic qualified by getting the better of Hibs in the other section, and the Second Division qualifiers were Clyde, Hamilton, Morton and our old friends East Fife who had had a struggle to get the better of section nine winners Forfar Athletic.

Hamilton's qualification had been on goal average over Stranraer and their section had a new team in it going by the geographically absurd name of East Stirlingshire Clydebank. It was the result of an amalgamation of the perpetually struggling East Stirlingshire and a new team called Clydebank who offered them Kilbowie Park for their home games, even though Falkirk and Clydebank are many miles apart. The crazy idea did not go down well with supporters of either side, particularly those of East Stirlingshire, but it lasted a year until the clubs separated.

The quarter-finals were played on Wednesdays, 9 and 16 September (Rangers were involved in European action on 9 September against Red Star Belgrade, so did not play their first leg against Dunfermline Athletic until Monday, 14 September) and the first legs were all predictable apart from one. This was at Bayview where East Fife, conscious of their glorious past in this competition and hinting at a return, beat Celtic 2-0. The defeat was comprehensive and unexpected (Celtic had beaten Rangers 3-1 in the league the Saturday before) but the second leg saw an early blunder by East Fife's goalkeeper and a predictable 6-0 drubbing. The other three games were settled in the first leg, with Dundee United's 8-0 tanking of Hamilton Accies being particularly impressive, but Clyde did put up a fight in their second leg, although not enough to beat Morton on aggregate.

The semi-finals were played on consecutive nights at the end of September, Celtic v Morton at Ibrox and Rangers v Dundee United at Hampden. In the event, the Old Firm won through, but neither of them convincingly, with Rangers lucky to get the better of Dundee United. Celtic won 2-0 against Morton, who might have played differently if their star striker Allan McGraw had not been injured. As it was, Morton were perhaps just a little too timid, and Bobby Lennox and Charlie Gallagher scored the goals for Celtic at the appropriate moments.

For Dundee United a League Cup semi-final was unfamiliar territory and perhaps they were fazed by Hampden and the big occasion. They froze, as they say, but so did Rangers, for the *Glasgow Herald* is unusually critical of the football using words like 'colourless' and 'drab' and saying that few Rangers players emerged with their reputation untarnished. A little more self-belief might have worked wonders for Dundee United but, as it was, the game meandered on to extra time, then reached half-time in extra time, and a genuine fear was expressed that there might have to be a replay. But then Jim Forrest, the target of a great deal of recent criticism from the Rangers support, suddenly showed what he could do by beating a few men and hammering home. Forrest was reinstated as a hero and Rangers were in the League Cup Final for the eighth time.

It would be the second Old Firm League Cup Final, the previous one having been the famous or infamous 7-1 of 1957. That was Celtic's last major honour, such had been the dreadful few years that the Parkhead management had inflicted on its fans. Rangers, on the other hand, seemed to be winning everything and radiated confidence, even when it was not justified. On form there was little doubt that Celtic were the better side, for there was a youthful enthusiasm about them, but questions were frequently asked about their mental approach to games, something that frequently let them down in their profligacy in front of goal, for example.

The final was scheduled for 24 October. Some nine days previously, Labour had won the general election, ending 13 years of mainly benign Tory rule of aristocrats, earls and grouse shooters. Celtic and their supporters certainly felt that the collapse of one *ancien regime* at Westminster could lead to the downfall of another in Glasgow. The weather was good and optimism was in the air.

A minor mystery surrounded the crowd, which was given as 91,423. It was a good crowd by any standards, but some 14,000 short of last year's attendance at the Rangers v Morton League Cup Final. There seemed to be no logical reason for this. Did Morton really have more supporters than Celtic? Were the Rangers fans so disgusted with their team that they refused to come and watch them? Neither explanation was convincing. Not for the first time, people wondered about that figure and permitted themselves unworthy thoughts that the figure given may have been minimised to reduce the entertainment tax payable. Never!

Both teams started playing towards their own supporters. Rangers had an early half-hearted shout for a penalty for handball turned down by referee Hugh Phillips and Celtic had a better one turned down for a tackle on Jimmy Johnstone by Dave Provan, but the pattern of the first half was one of Celtic on top but, crucially, unable to convert chances with Bobby Murdoch and Jimmy Johnstone both missing very good ones. At half-time, the Rangers end was noticeably more confident than the Celtic one, for they felt that Celtic had blown it. The Celtic end silently agreed.

Yet battle raged in the second half until crucially Jim Forrest scored an opportunist goal. Celtic then claimed unconvincingly that a shot had crossed the line at the other end – photographs clearly show that it didn't – and then Forrest scored again, triggering a mini-exodus from the dispirited Celtic end. Celtic, however, fought back, changing wingers so that Johnstone faced Caldow and Hughes faced Provan and scoring through Jimmy Johnstone to give them a lifeline.

Rangers counteracted that move by changing their full-backs and that tended to snuffle out Celtic's attacks. Most neutral observers agreed that Celtic were worth a draw and extra time, but when Hugh Phillips blew for full time, Rangers had won the Scottish League Cup for the sixth time and for four seasons out of five.

Yet in many ways this game was a watershed. Rangers' cavorting with the League Cup did not really disguise the internal problems that existed at Ibrox. The League Cup would be their only honour this year and, for Celtic, things went from bad to worse with an appalling run of form in autumn and winter 1964/65. It became so bad that a drastic change at the top simply had to be made. And Scottish football would never be the same again.

The teams were:

Rangers: Ritchie, Provan and Caldow, Greig, McKinnon and Wood, Brand, Millar, Forrest, Baxter and Johnston

Celtic: Fallon, Young and Gemmell, Clark, Cushley and Kennedy, Johnstone, Murdoch, Chalmers, Divers and Hughes

Referee: H Phillips, Wishaw

CHAPTER FIVE

CELTIC'S FIVE IN A ROW
1965–1969

THAT SCOTTISH football changed seismically on 31 January 1965 is in no real doubt. This was the day on which Celtic appointed Jock Stein to be their manager. It should have happened years before but was delayed by the chairman's archaic and bizarre concern that the supporters might not take kindly to a manager who was not a Roman Catholic. The supporters showed scant respect for such religious tribalism by accepting Stein immediately and Celtic never looked back. Indeed, the problem may well have been that the chairman was reluctant to appoint a manager who would not have been content to remain a glorified office boy.

Celtic won the Scottish Cup in 1965 (Kilmarnock won the league), but their League Cup section in season 1965/66 was a tricky one against both Dundee teams and Motherwell. It was a thriller from start to finish with every team in with a chance from time to time and Celtic owing their qualification to a great fightback and one of the best goals ever seen at Dens

Park. At the halfway stage, Celtic had lost to both Dundee teams and their chances of qualification looked slim, but they fought back, earned a little luck when all the other teams took points off each other and needed at least a draw at Dens Park on the last day (4 September 1965) to qualify. The crowd was massive on a hot day and Celtic won 3-1 with John Hughes scoring the best goal anyone would ever wish to see, charging across the field and then hammering home from well over 25 yards.

Rangers too struggled for a spell. In a strong section containing Hearts and Aberdeen, they also lost two of their first three games, but rallied to beat Aberdeen 4-0 on the last day. Aberdeen had seemed home and dry at one point but the old Pittodrie fault of failing to win the games that they really had to win, particularly at Ibrox, resurrected itself once again. Hibs and Dunfermline also qualified, both with a certain amount of comfort.

In the Second Division sections, although no one realised it at the time, the League Cup probably represented one of the last chances for that grand old team called Third Lanark to make some sort of a name for themselves. They did indeed win their difficult section of Berwick Rangers, Cowdenbeath and Hamilton Accies but lost in both legs of the supplementary round to Ayr United. Alloa Athletic and Airdrieonians joined them as well, Raith Rovers made a welcome return to the quarter-finals, but their neighbours East Fife, normally reliably consistent, finished bottom of their section.

The quarter-finals were very one-sided. Hibs, Rangers and Celtic saw off Alloa, Airdrie and Raith Rovers with no problem whatsoever, although we did have a hint of closeness in the Ayrshire derby. Kilmarnock won 2-0 in the first leg at Rugby Park, and they needed their lead because Ayr held them to 2-2 at Somerset Park and would have done a great deal better but for poor finishing.

The semi-finals paired Celtic v Hibs at Ibrox and Rangers v Kilmarnock at Hampden, but the new Celtic regime was not above a little mischief-making about the choice of venues. The *Celtic View*, a new publication and the first of its kind in the world, led a campaign to get their venue changed to Hampden instead of Ibrox, pointing out that it was only fair that both semi-finals should be at the same venue as the final. In addition, they claimed that the Ibrox floodlights were substandard.

This seems to have been a deliberate attempt to rile and unsettle Rangers. No one else, even after European games, had ever made a serious complaint about the Ibrox floodlights and the complaint was unfounded, but the campaigners did persuade Hibs and their supporters (who also enjoyed having a pop at Rangers) to join in, with the Hibs supporters also making the dubious claim that Hampden was a lot easier to get to than Ibrox for supporters coming from Edinburgh (one of the many complaints about Hampden had been its inaccessibility by road). The complaints intensified when the first game ended in a draw and the tie went to a replay, but the Scottish League stuck to their decision. Although clearly unnerved and upset, Rangers retained a dignified silence, and no more was heard, especially after Celtic, poor floodlights or not, managed to beat Hibs 4-0 in the replay.

Celtic were extremely fortunate to earn a replay because in the first game, on Monday, 4 October, Hibs were the better team for long spells in the game. The Ibrox pitch was sodden and, as was often the case between Celtic and

Hibs, the football was superb with Celtic scoring first, then Hibs equalising and going ahead, before in the 90th minute, Celtic, with the weaker brethren of their support already at the Copland Road tube station on their way home, equalised through Bobby Lennox after Hibs' goalkeeper had failed to hold a fierce Gemmell drive. Thirty minutes of extra time was played in energy-sapping conditions but no further scoring took place.

Because of international commitments it was not possible to have the replay for another two weeks. The game went ahead on 18 October, only five days before the final itself. This time it was a totally different story with Celtic well on top from beginning to end, winning 4-0 over a Hibs side which was barely recognisable from the one which had done so well two weeks previously. Two goals were scored in each half and Hibs centre-half John McNamee, an ex-Celtic player, was sent off for a foul which earned him a booking. He kept arguing about it and picked up a second yellow card.

This put Celtic into the final to play, for the second year in a row, Rangers. Rangers' semi-final, played on 6 October against Kilmarnock, had been a remarkable game as well. Rangers, playing with a flair that had been absent all season, simply outplayed Kilmarnock for about two-thirds of the game to lead 6-1 at about the hour mark. The delight of their fans, however, turned to horror as they took their foot off the pedal, and Kilmarnock came back into the game with young Tommy McLean scoring three times to make the final score 6-4. It was a great game for the crowd to watch, but the Rangers supporters were in many ways relieved to hear the full-time whistle in a game in which both defences seemed to have totally lost control.

It was the Old Firm again. Last year's League Cup Final had been a watershed that indicated the end of an era for Rangers; this year's was a pointer to the future. The pressure was on Celtic to prove that last year's success in the Scottish Cup Final was not a one-off. They had to prove that they were here to stay. For Rangers on the other hand, now without their talismanic Jim Baxter, it was no less vital. Their crown was slipping. They had to restore matters. And Celtic were radiating confidence, with a piece of writing by Sean Fallon in the *Scottish Daily Express* a few days before the final giving the impression that Celtic were going to win handsomely.

The final was played in fine autumn sunshine on 23 October before a League Cup record crowd of 107,609, just beating the Rangers v Morton attendance of two seasons ago. It was an unsatisfactory game in several respects. It maybe did not quite warrant the phrases like 'orgy of crudeness' and 'X certificate' bestowed on it by some sections of the press, but tackles were full-blooded and it was no place for softies, the tone set by a scything tackle by Celtic's Ian Young on Willie Johnston of Rangers early in the game. The message was clear. No more Mr Nice Guy from Celtic, whose chairman, Mr Kelly, had often given the impression in the past that he was more concerned with his team acting in a sportsmanlike fashion than actually winning. The final was well controlled by referee Hugh Phillips who booked five men and prevented things from getting silly, by being on the spot and always in command.

What was totally unacceptable was the invasion of some not very bright Rangers supporters at the end who tried to attack the Celtic players on their lap of honour with the League Cup. It was a mercy that the Celtic players did not turn on them – fully trained professional football players would have done well against undernourished brainless youths fuelled and enervated by drink – and even more of a mercy that the Celtic fans did not launch a counterattack. From this point of view, it was a very sad day in the history of the Scottish League Cup and, for some time after this, laps of honour would be banned.

The game itself hinged on two penalty kicks in the first half, both sunk by John Hughes, one for a handball inexplicably committed by Ron McKinnon and the other when Jimmy Johnstone was brought down by Dave Provan – by no means a clear-cut penalty. Rangers pulled one back with an own goal late in the game but the Celtic defence, well marshalled by veteran goalkeeper Ronnie Simpson, held out.

The teams were:

Celtic: Simpson, Young and Gemmell, Murdoch, McNeill and Clark, Johnstone, Gallagher, McBride, Lennox and Hughes

Rangers: Ritchie, Johansen and Provan, Wood, McKinnon and Greig, Henderson, Willoughby, Forrest, Wilson and Johnston

Referee: H Phillips, Wishaw

It was Celtic's third League Cup victory and much celebrated by their fans. The Scottish League Cup had now celebrated its 20th birthday. It was still a very successful competition from the point of view of making money and, far more importantly, providing entertainment for the public, the much larger public now that television was allowing everyone to see more football, albeit still in edited highlights form. Seven teams had won the trophy – Rangers, East Fife, Motherwell, Dundee,

Aberdeen, Hearts and Celtic – but there were still quite a few absentees from the winners engraved on the trophy.

The season 1966/67 was, as everyone knows, Celtic's greatest year, but at the start of the season, no one really knew just how good it was going to be and one could argue that it was the League Cup which proved the most difficult competition for them, not least in the final. They had no problem winning their section beginning from the opening day at Tynecastle, a day of foul weather, when they beat Hearts 2-0 and never really looked back after that.

They were not the only team to take maximum points from their section, joined on that mark by Aberdeen, a team making a welcome and long-overdue return to form by beating both Dundee teams and St Johnstone in a very geographically localised section. On the eve of the season Aberdeen had antagonised most of their support by selling wing-half Dave Smith to Rangers, but they won them back with this fine form. Under Eddie Turnbull, things were beginning to look good for Aberdeen.

Rangers' qualification was a great deal tighter, requiring a last-day win at Kilmarnock to clinch the section on goal average following a spirited fight from Hibs. The problem was that Hibs had conceded rather too many goals, even in games that they won. They beat Rangers at Easter Road by the score of 3-2 and they also conceded two goals to Stirling Albion in their 4-2 triumph. This would eventually count against them. Rangers, on the other hand, managed to qualify to a large extent by taking advantage of the new law on substitutes and sending on Davie Wilson in place of the ineffective Willie Henderson in their last game. It is important to remember that in season 1966/67, Rangers were no bad side. Clearly they won nothing and had one shocker at Berwick in January 1967, but they did reach the final of the European Cup Winners' Cup (and only lost because the final was played in Germany against Bayern Munich), and the fact that they stayed so close to Celtic said a great deal about them as well. Dunfermline also won through and they were joined by Montrose, Airdrie, Ayr United and, eventually, Morton who beat Brechin City in the supplementary round. Ayr United were another team who qualified on goal average, beating Cowdenbeath 3-0 on the last day.

The quarter-finals saw Celtic beat Dunfermline Athletic in a high-scoring tie, Rangers beat Ayr United in a second-leg performance which was a great deal more impressive than the first leg, and Airdrieonians eventually triumphed over a gallant Montrose side, but the most exciting tie was between Morton and Aberdeen.

In the first leg at Cappielow, the prodigiously talented Jimmy Smith scored first for the Dons before Morton scored three times. The value, however, of the Aberdeen goal became apparent in the second leg at Pittodrie when Aberdeen turned the tables to win 3-0 and 4-3 on aggregate. The game was tense throughout with Morton defending brilliantly in the first half and their goalkeeper Erik Sorensen in particularly good form. Pittodrie's old warhorse Ernie Winchester scored early in the second half but, with five minutes to go, Morton were still leading on aggregate until Jimmy Smith scored from a rebound to take the game to extra time – apparently. With time running out and the Morton defence still reeling from that late blow and the whole second-half pounding, Jens Petersen scored for Aberdeen to win the tie.

The draw for the semi-finals paired Celtic with Airdrie and Rangers with Aberdeen, the games to be played on Monday,

17 October and Wednesday, 19 October, both at Hampden. Tuesday tended to be avoided in the 1960s because it was the traditional night for overtime in shipyards and other workplaces. The fact that both semis were to be played at Hampden Park seemed to indicate that Celtic had won their point from the previous year about the floodlights at Ibrox and was a pointer to the increasing influence that a successful Celtic club were beginning to exercise over the authorities. Curiously, it was not a point that was made much of by the press.

Celtic won the first semi-final 2-0 after having had to work hard to break down the solid Airdrie defence. Eventually goals by Bobby Murdoch and Joe McBride saw them through, then attention turned to the other semi-final between Aberdeen and Rangers. This game, a couple of nights later, attracted a marginally larger crowd. They saw Rangers twice go ahead but, in each case, Aberdeen equalised. Willie Henderson did the scoring on both occasions for Rangers, Jimmy Wilson and Ally Shewan scored for the Dons; it was generally agreed that Rangers had been the better team but had suffered from poor finishing and bad luck.

Extra time failed to resolve the issue so it was back to Hampden the following Monday. Once again, there was a surprisingly good crowd of 38,000 with a large contingent from the north but this time Rangers made no mistake and took the tie with goals from Willie Johnston and Alec Smith. This time there was no comeback from the dispirited Aberdeen side and Rangers fans now looked forward with increasing confidence to their fourth successive League Cup Final, and the third in a row against Celtic.

A total of 94,532 attended this game on a dull but dry day on 29 October. Possibly the reason for the slight decline in attendance from last year was because Rangers fans did not know until the previous Monday night that they would be involved and their fans from a distance couldn't make plans. The run-up to the game involved Jock Stein trying to play down the importance of it all. This was Stein's kidology at its best. It fooled no one. All Old Firm games are crucial and silverware was at stake.

Celtic's recent splendid form (they had a 100 per cent record in all competitions and had already beaten Rangers 2-0 at Parkhead in the league) made them the clear favourites, and they did indeed win, but not without a mighty scare. It is a curious fact that the team who is on top tends to get the breaks in the shape of refereeing decisions and so forth. That was certainly the case in the League Cup Final of October 1964 when the better team lost; now Rangers supporters could make out a case for a similar thing happening in October 1966, but in reverse. On the other hand, they had their own forwards to blame for squandering chances and the plain fact of the matter was that Celtic won the game 1-0.

The only goal of the game came in the first half, and a good goal it was. It was a traditional three-card trick. A long ball from Bertie Auld found the head of Joe McBride, who nodded into the path of the inrushing Bobby Lennox, and he made no mistake. Shortly after that came the moment of controversy when Rangers seemed to have equalised in the aftermath of a free kick which found Bobby Watson. He scored but the goal was disallowed when referee Mr Wharton saw a foul on Celtic's goalkeeper Ronnie Simpson. The infringement was not immediately apparent to the Rangers fans behind that goal (nor to the press and TV after the game) and crowd trouble resulted. Bottles were thrown, although this being

Hampden, the bottles fell a good 20 yards short of the pitch. But then again, bottle throwing and intelligence are things that do not naturally go together. The second half saw more Rangers pressure and a Celtic defence able to cope with it. Robust penalty claims for each side (minutes after each other) were disallowed by the obdurate Mr Wharton. Then came the occasion which almost defined the life of Celtic's Willie O'Neill, who was on the spot to clear a miskick from Rangers' Alec Smith off the line. By full time, Celtic had ridden the storm and were delighted to hear the final whistle in what was regarded as being one of the better Old Firm games.

The teams were:

Celtic: Simpson, Gemmell and O'Neill, Murdoch, McNeill and Clark, Johnstone, Lennox, McBride, Auld and Hughes (Chalmers)

Rangers: Martin, Johansen and Provan, Greig, McKinnon and D Smith, Henderson, Watson, McLean, A Smith and Johnston

Referee: T Wharton, Clarkston

One likes to talk about watersheds and critical moments. In this case, one wonders whether life, including Lisbon, would have been quite the same for Celtic if they had lost this one. Certainly for Rangers, obsessed as always by Celtic, the season never really recovered, even though most people would agree that this could have been one of the better Rangers sides. They lost infamously to Berwick Rangers and (because of a crazy team selection) Bayern Munich to render their season empty, but everyone knew that it was Celtic who had really beaten them. It remains important, however, to recognise that 1967 was a good year for Scottish football, for in addition to the success of the Glasgow teams, Kilmarnock reached the semi-final of the Inter-Cities Fairs Cup (the equivalent of the modern Europa League) and Scotland beat England at Wembley to become the first team to dethrone the World Cup winners.

Summer 1967 was therefore spent on a high, and when the season started again, there was no let-up in the excitement of it all. The standout section was the one which contained Celtic, Rangers, Aberdeen and Dundee United. Celtic scored with literally the last kick of the ball, through Jimmy Johnstone, to beat Dundee United on opening day but, from then on, every game was close-fought. In the two Old Firm games, Rangers were perhaps unlucky to be held to a draw at Ibrox, but for sheer drama, the return game at Celtic Park was hard to beat.

It was played on 30 August 1967, known as the 'Night of *The Fugitive*' for an American serialised drama came to its conclusion that night on TV. But Celtic Park was the place for football. There were controversial refereeing decisions and exciting moments galore. Rangers found themselves 1-0 up with about 15 minutes to go when they were awarded a penalty kick. Kai Johansen took it, hit the bar, then illegally touched the ball again. Correctly, Mr Wharton awarded an indirect free kick to Celtic. Celtic then ran up the field and scored three times before full time as Rangers completely lost their composure and collapsed under the onslaught.

That section was the best attended and the one which earned the most media attention, but the other sections were equally interesting and the form of Dundee was impressive as they dropped only one point in qualification from their section which included Hibs. St Johnstone won their opening-day fixture against Hearts at Tynecastle, then survived a late dip in form to qualify, while the strong-going Kilmarnock got the better of Dunfermline.

From the Second Division sections came East Fife, yet again drawing on their somewhat distant League Cup glory of nearly 20 years ago, Morton with a far better recent pedigree in the League Cup, Ayr United and the grand old Glasgow team Queen's Park. It was sad to note, in passing, that there was no longer Third Lanark this year. The club had finally folded in the summer with unsurmountable debt and a great deal of internal corruption, but it had been heading that way for a while. They had never won the Scottish League Cup but appeared in the final of 1959/60. They were much missed.

Their place was taken by Clydebank, now a separate entity from the absurd idea of amalgamating them with East Stirlingshire. The Bankies won section nine but lost out to Ayr United in the supplementary round, so the draw read Celtic v Ayr United, Dundee v East Fife, Queen's Park v St Johnstone and Morton v Kilmarnock. Of these ties, the only one that was close was the Morton triumph over Killie, but there could be no argument about it, for the Greenock men won both games. Dundee finished off the job a week before everyone else because of European commitments and remained very impressive, St Johnstone were far too good for the amateurs of Queen's Park, while Celtic, although suffering a form slump (perhaps inevitably after last season's greatness) were still well on top of the honest men of Ayr.

Morton's victory was possibly unexpected, for Kilmarnock had been doing well and it was generally believed that Morton's 3-2 win at Greenock would be overturned at Rugby Park. Not a bit of it. Morton went about their business in the right way, did not make the fatal mistake of trying to defend, passed the ball around well to each other with Danish right-half Preben Arentoft particularly outstanding, and got their reward in the shape of two goals to the one of Kilmarnock.

Their reward was a semi-final appearance at Hampden on Wednesday, 11 October against Celtic while Dundee took on St Johnstone at Tannadice Park, only 100 yards from Dundee's front door, but nevertheless the logical place for this fixture which attracted a crowd of 18,000 to provide a tremendous atmosphere in that small, compact stadium. Hampden would have attracted fewer people and the atmosphere would have been dead.

It was a great game for Dundee who thus reached their third League Cup Final, but a nightmare for St Johnstone's George Millar who managed to score two own goals after Gordon Whitelaw had put the Saints ahead. But Dundee took advantage of their gifts, scored again through a penalty and finished well on top.

The other semi-final saw Celtic at their devastating best. It is often said that, although the Scottish League Cup is Celtic's least-favourite tournament in terms of winning the actual trophy, they nevertheless play their best football in individual games in this tournament. They have had two super finals – the 7-1 win over Rangers in 1957, and another win in the final in 1969 over Hibs – and this semi-final was at least the equal of these two in terms of goals scored.

Celtic had a point to prove. Since winning the European Cup, all had not gone smoothly. There had been a few poor results in the league and they were out of the European Cup of 1967/68 at the first time of asking. Arguably, they had been unlucky in Kiev where the refereeing had not been good, but that was no excuse after a very poor first leg at Celtic Park. People now asked whether they were just one-season wonders and pointed to the undeniable fact that one or two heads had swollen out of all proportion.

But it was a chastened Celtic this night at Hampden; 45,662 (considered a poor crowd for Celtic in 1967) on a fine dry night saw football of the highest order with John Hughes having a great game and scoring a marvellous individual goal. Even full-back Jim Craig got into the act and scored two goals. The 7-1 scoreline was a fair reflection on the flow of the play.

Celtic were into their fourth consecutive Scottish League Cup Final but could be excused if they took their eye off the ball, for they were at this time embroiled in the World Club Championship against Racing Club of Argentina. They won the first leg at Hampden 1-0 but were due to fly out to South America on the night of Saturday, 28 October, a matter of hours after the League Cup Final!

The game itself was a remarkable one and the score was 5-3 in Celtic's favour. Celtic were without Jimmy Johnstone who was suspended for a list of misdemeanours, but that did not prevent the forwards scoring five times. Dundee deserved a great deal of credit for they clearly decided that they were going to have a go at Celtic and they refused to give up, even when their cause seemed lost. The goals came thick and fast, so much so that some spectators, on their buses home, were heard to be arguing with each other about what the actual score was. Certainly it was difficult to remember in which order they came.

The crowd was a disappointing one of 66,660. There were several reasons for this. Celtic's supporters were perhaps sated with success and even a cup final was in danger of becoming an ordinary occasion, particularly when the club had other fish to fry. Dundee supporters also were reluctant to travel to Glasgow to see a team whose directors had tunnel vision about selling their best players. There was also the undeniable fact that there was a whole programme of football that afternoon in competition with the final.

Celtic's forward play was fine but their defending less so – a criticism frequently voiced about them in the late 1960s. Such was their obsession with attacking football that they pushed men forward and did not concentrate enough at the back. Steve Chalmers and John Hughes put them two up, then George McLean pulled one back for Dundee. It stayed like that until 17 minutes from time when, in quick succession, Steve Chalmers for Celtic, Jim McLean for Dundee, Bobby Lennox for Celtic, Jim McLean again for Dundee and then Willie Wallace for Celtic all scored to make it 5-3.

Dundee deserved all the plaudits for their part in the game but Celtic had now done what no one else had done in the League Cup and registered a hat-trick of consecutive wins. Photographs were taken quickly and celebrations were muted, for the team's departure was almost immediate. The South American adventure would turn out to be a total disaster for Celtic, causing them immense loss of prestige and a great deal of embarrassment. They would also go out of the Scottish Cup early that season and struggle to retain the league championship, but at least, in the midst of their self-inflicted trauma, they had one piece of silverware in the Scottish League Cup. It would soon look as if it was beginning to take up permanent residence on the Parkhead sideboard.

The teams were:

Celtic: Simpson, Craig and Gemmell, Murdoch, McNeill and Clark, Chalmers, Lennox, Wallace, Auld (O'Neill) and Hughes

Dundee: Arrol, Wilson and Houston, Murray, Stewart and Stuart, Campbell, J McLean, Wilson, G McLean and Bryce

Referee: RH Davidson, Airdrie

Season 1968/69 opened in glorious sunshine on 10 August, and Celtic had an early success against Rangers by beating them 2-0 at Ibrox, something that ensured that the Ibrox inferiority complex would remain in full force. Even when Rangers in the return leg at Parkhead were at least the equals of Celtic in terms of possession, they would nevertheless obey the apparent law of destiny and lose 0-1. Partick Thistle and Morton did little other than make up the numbers in that group.

The fast-developing Hibs team also qualified, recovering from a surprise opening-day defeat at the hands of St Johnstone at Easter Road to get the better of Falkirk and Raith Rovers. Their draw at Perth in the return leg was enough to get them through because St Johnstone did not do as well in the other group matches as they did.

Dundee also qualified from a tight section thanks to a comprehensive 4-0 demolition of Hearts at Dens Park in the penultimate game, a result which had their fans and the local press purring about a return to the old days, while surprise qualifiers were Clyde, a team of limited resources but good management under Archie Robertson. They delighted their fans by getting the better of strong eastern teams like Aberdeen, Dundee United and Dunfermline.

Ayr United, Hamilton Academical and East Fife (again!) qualified from the Second Division sections, and they were joined by Stranraer who won section nine and defeated Albion Rovers in the supplementary round.

All this was going on in pleasant weather but with a horrifying geopolitical scenario unfolding in the background. Czechoslovakia had been invaded in late August by the Soviet Union because it had shown rather too many signs of failing to adhere to the party line. The ruthlessness caught the western world by surprise, but short of starting World War III, there was little that could be done about the situation other than diplomatic disapproval (including redoing the draw for the European Cup!) and sympathy for the Czechs. In any case, the USA had lost what little moral credibility that it had by its continuing involvement in Vietnam where the daily butchery was a great deal worse than in Czechoslovakia.

The world may have been a great deal scarier than of late, but the Scottish League Cup continued. The quarter-final ties were, with one exception, rather boring and predictable as Celtic, Hibs and Dundee beat Hamilton, East Fife and Stranraer so comprehensively on the first time of asking that the second legs were all irrelevant. The exception was the tie between Clyde and Ayr United. Clyde were 1-0 up from the first leg at Somerset Park but then, on a rainy night at Shawfield before a small but enthusiastic and noisy crowd, Ayr United showed what they were made of and really should have scored on several occasions before Clyde, through Harry Hood and Ian Stewart, scored twice at the death. The heroes of the night were Ayr United, but it was Clyde who went through to play Celtic in the semi-final at Hampden while Dundee faced Hibs at Tynecastle on 9 October. Ayr United, however, who had done consistently well for several years in the Scottish League Cup, would have their moments of glory yet.

The semi-final at Tynecastle was a thriller with Dundee, arguably the better team of the two, unlucky not to win at the end. But Hibs had one hero in Allan McGraw, a man who had now joined them from Morton where he had made his name. Twenty thousand fans saw George McLean score for Dundee and then Colin Stein equalise for Hibs, but the game was very equal with Dundee possibly having the better of exchanges. Only 15 minutes remained when the game seemed to swing decisively in favour of Dundee as Allan McGraw was carried off on a stretcher, thereby reducing Hibs to ten men since they had already committed their substitute (only one substitute was allowed in 1968). Then Dundee should have scored when Sammy Wilson was through on goal and fired from eight yards, only for Billy Wilson in the Hibs goal to bring off the save of his life.

Then Hibs manager, Bob Shankly, having satisfied himself that Allan McGraw could at least walk, put him back on the field and told him to hang about and poach a goal. This was exactly what happened in the very final minute of the game when McGraw was on hand to prod home a loose ball in injury time, so late as to deny Dundee the chance to fight back.

The other game saw Celtic v Clyde. The conventional wisdom is that when Glasgow's two East Enders meet, you do not get a good game. This was only half true on this occasion. Clyde played superbly well yet Celtic, whose supporters in the 34,767 crowd were not slow to express their feelings of dissatisfaction, chose to play very poorly with their forwards in particular playing distinctly fecklessly and Ronnie Simpson being called upon to do far more work than he was accustomed to in the Celtic goal.

However, when the goal did come, it was a cracker scored by George Connelly, a man beginning to make his mark on the team. He had come on to replace Joe McBride and scored from a cross from the hitherto ineffectual John Hughes. He hit the ball on the volley and it went in off the bar. Even then Celtic were not entirely safe, but had enough defensive know-how to prevent an equaliser. Thus began a Celtic tradition of playing badly in League Cup semi-finals against smaller teams but still winning. Clyde's performance was good enough for Gair Henderson, the respected journalist of the *Evening Times*, to appeal to the Glasgow public to go to Shawfield a little more often to support Glasgow's third force.

It was Celtic v Hibs for the Scottish League Cup Final on 26 October – or so we thought. The night of Monday, 21 October saw a fire at Hampden Park caused by an electrical fault which damaged the dressing rooms and the League Cup Final was postponed to the spring. Fortunately, no one was around at the time, and no one was injured. There was a copycat fire the following night at Ibrox which was clearly deliberate but the Hampden one was a pure accident which perhaps said something about the antiquity and general neglect of the old stadium.

But then Hibs did something so bizarre and so betraying of their supporters that it was difficult to avoid the charge of money-grubbing. Colin Stein (no relation of Celtic's Jock) had been playing well for Hibs, scoring goals regularly. His problem was a poor disciplinary record meaning he was suspended and would have been ineligible for the Scottish League Cup Final on 26 October. He would have been available for April when the final was eventually played but Hibs staggered the footballing world by selling him to

Rangers for £100,000 in November. Why there were no boycotts and rebellions among the Easter Road support is a mystery, particularly when Rangers then beat Hibs 6-1 soon afterwards, and Colin Stein scored a hat-trick. In the long and lamentable catalogue of Hibs' betrayals of their supporters, this one was a collector's item. On 5 April 1969, with the damage at Hampden repaired, the final eventually took place. Whether Colin Stein would have made any difference or not is open to question, but the day certainly belonged to the other Stein, for Celtic played one of the best games of football that one could have imagined. And yet Hibs did not play badly, entering into the spirit of flowing attacking football and helping to produce a display in the fine Easter sunshine that none of the 74,240 crowd would forget for a long time.

Celtic, with a point to prove for they had recently gone out of the European Cup in heartbreaking fashion to AC Milan, started playing towards their own supporters at the King's Park end and were 3-0 up at half-time with Willie Wallace, Bertie Auld and Bobby Lennox scoring. In the second half they began to play even better. Lennox completed his hat-trick (joining Billy McPhail, Willie Bauld, Davie Duncan and Jim Forrest in the Hall of Fame of League Cup Final hat-trick heroes), then full-back Jim Craig scored as well before Hibs added two late goals to make the score 6-2.

The teams were:

Celtic: Fallon, Craig and Gemmell (Clark), Murdoch, McNeill and Brogan, Johnstone, Wallace, Chalmers, Auld and Lennox

Hibs: Allan, Shevlane and Davis, Stanton, Madsen and Blackley, Marinello, Quinn, Cormack, O'Rourke and Stevenson

Referee: W Syme, Airdrie

The clear success of having the final in spring made the authorities think about whether this might be the best time in any case. It would happen eventually, but the Scottish League still believed (and they were right) that there was merit in finishing the competition before the winter began at the end of October, usually on the day that, symbolically, the clocks changed. So the competition stayed an autumn one for the time being and, when Celtic won it again in October, they had achieved the unlikely feat of winning the trophy twice in the one calendar year. And that wasn't all they won, for 1969 also saw them win the Scottish League and the Scottish Cup. They thus won, in the calendar month of April, the three Scottish trophies.

The draw for the sectional stage for the 1969/70 tournament paired Celtic and Rangers together with Raith Rovers and Airdrie making up the numbers. In an attempt to appease the more gullible of their unhappy support, Rangers bought back Jim Baxter whom they had sold in 1965, but any hopes of Slim Jim making a difference dissipated almost as soon as they saw him, for he was no Slim Jim anymore. Indeed, the Celtic end started shouting things like 'Fatty' and 'Billy Bunter' at him. Nevertheless, Rangers scored an early success in a 2-1 victory on the first Wednesday night at Ibrox.

In a move that made little sense and betokened the first 'playing about' which would bedevil the tournament all through the 1970s and 1980s, the return fixtures were played the following Wednesday. There was no midweek off (during which a league fixture had been played in the past) and the section now finished on the third Wednesday of the season. No one understood the logic, but everyone understood that when Celtic beat Rangers 1-0 at Celtic Park through a

Tommy Gemmell header, the pressure would be on Rangers and that they would crack. They did so when they failed to beat Raith Rovers at Ibrox and Celtic duly qualified, albeit by a narrower margin than of late. Rangers then imploded and Jim Baxter and his manager Davie White were out the door before Christmas.

St Johnstone under Willie Ormond of Hibs' Famous Five fame had a very impressive early season and topped their group of Kilmarnock, Dundee and Partick Thistle with maximum points. Aberdeen, who had shown a quiet but steady improvement under Eddie Turnbull (another part of the Famous Five) over the past few seasons but without ever achieving anything in terms of trophies, qualified as well, drawing both games against Hibs but doing better against Clyde and Dunfermline Athletic. The last game of the section was at Easter Road, and was a 0-0 draw with Aberdeen defending resolutely, surprising everyone by naming Bobby Clark, their goalkeeper, as 12th man on the grounds that he was a good outfield player as well. He would get a few outings in that role.

The tightest group was that involving Dundee United, Hearts, Morton and St Mirren. Fortunately for Morton it was goal difference (rather than goal average) that was now the determining factor, and although they lost 2-0 to Hearts in the final game at Cappielow, they had a difference of +3 as distinct from Hearts' +2. Ayr United also qualified on goal difference over Queen of the South and were joined by Motherwell (who beat consistent qualifiers East Fife), Falkirk and Dumbarton after the men from Boghead disposed of Brechin City.

Aberdeen's success had lain in a well-organised and drilled defence which conceded few goals, often relying on an offside trap to frustrate opponents. Such tactics did not always go down well with supporters, not least their own traditionally very hard-to-please home fans, but it was successful. Now in the quarter-finals, they had Celtic to deal with. The first leg at Pittodrie was a goalless draw with defending of the type that Celtic faced in Europe, but the second leg at Celtic Park was an exciting affair in which Aberdeen went ahead through Jim Forrest but Celtic pulled them back with goals by Bobby Lennox and Willie Wallace to win 2-1 before a crowd of 47,000. The star of the game was Jimmy Johnstone, playing, theoretically at least, at centre-forward. That was not, however, the most thrilling of the quarter-finals. That honour must be bestowed on the Morton v Motherwell tie where both sides won their home legs 3-0 and a play-off was decreed at Ibrox. It was a tremendous anti-climax in front of a poor crowd in a large stadium, and Motherwell sneaked a late goal for a scarcely deserved victory. Play-offs at neutral venues were seldom a success but no one had, as yet, thought of the penalty shoot-out to decide ties. In the other two games, the free-scoring St Johnstone, whose forward play was now attracting all sorts of admirers, hammered Falkirk 11-3; Ayr United, under a bouncy extrovert called Ally MacLeod, beat Dumbarton 5-1.

The first semi-final was played at Ibrox on Monday, 6 October, and those who were there were very impressed by the sheer competence of St Johnstone who won 2-0 over Motherwell through goals from Bill McCarry and Fred Aitken. This performance earned the Saints their first-ever Hampden cup final in either the Scottish Cup or the Scottish League Cup. That it was totally deserved was in no doubt, and praise was heaped on manager Willie Ormond, as English clubs began to pay attention to some of the talent on view at Muirton Park.

Perth, for all that it is one of Scotland's finest cities, is anything but a hotbed of Scottish football. One would think of curling, whisky, craft shops, horse racing and cricket to associate with the Fair City before one came up with football. St Johnstone had enjoyed moments of triumph in the past, not least against Celtic whom they dumped out of the Scottish League Cup in 1961/62 and out of the Scottish Cup in 1936, but a large part of their existence had been spent in the Second Division. Nevertheless, it was generally agreed that Muirton Park (now sadly demolished but still very much in use until 1969) was one of the best playing surfaces in Scotland.

The other semi-final at Hampden between Celtic and Ayr United on Wednesday, 8 October looked at first glance to be easy for Celtic. It turned out to be anything but. Without Jimmy Johnstone, but with a young Kenny Dalglish on board, Celtic were held to 2-2, then went behind in extra time before Bertie Auld rescued them; 33, 000 spectators were impressed by Ayr United. In the Monday night replay, before a far larger crowd of 48,000, Ayr went ahead in the early stages of the game through Alex Ingram before Harry Hood and Steve Chalmers won the day for Celtic. Ronnie Simpson was injured in that game and had to be carried off but Celtic, with Tommy Gemmell in goal, limped through to the final. All the glory, however, belonged to Ayr United, whose promotion to the First Division last season was now seen to be totally deserved. For Celtic, it was a poor performance in a League Cup semi-final.

That, plus the fact that Celtic had not been playing too well generally, gave the Saints a great deal of hope for the final. Perth was swept away in an unusual tide of passion. Bus companies did a roaring trade and it was nice to see such a well-behaved collection of supporters with a large proportion of ladies among them. Neutral support favoured St Johnstone with even a few Celtic supporters being heard to say that it would not be the worst thing in the world if St Johnstone won the League Cup. But for Celtic, there was also a sideshow.

It concerned Tommy Gemmell. Scotland had exited the qualifying competition for the Mexico World Cup the previous Wednesday. They had lost narrowly in Germany and, such was the frustration of Tommy Gemmell, he was sent off for a clash that was more like an assault than a tackle. Jock Stein had watched the game, been black affronted and decided that Tommy Gemmell would not play in the Scottish League Cup Final, to be replaced by young David Hay.

The trouble was that Stein forgot (or deliberately chose not) to tell Gemmell, and Tommy came into the dressing-room to discover Davie Hay in his place and getting ready for the game. Relationships between Gemmell and Stein were never quite the same again after that.

A total of 73,067 were attracted to Hampden to see the game with the St Johnstone fans clearly enjoying their big day out. It was ironic that the two most free-scoring teams in the country should produce a game which only had one goal in it. Bertie Auld scored for Celtic early on, poking home a rebound from the bar, and the rest of the game, although bereft of goals, was a good game as Celtic held out to win their fifth Scottish League Cup in a row. Bobby Murdoch, who had been away on a health farm to lose weight, was back and in command of the midfield, but everyone in the Celtic camp played tribute to St Johnstone for the way that they played. Twenty-four League Cups had been played for, and Celtic were now clearly top of the pile with seven victories, ahead of Rangers with six.

The teams were:

Celtic: Fallon, Craig, Hay, Murdoch, McNeill, Brogan, Callaghan, Hood, Hughes, Chalmers (Johnstone), Auld

St Johnstone: Donaldson, Lambie, Coburn, Gordon, Rooney, McPhee, Aird, Hall, McCarry (Whitelaw), Connolly, Aitken

Referee: J Paterson, Bothwell

CHAPTER SIX

CELTIC KEEP LOSING HABIT
1970–1978

THE YEAR 1970 has been described by eminent Celtic historians Pat Woods and Tom Campbell, who also have a detailed knowledge of Charles Dickens, as 'the best of times, the worst of times'.

On the one hand Celtic had won the Scottish League and the Scottish League Cup and were the undisputed champions of Great Britain after defeating Leeds United; on the other they had lost two cups in spring 1970. The Scottish Cup Final of 1970 may possibly be explained away, in part, by poor refereeing; there was no excuse whatsoever for the European Cup Final.

Things had changed in other respects as well. Edward Heath's Conservatives won the general election, ending Harold Wilson's first stint as Prime Minister, and England were no longer the World Champions, for the World Cup held in Mexico was won by Brazil who played marvellous football throughout.

Serious player unrest followed Celtic's defeat in Milan in the European Cup Final, particularly when the club went on a pointless tour of the USA which would have been a great success if they had the European Cup with them. Jock Stein suddenly departed back to Scotland amid rumours that he was about to resign and two players, Gemmell and Auld, were sent home for bad behaviour. Everything was in total confusion until the season started and some sort of normality returned, but there was to be further disappointment for their supporters in the Scottish League Cup, a trophy that they had won five years in a row, but which was now destined to give them a fair amount of grief throughout the 1970s and for most of the rest of the century.

Celtic's qualification was unspectacular and uneventful following an opening-day win at Tynecastle. Rangers, admittedly in an easier section, dropped only one point in an otherwise successful campaign, even though their fans were far from happy at some performances. Aberdeen, who should have been on a roll after their Scottish Cup triumph of last April, failed to maintain their success. They were neck and neck with Hibs until the last day of the section and an astonishing game in which Hibs simply ripped apart Aberdeen's much-vaunted defence and were 4-0 up at half-time with their 25,000 fans in rapture. It was then the turn of Hibs' defence to show how good they were and frantic Aberdeen pressure proved futile. Poor St Johnstone, the heroes of last year's campaign, failed badly and earned only one point.

Dundee qualified from their section without very much bother and they were joined by Partick Thistle, Cowdenbeath, Dumbarton and Falkirk. Cowdenbeath had been promoted to the First Division and proved their mettle by getting the better of Montrose and Queen of the South in their section, whereas Partick Thistle, relegated for the first time and determined to fight back, did so, eventually getting the better of these League Cup specialists East Fife and qualifying on goals scored when goal difference proved equal. Their qualification was despite a last-day defeat to East Fife at Firhill. The margin was only 1-3, however, and the Fifers simply couldn't get the fourth goal which would have changed things.

Partick Thistle were the team who had to play in the supplementary round. They won, but not without a struggle, against gallant Stranraer who lost narrowly at Firhill but drew 2-2 at Stair Park and might just have snatched a winner. Partick were now paired against Dumbarton, Falkirk against Cowdenbeath, while the two crowd-pullers were Rangers v Hibs and Dundee v Celtic.

Sometimes the quarter-finals of the Scottish League Cup could be predictable, so much so that a movement was growing that the two-legged format should be ditched but, in this case, three games were very exciting indeed. The exception was, funnily enough, the game that looked the closest, namely Rangers v Hibs. Hibs disappointed their fans in the 37,000 crowd at Easter Road in the first leg by going down 1-3 to a competent Rangers side and, although there were hopes for a fightback at Ibrox, at a key point a penalty was missed. Rangers, playing better than they had done at any point so far this season, won 6-2.

The first leg at Dens Park was a thrilling affair which ended 2-2. Jimmy Johnstone scored twice for Celtic in the first half, but then in the second half Dundee levelled things and either team could have won the game. Dundee and

Celtic usually served up good games but on this occasion the second leg was very one-sided with youngsters Lou Macari and Danny McGrain showing that they were worth a place in the Celtic side as they won 5-1.

Partick Thistle and Dumbarton provided tremendous entertainment in a 3-3 draw at Firhill, and there was scarcely less interest in the return leg at Boghead when the Sons of the Rock won through to their first-ever Scottish League Cup semi-final by beating Thistle 3-2 with a little more comfort than the narrow scoreline would have suggested. Only one goal separated the two teams in the other quarter-final between Falkirk and Cowdenbeath, and that was scored by Cowdenbeath on a foul night at Brockville in the first leg. The word 'stubborn' was used to describe Cowdenbeath's performance in the second leg at Central Park. It was a 0-0 draw and hardly Scottish football's game of the season, but Cowdenbeath won through in a game where seven players were booked, and one or two of them were lucky not to get the long walk to an early bath.

The semi-final draw paired Celtic with Dumbarton and Rangers with Cowdenbeath. Knowing smiles were exchanged, for this seemed to guarantee an Old Firm League Cup Final. Certainly, bookmakers were known to offer odds of 500-1 against a Dumbarton v Cowdenbeath final, but at least one of the members of the Old Firm came perilously close to not making it.

Celtic had, for the past two years, had some trouble in dealing with so-called minor opposition at the semi-final stage, and this year was no different. A small attendance of 25,838 was at Hampden on 7 October to see a great game between Celtic and Dumbarton. Oddly, both goalkeepers were called Williams and Dumbarton had two Gallaghers; one of them was ex-Celtic favourite Charlie. Dumbarton also had ex-Ranger Davie Wilson in their ranks and were well worth their 0-0 draw. Things could have been a great deal better for Celtic had Willie Wallace scored an extra-time penalty harshly awarded by referee Mr Gordon. Celtic's only real excuse was a bad injury to Bobby Murdoch.

Another great performance by Dumbarton was witnessed by the somewhat larger crowd of 32,913 the following Monday night. Once again, they took a lacklustre Celtic side to extra time after levelling things at 2-2. By this time the impatient Celtic crowd gave every sign of turning on their team, but Celtic then scored two goals in extra time through Willie Wallace and Lou Macari. Even then they were not safe, for Dumbarton scored again near the end and Celtic were mighty glad to hear the full-time whistle. All the glory went to Dumbarton and they were well acclaimed by the Celtic crowd, even Davie Wilson being given a grudging round of applause!

Rangers beat Cowdenbeath 2-0 in the other semi-final on 14 October. They were a shade more competent than Celtic were over Dumbarton, but that is not to say they were brilliant, nor is it to denigrate the way that Cowdenbeath played. But Colin Stein and Willie Johnston (with a penalty) scored the goals which put Rangers through to play Celtic, a game which triggered off a scramble for tickets and saw 106,263 attend the 25th Scottish League Cup Final on 24 October 1970.

Neither team was really pleasing their supporters, and the fact that Celtic were made clear favourites with the bookmakers and in the press owed more to Celtic's aura of apparent invincibility and their 2-0 win over Rangers at Parkhead a month ago rather than any recent form, for their semi-final form against Dumbarton had been far from impressive. Rangers were not great either and went into this final without Dave Smith and John Greig.

The game was close but it was Rangers who won with a goal scored by 16-year-old Derek Johnstone. It came from a cross sent over by Willie Johnston near half-time at the Rangers end of the field. The second half was a long one for Rangers supporters and both teams might have scored, but Rangers on this occasion were the better side and won their first trophy for Willie Waddell, who had been their manager for almost a year now.

The teams were:

Rangers: McCloy, Jardine, Miller, Conn, McKinnon, Jackson, Henderson, MacDonald, D Johnstone, Stein, W Johnston

Celtic: Williams, Craig, Quinn, Murdoch, McNeill, Hay, Johnstone, Connelly, Wallace, Hood (Lennox), Macari

Referee: T Wharton, Clarkston

It was Rangers' first trophy since Kai Johansen had won the Scottish Cup for them in 1966 and no one would grudge them it, but even their greatest fans had to admit that it was unexpected and unusual. It would be the only trophy that they would win this season (which contained the tragic Ibrox Disaster in the New Year) since Celtic, in the course of rebuilding, fought back and regained their position of superiority. But not in the Scottish League Cup, which would now become a major source of heartbreak for their fans.

Yet the League Cup of 1971/72 started so well for Celtic. They were drawn in the same section as Rangers and it was decided that, with Celtic Park being renovated (particularly the main stand), the two Old Firm games should be played at Ibrox, although Celtic's games against Ayr United and Morton could go ahead at Celtic Park. Celtic won both Old Firm games with a degree of ease, the first one being the famous occasion when 'young Ken [sic] Dalglish' was given the task of taking a penalty kick and famously bent down to tie his laces before doing the needful. His Rangers-supporting father looked on with mixed emotions.

But before all this happened, the Scottish League Cup suffered a serious blow to its dignity; 1971 saw the introduction of a tournament sponsored by a brewing firm beginning in July before the start of the League Cup. The League Cup, therefore, did not have the honour of kicking off the new season. The new tournament involved the teams who scored the most goals the previous season and because this was inevitably teams like Celtic, Rangers, Hibs and Aberdeen, it attracted large attendances. It did, however, detract from the League Cup and was the first step to the destructive effect that constant mucking about with the format would bring. The sponsored tournament would only last four seasons, for the sponsors tired of the idea, something that says a great deal about the concept of sponsorship and often happens when there is no real or lasting love or concern with the tournament. The Scottish League Cup itself would suffer in this regard in later years.

Diminished in status or not, the Scottish League Cup, now in its 26th year, saw St Johnstone join Celtic after a tough fight with Hearts, Airdrie and Dunfermline. Hibs also qualified, in their case easily over Motherwell, Kilmarnock and Dundee United, but the surprise qualifiers in a section which contained Dundee and Aberdeen were Falkirk who beat the Dons on the last Wednesday night 3-1 at Brockville after Aberdeen had been 1-0 up at half-time. Clydebank and Stirling Albion joined them, as did two teams whose history in Scottish football was rich but who had fallen on bad times: St Mirren and Partick Thistle.

Sometimes relegation can work to the long-term good of the club. Thistle had fought their way back from the Second Division in 1971. In their section they swept aside their east-coast challenge of Raith Rovers, Arbroath and East Fife, then Alloa in the supplementary round. They looked good, but no one could predict how good they would become in this year's tournament.

Of the quarter-finals, two proved predictable and uneventful, the other two weren't. Celtic beat Clydebank 5-0 and 6-2, St Mirren beat Stirling Albion 2-0 and 3-0. But Falkirk added to their already growing reputation with a fine performance against Hibs. Willie Cunningham, their manager, had recently turned down the offer of employment with the Scotland team and his decision to stay with the Bairns was rewarded by a packed and possibly overcrowded Brockville to see the team beat Hibs 2-0, inflicting Hibs' first defeat of the season.

But that was only the first leg. The second leg at Easter Road on 22 September in front of 23,000 was an even better night for Falkirk. They lost 1-0 thanks to a Bertie Auld goal but managed to hold out for the rest of the game with a combination of vigorous defending and a bit of luck, as is always required, for goalkeeper Rennie and the rest of his defence.

For the fourth quarter-final between St Johnstone and Partick Thistle, the first leg could not be played until Monday, 22 September because of St Johnstone's European commitments (a phrase that would have been almost unbelievable a few years earlier) but the 8,000 crowd at Muirton saw a 2-0 victory for the Perth side and things looked bleak for Partick Thistle. But the second leg, only two days later, proved the adage 'Firhill for thrills'. Thistle roared into the attack, played brilliant football and turned the tables on St Johnstone with a 5-1 victory.

The semi-finals were both played at Hampden, on Monday, 4 October and Wednesday, 6 October. The first game was a thriller between Partick Thistle and Falkirk. It was the Glasgow team which prevailed thanks to a couple of goals from Denis McQuade. For a long time it was only 1-0 and the tie was in the balance but, late in the game, a mistake by a Falkirk defender lost the game for his side. Partick were now in their fourth League Cup Final, having lost in 1953/54, 1956/57 and 1958/59. They had never won it and their only success in any national competition was some 50 years ago in 1921, when they won the Scottish Cup.

Celtic, on the other hand, had won the trophy seven times. This year they had St Mirren to contend with in the semi-final. For the past three years they had been lucky to get past the semi-final stage, and this year they got a break when St Mirren's Hugh McLaughlin committed two bad fouls and was dismissed by referee Mr JRP Gordon of Tayport. Celtic then scored three goals in a short spell through David Hay, Harry Hood and Bobby Lennox. No one would say that this was a vintage Celtic performance, but it was competent, and the Parkhead side were now in the Scottish League Cup Final for the eighth successive season!

The game on 23 October 1971 is probably still one of the most talked about games in Scottish football history. Frankly, Partick Thistle didn't seem to have a hope or a prayer. Celtic hadn't always been all that impressive, and now Billy McNeill was out injured. But they were still Celtic. Thistle were halfway up the league, but they were and always had been the unpredictables of Scottish football. Willie Ormond, the manager of St Johnstone whom Partick had beaten en route to the final, tipped Thistle. The *Evening Times* agreed it was possible, but perhaps said so with tongue in cheek. The bookies made Celtic 1-5 on for the trophy.

The facts are well known. Thistle scored four before half-time through Rae, Lawrie, McQuade and Bone while Kenny Dalglish pulled one back in the second half. Jimmy Johnstone had to be taken off injured, but that hardly explains matters as far as Celtic were concerned. Perhaps they underestimated Thistle, perhaps they missed McNeill more than they thought they would, perhaps there was some internal strife involving the recent transfers of Willie Wallace and John Hughes to Crystal Palace ... all these are possible explanations, but the most likely is that Partick Thistle simply played well and credit must be given to Davie McParland, their manager.

Like most famous games, this one has attracted a great deal of historical myths, usually involving TV presenters reading it as Celtic 4 Partick Thistle 1 on the grounds that there had to be some mistake. Another one concerns the so-called Rangers fans at Ibrox who left at half-time to see the slaughter at Hampden. No, they didn't! It would have been more or less impossible, given the logistics of Saturday afternoon transport, to get there in time. They stayed at Ibrox to watch Rangers (no doubt buoyed up by the news from Hampden) beat Motherwell 4-0.

Some Celtic fans, however, left the rest of the 62,740 fans at Hampden to go home. Their moment would come at the end of the season, for they would rebuild from this disaster, but they had now lost two League Cup finals in a row. And it would get worse in this competition. Partick Thistle had their moment of glory and Maryhill would never be the same place again.

The teams were:

Partick Thistle: Rough, Hansen, Forsyth, Glavin (Gibson), Campbell, Strachan, McQuade, Coulston, Bone, Rae, Lawrie

Celtic: Williams, Hay, Gemmell, Murdoch, Connelly, Brogan, Johnstone (Craig), Dalglish, Hood, Callaghan, Macari

Referee: W Mullan, Dalkeith

'If it ain't broke, don't fix it.' Oh, how one wishes that the Scottish League had listened to that maxim in 1972! The League Cup had now been going strong for 26 years, had made loads of money, had given several teams the chance to win honours (Partick Thistle being the most recent example) and it was generally agreed by the fans that there was little wrong with the format, except perhaps that the quarter-finals did not need to be home-and-home affairs, for one leg would have been enough.

That, however, was only a small gripe. The tournament was a success and everyone appreciated the final being played at the end of October, usually on a crisp autumn day before the advent of winter on the weekend, normally, that the clocks changed.

But sadly, under the misguided banner of progress and making a few vague statements about 'this will make the tournament a little more interesting' and 'the crowds will come back', the tournament was expanded so that two teams qualified from the sectional stage (which would now be a free-for-all draw) and there would be a second round (over two legs) before we got to the quarter-finals (also two legs). The final would be delayed and would, in 1972, be played in December.

The advantage was that more teams would play in the tournament for longer. But, on the other, hand there were far too many foregone conclusions. Celtic were drawn in the same group as East Fife, Stirling Albion and Arbroath, and two qualified. Most people could guess who one of the qualifiers might be. Rangers similarly had St Mirren, Clydebank and Ayr United and (surprise, surprise) they qualified as well.

The trouble with more games and home-and-home fixtures was that it minimised the chance of a surprise. The League Cup had hitherto been rich in the phenomenon of smaller teams doing well. East Fife were legends in the early years, Partick Thistle were the recent examples in 1971. Third Lanark had been in the final, as had Dunfermline, Falkirk, Raith Rovers and, recently, St Johnstone. Brechin, Cowdenbeath, Ayr United, Clyde and Dumbarton had all reached the semis. It would now be some time before another smaller team had their moment of glory – Raith Rovers in 1994/95 – but by then the format had changed yet again.

This year's second round did see Stenhousemuir beat Rangers at Ibrox 2-1. The only problem was that Rangers had won 5-0 at Ochilview. To some observers, the Rangers team seemed to contain more than a few fringe players that night.

For their part Stenhousemuir apparently had major financial problems paying their men the bonus in the aftermath.

The semi-finals, played in late November, were Celtic v Aberdeen and Rangers v Hibs with not a wee team in sight. Hibs had beaten Airdrie 10-3 to get there in the two-legged quarter-finals, Aberdeen 7-1 over East Fife. Rangers had more of a struggle to beat St Johnstone and Celtic's tie against Dundee was an absolute epic with Dundee a little unlucky on more than one occasion.

Dundee won the first leg at Dens Park narrowly but deservedly 1-0 with a goal from Gordon Wallace. The second leg at Celtic Park on 1 November before 39,000 was controversial with two old rivals, Jock Stein and referee Bobby Davidson, crossing swords not for the first time. Stein was fined for a public show of dissent after 90 minutes. The history went back to the Scottish Cup Final of 1970 – possibly even earlier – and since, Mr Davidson and Celtic tended to be kept away from each other. Both teams had cause for complaint about a goal given to the other side, but the game finished 3-2 after extra time and there could be little doubt that it was one of the best games seen for a while. On the away goals rule, now prevalent in European football, Dundee would have won; as it was, a replay was decreed for 20 November at Hampden.

It was a remarkable game. Dundee scored first. Then Celtic scored four, all in the space of six minutes – all headers too, from Hood, Dalglish and Deans twice – then the game lapsed into an appallingly boring occasion with both teams having apparently given up in a curious anti-climax with Celtic fans amusing themselves by shouting and chanting inanities about Bobby Davidson to pass the time. Two days later Rangers and Hibs met in the first semi-final; 46,513 saw a foul-tempered, unpleasant affair with one or two vendettas and the history of previous meetings being played out. The two teams had played each other at Easter Road the Saturday before in the league and it had been equally tough. Five players were booked by referee Mr Gordon, quite a few more deserved to have been too, with jersey pulling seeming to be the speciality of the night in the opinion of Ian Archer of the *Glasgow Herald*. Only one goal separated the teams and it was scored by John Brownlie of Hibs who, in the 72nd minute, ran through, evading attempts to grab his jersey and a few scything tackles, to score. Rangers then hit the bar in injury time but there could be little doubt that the better team won on the night.

The other semi-final was on Monday, 27 November, also at Hampden. The weather was foul but the crowd was a creditable 40,000 in the circumstances, including a knot of Aberdeen supporters who had travelled 150 miles for the privilege of seeing their team battle for a place in their third Scottish League Cup Final. It would have been a wet and miserable trek back for them, for they had the mortification of seeing their team twice take the lead, twice lose it (the first time was through a penalty kick needlessly conceded), then see Celtic grab a late winner. At times Aberdeen looked the better team, but Celtic's winner was a sight to behold and showed the football brain that young Kenny Dalglish possessed. A cross came from Harry Hood, Dalglish ran for it knowing that he had no realistic chance of reaching it, but he took two Dons defenders with him and left the way clear for Tommy Callaghan to lash home.

Celtic had played 12 games to reach Hampden and the final was scheduled for 9 December. Some newspapers suggested, not unreasonably, that December was no time to play a cup final and that a postponement to the spring was an idea not without merit. Some people within both clubs agreed, but the Scottish League decided that 9 December was when it should be for the second all-green League Cup Final in four years. The teams had also met in last year's Scottish Cup Final, the day of Dixie Deans' hat-trick and his famous somersault. But Dixie was not playing this time because of an injury and Hibs felt that they now had a chance.

Hibs were generally agreed to be the most annoying team to support. No club had a more dismal record of failing to win when they needed to or of selling off their star players, sometimes at crazy times of the season and when there was no obvious need of money. Their support was solid, however, and it was clear that they were now the better team in Edinburgh, something that they would prove spectacularly a few weeks after the League Cup Final.

They now had an energetic and committed manager in Eddie Turnbull who had built up a strong team, called Turnbull's Tornadoes, with a great defence built around Pat Stanton and forwards like Alex Edwards and Jim O'Rourke with the ability to take a goal. All that was needed, one felt, was a certain belief in themselves, but facing Celtic who had beaten them 6-1 in May at Hampden made it difficult to engender any great optimism in their support. There was also the undeniable historical fact that Hibs had won nothing of importance for over 20 years since they won the Scottish League in 1952. As far as the League Cup was concerned, they had appeared in only two finals and had lost the pair of them. Phrases like 'trophy shy' were beginning to be applied to Hibs by the press.

Celtic had exited from Europe a month previously but had played well since, and although everyone agreed that Hibs would put up a good performance, it was generally felt that Celtic would just have the edge. The 71,696 crowd made their way to Hampden in what seemed a most unlikely sort of day for a cup final. The weather was dull and cold, but fortunately there was no snow or ice (there would be the following year). December darkness was beginning to fall even as the teams took the field and people questioned the wisdom and even the sanity of those who arranged the League Cup Final – a showpiece of the season – on such a day.

The first half mirrored the weather, dull and drab with little to warm the fans, and it was the 60th minute before anything happened. Celtic conceded a free kick on the edge of the box. It came to Stanton who ran across the Celtic penalty area before squeezing the ball home. Six minutes later, Hibs took a grip of the game and Stanton was involved again, charging down the right wing before crossing for O'Rourke to score. Celtic, to their credit, fought back and scored through Dalglish to set up what would have been a grandstand finish, but Hibs and Stanton took control again and finished quite clearly the better side.

So ended the 27th Scottish League Cup and Hibs headed back to Edinburgh in the darkness to celebrate their first triumph in this competition, some 70 and a bit years after they had won the Scottish Cup in 1902 against the same opponents. Life got even better for Hibs and their supporters on New Year's Day 1973 when they beat Hearts 7-0. There were those who felt this Hibs team might have spearheaded the start of a permanent shift of power from Glasgow to Edinburgh. This was not to be, but in the meantime, Celtic had to reckon with the fact that they had now lost three League Cup finals in a row. And they had not finished yet.

The teams were:

Hibs: Herriot, Brownlie, Schaedler, Stanton, Black, Blackley, Edwards, O'Rourke, Gordon, Cropley, Duncan

Celtic: Williams, McGrain, Brogan, McCluskey, McNeill, Hay, Johnstone (Callaghan), Connelly, Hood, Dalglish, Macari

Referee: A McKenzie, Larbert

The year 1973 had more than its fair share of problems throughout the globe. Rampant inflation all over the developed world, particularly in Great Britain, war still raging in Vietnam, another war in the Middle East which had a major impact on Europe and the USA, the US President under more and more pressure for telling lies about his involvement in the Watergate affair, major labour problems in the UK leading to a three-day working week and power cuts. All this had its effect on the Scottish League Cup, believe it or not, and this particular cup final is generally reckoned to have been the worst of the lot – unless you are a supporter of Dundee FC.

Apart from all the other things that went wrong with the League Cup this year, there was also an experimental offside rule which stated that a man could only be offside in the last 18 yards of the park. To this effect the penalty box line was extended to the touchline. This was a basically well-intentioned plan to create more goals and an ill-disguised riposte to the offside trap practised by Aberdeen and a few other teams in the early 1970s. It did not work because it was a poachers' charter. We had the phenomenon of players standing on the edge of the penalty box waiting for a long ball, knowing that they could not be offside. Nor was there an appreciable increase in the number of goals scored.

The general idiocy of the League Cup sectional format was made apparent when one looked at a section which contained Celtic, Rangers, Arbroath and Falkirk from which two teams qualified. Now which two would that be? As if by agreement, Celtic beat Rangers at Ibrox and Rangers triumphed at Parkhead. Small wonder that attendances began to drop, even at those Old Firm games. But, amid all this gloom and self-inflicted tedium, Scotland qualified for the 1974 World Cup!

Two teams now qualified from section nine and therefore there had to be two games in the supplementary round. Albion Rovers and Clyde duly beat East Stirlingshire and Forfar Athletic and took their places in the second round. Some games were over almost before they started. Rangers, for example, beat Dumbarton 8-1 and Aberdeen beat Stirling Albion 6-0 over two legs, but other games were surprisingly competitive. Hibs eventually got the better of Raith Rovers but not before the Kirkcaldy men had put up a good fight in the first leg at Easter Road. The two games between Dundee and Dunfermline were absolute crackers before Dundee eventually edged through 5-4 in a performance that was gritty rather than classy and has the *Glasgow Herald* making one of its less-successful prophecies by affirming that 'few of the 5,000 crowd will rate their [Dundee's] future chances very highly'. It also suggested that Dunfermline Athletic, after a glorious decade in the 1960s, were now on the slide.

The best game of the second round was between Celtic and Motherwell. Celtic won the first leg at Fir Park but then Motherwell, managed by Ian St John, equalised the tie at

Celtic Park and the game had to go to a replay. Celtic won the toss for the venue, and so we had the remarkable spectacle of Celtic playing Motherwell on the night of Monday, 29 October and winning 3-2, then playing Aberdeen on the Wednesday in the quarter-final of the same tournament, also at Parkhead, and also winning 3-2. Both games provided great entertainment and both attracted attendances of 25,000, but there was still a second leg of the quarter-final to come!

There was a fair amount of criticism in the press, but given European commitments and Scotland internationals and the insane desire of the Scottish League to finish this now overcrowded tournament before the turn of the year, they could do little else. It is difficult to imagine players of the modern era putting up with all this, but cynics were not slow to point out that, for teams like Celtic, the money kept rolling in!

In the other quarter-finals, there was a major shock when Albion Rovers defeated Kilmarnock 2-0 in the first leg. This game was played on Tuesday, 30 October. The other three first legs played the following night on Halloween were all narrow wins for the home sides: Celtic beating Aberdeen 3-2, Rangers beating Hibs 2-0 and Dundee beating Clyde 1-0.

The second legs had an element of farce about them: on 21 November in midwinter darkness, and the miners' overtime ban had compelled the Government to put the country on a three-day week. It was a political overreaction, but we at least had not been put on a nuclear alert as the US military had been a month earlier as a result of events in the Yom Kippur War in the Middle East. The world was crazy in late 1973 and the Scottish League Cup joined in the madness. We had the spectacle of Celtic and Rangers both qualifying for the semi-final of the League Cup by playing away from home in the afternoon, at Aberdeen and Hibs respectively, and boring the pants off small crowds by drawing 0-0 in both cases. All this in the interests of saving power. Meanwhile, Clyde hosted Dundee in the evening in front of Scotland's only floodlit game (why were they able to use floodlights when both Aberdeen and Hibs weren't?) and drew 2-2, but Dundee's goal at Dens Park in the first leg was enough to see them through.

Then, for some reason, Kilmarnock and Albion Rovers played their game on the Saturday (having played each other in the league at Cliftonhill on Wednesday) at storm-swept Rugby Park. Killie, by winning 5-2, squeezed through 5-4 on aggregate. The historian is sometimes at a loss to understand the dates and times of football matches during these mad times, but the three-day week meant that half the country worked from Monday to Wednesday, the other half from Thursday to Saturday. Everyone was asked to save power, TV was stopped at 10.30pm every night, the Tories blamed the miners, the miners blamed the Tories, petrol was becoming scarce and expensive because of the Middle East war and everything seemed to get more and more incomprehensible and gloomy by the day.

But the League Cup continued. Once again, sensible appeals were made to postpone things until the spring, but once again the decision was taken to go ahead. The Dundee v Kilmarnock semi-final due to be played on 28 November at Hampden was postponed because of bad weather and rearranged for Monday, 3 December. It was cruelly described by the *Glasgow Herald* as the 'ghost' semi-final, for it was attended by a crowd of 4,682 and those who braved the conditions saw Dundee beat Second Division Kilmarnock 1-0 with a goal from Tommy Gemmell.

Two nights later came the Old Firm semi-final. It was not like other games between these two. Extra generators were deployed to get the floodlights going, while transport and weather problems of rain and sleet restricted the crowd to 54,864. It was the Celtic fans on the uncovered terracing who sang songs like 'Raindrops Keep Falling on My Head' and 'Singing in the Rain' as they beat Rangers 3-1 with a hat-trick from Harry Hood. Celtic reached their tenth League Cup Final in a row.

And so we come to the dire Scottish League Cup Final of 15 December 1973. If ever there was a game that should have been rearranged, it was this one. If it had been in Ancient Rome, the omens would have been against it. The weather was awful and, because of power restrictions and the need to allow for extra time in midwinter, the game had to kick off at 1.30pm. Referee Bobby Davidson might have solved the Scottish League's problem for them by calling the game off in the morning, but he decided that Hampden was playable, a decision not universally agreed with and for which he was severely criticised. Events would suggest that the pitch was playable – just – but conditions did not lend themselves to a good game.

Everyone favoured Celtic as winners but Dundee, under Davie White (one-time manager of Rangers), had done well to reach this stage. A club which had gone out of its way to upset its own supporters by their policy of selling star players in the 1960s had nevertheless fought back and they had a tremendous asset in Tommy Gemmell, a man who knew how to win football matches. Ebullient as always and now with a point to prove over Celtic and his ex-manager Jock Stein, Tommy had his revenge that day.

Staging a game in circumstances like this usually brings its own reward in terms of attendance but only 27,924 turned up, by any standards a shocking crowd for a national cup final, particularly one involving Celtic and Dundee who had attracted 66,660 to see the League Cup Final in October 1967. Most of the spectators huddled under the cover on the West Terrace, while the East Terrace, normally thronged and packed with excited humanity, was bare, windswept and wet. In the circumstances the teams deserve a great deal of credit for playing any kind of football at all, and it was an even game until Gordon Wallace scored for Dundee 15 minutes from the end with a fine shot from the edge of the box. Dundee were able to hold out and resist a desperate late Celtic effort to equalise.

The teams were:

Dundee: Allan, Wilson, Gemmell, Ford, Stewart, Phillip, Duncan, Robinson, Wallace, Scott, Lambie

Celtic: Hunter, McGrain, Brogan, McCluskey, McNeill, Murray, Hood (Johnstone), Hay (Connelly), Wilson, Callaghan, Dalglish

Referee: RH Davidson, Airdrie

It was Dundee's third Scottish League Cup, but it would bring a great deal less happiness than their two epic ones in 1951 and 1952. One was almost sorry for the small knot of Dundee fans who should have been enjoying their best day out for years, but celebration and December 1973 did not go well together. 'It's no' a day for a tree tae be oot in,' one of them said. As for the Celtic fans, sadly diminished in numbers and reduced by the end to singing old offensive Rangers chants about Tommy Gemmell, it was a day for them to forget. They were aware that they had lost four League Cup finals in a row. Oddly enough, these four seasons always saw them come back to win the Scottish League. It was almost as if a Celtic supporter had to go through purgatory in the autumn and winter in order to reach paradise in the spring.

But lessons were learned, at least for a while. The experimental offside rule was persevered with for another year but major restructuring was ordered for 1974/75. The nonsense of two teams qualifying was done away with and the final was scheduled for the sensible date of 26 October. It was a return to common sense, although there was still the slightly strange sectional set-up of games being played on Saturday, Wednesday, Saturday, Wednesday, Saturday, Wednesday rather than having a break on the middle Wednesday when a league fixture could be played.

The world was in a slightly better place than a year before. There was now a minority Labour Government under the benign and conciliatory Harold Wilson, but inflation was now at a silly level. The Middle East had settled down a little, but on the very eve of the football season was the unprecedented resignation of the US President. Richard Nixon's men had been involved in a burglary at Watergate and the President had lied about it. He had said, 'There will be no whitewash at the White House.' Oh dear! He had to go but he fought to the end, resigning only days before he would have been impeached and removed from office.

Scotland performed creditably at the World Cup in the summer and came home with heads held high. The season would be a vital one in that it would determine who would qualify for the new Premier League, to be launched in 1975, and which the gullible believed would solve everyone's problems. And Meadowbank had now joined the fun.

It was extremely rare for both Edinburgh teams to qualify for the League Cup quarter-finals, but Hearts and Hibs duly did so in 1974/75. Hibs beat Rangers on opening day and never looked back until they lost on the last Wednesday, by which time qualification was assured. Rangers, to whom 1974 had not been kind, also lost to Dundee, but Dundee themselves were unable to raise their game in this section and emulate their feat of last year.

Without in any way setting the heather on fire or even getting their supporters excited about them, Hearts qualified in a tight section by beating Aberdeen at Tynecastle 2-1 on the last Wednesday. It was the first time that Hearts had qualified since they won the trophy in 1962/63 and the sigh of relief from the 14,000 fans was a loud and happy one.

Celtic survived an early scare at Ayr United to qualify again and Partick Thistle joined them by beating Arbroath 4-0 on the last night while challengers Clyde and Dumbarton drew. Falkirk, Hamilton, Kilmarnock and Airdrie also made it, Airdrie's qualification being particularly impressive. At the halfway stage they had lost twice and didn't appear to have a hope until a spectacular 6-0 demolition of St Mirren at Love Street set them on their way.

Both Edinburgh teams were kept apart in the quarter-final draw, but Hibs were given the difficult task of beating Kilmarnock, now managed by ex-Celt Willie Fernie. Hearts took on Falkirk, Celtic were given Hamilton and what seemed to be the tie of the round was Partick Thistle v Airdrie. Celtic had little bother in disposing of Hamilton Accies, and Partick Thistle did not recover from their first-leg defeat by Airdrie. But the games involving the Edinburgh teams were thrillers.

Both first legs were drawn. The second legs were played on 25 September, a night of steady rain which certainly reduced attendances. Hearts went to Brockville to play before 8,000 spectators who saw a tremendous game of football in terrible conditions. Hearts had many chances which they spurned and it was Falkirk who scored the only goal of the game through Kirkie Lawson after Hearts had been reduced to ten men after when Gallacher was injured.

The mood of the Hearts supporters was hardly improved when they heard that their rivals Hibs had had a great night at Easter Road. They delighted their fans by beating Kilmarnock 4-1 thanks to an excellent second-half performance in the rain. This set up a semi-final against Falkirk, while Celtic played Airdrie, a team who were not as easy as they sounded for the Parkhead men.

The games were played on the evening of 9 October, the eve of 1974's second general election. That hardly explains the poor crowd of 19,000 at Hampden to see Celtic play Airdrie. The standard of play reflected the poor crowd and the lack of atmosphere in the Hampden bowl where one could often hear the shouts of the players. Celtic supporters were in some ways sated with constant success but were also a little disillusioned by their exit from the European Cup to a mediocre Greek team a week before. Tonight, however, the diehards saw their team (wearing an unusual green and black, vertical-striped jersey) reach their 11th successive Scottish League Cup Final with a second-half goal scored by Stevie Murray in a depressingly poor match.

There was a bigger crowd of 22,000 at Tynecastle to see a far better game between Hibs v Falkirk. Three players were booked but the tally should have been a lot higher as Second Division Falkirk punched well above their weight. Eventually Hibs wore them down, and a fine combination involving Alan Gordon and Joe Harper saw Harper score the only goal of the game.

For the third time, the Scottish League Cup Final was between Celtic and Hibs. Both teams had won one final each, and with goalscorers like Joe Harper in the Hibs ranks and Dixie Deans playing for Celtic, it was widely expected that there would be loads of goals. No one, however, could predict just what an entertaining game this would be. It was felt that Celtic had the edge, mainly because they had beaten Hibs in the league the week before, but it was a League Cup Final and Celtic had had a habit of losing them. They had lost the last four.

Overall, 53,848 were at Hampden on a coldish autumn day of 26 October 1974. Celtic supporters were still not there in the huge numbers that we would have expected, but there was a sizeable contingent from Edinburgh. Celtic scored first through Jimmy Johnstone. Dixie Deans, who had scored a hat-trick the previous week in the league game, scored one while surrounded by Hibs men. Joe Harper, however, pulled one back before half-time. Celtic then went further ahead through Paul Wilson, Harper scored again to make it 3-2, but after that Celtic took command with a couple of goals from Deans and another from Steve Murray before Harper scrambled another for Hibs to make the final score 6-3.

The fifth goal was a total marvel. Jimmy Johnstone shot for goal but the ball was sliced wide until Dixie Deans dived forward to score a remarkable reflex goal. Dixie had thus scored hat-tricks in successive weeks against Hibs to add to his famous hat-trick in 1972 in the Scottish Cup Final, again against Hibs. He would joke afterwards that he 'didn't like the green jersey'. And a word of sympathy was due for Joe Harper of Hibs who performed the rare feat (unique in a major cup final, it is believed) of scoring a hat-trick but ending up on the losing side!

The teams were:

Celtic: Hunter, McGrain, Brogan, Murray, McNeill, McCluskey, Johnstone, Dalglish, Deans, Hood, Wilson

Hibs: McArthur, Brownlie (Smith), Bremner, Stanton, Spalding, Blackley, Edwards, Cropley, Harper, Munro, Duncan (Murray)

Referee: JRP Gordon, Newport on Tay

Celtic had broken their run of losing League Cup finals. They had won the trophy eight times, edging ahead of Rangers. Twenty-nine League Cup finals had now come and gone. Celtic held all three Scottish trophies, something that was not bad for a team meant to have reached the peak and now in decline. One hopes that the Celtic supporters enjoyed this triumph, for the League Cup Final losing habit would soon return and Celtic would never again win the trophy in the 1970s. They would win the trophy only twice more in the 20th century.

Rangers won the Scottish League in March 1975, although Celtic added the Scottish Cup to the Scottish League Cup. But a significant event happened in early July 1975 when Celtic manager Jock Stein was involved in a life-threatening road accident in the Scottish Borders and was ruled out of action for a whole season. Without Stein, Celtic struggled and Rangers who, frankly, had been afraid of and intimidated by him took full advantage.

It was not a great era of Scottish football. A great deal depended on the new Premier League, but there were more problems in Scottish football than the league structure. Not the least problem was the look of things. Stadia were run-down and antiquated and there was not nearly enough cover. No one seemed to have the courage or conviction to tackle the problem of hooliganism. And the players with their long hair and hideous fashions of the 1970s did not really look like athletes.

The Scottish League Cup reached its 30th birthday this year and, once again, it provided its fair share of entertainment and excitement. The most interesting section was that which contained Celtic, Aberdeen, Hearts and Dumbarton. The first day was possibly the most vital one, for Hearts lost to Dumbarton and, although they then immediately beat Celtic at Tynecastle on the Wednesday night, Celtic beat them at Celtic Park and duly qualified. This was no insignificant achievement for the Parkhead side who were not only without Jock Stein but had also lost to retirement their centre-half and captain Billy McNeill.

Rangers qualified without a great deal of bother. They drew twice with Motherwell but the Fir Park men did not do as well against Airdrie as Rangers did. Hibs too qualified against Dundee, Dunfermline Athletic and Ayr United, but the team of the qualifying sections were Partick Thistle, dubbed 'the people's champions' by the *Glasgow Herald*. Managed by the irrepressible Bertie Auld, a Maryhill man himself, Thistle finished their section with maximum points beating Dundee United, Kilmarnock and St Johnstone to encourage hopes of another 1971.

The other sections involving the teams from the lesser divisions (as from 1975 there were three divisions in the Scottish League) were far more exciting affairs. Clydebank and Stenhousemuir won through by victories on the last night, but possibly the most exciting finish came in section five when Queen of the South beat Stirling Albion 3-2 at Annfield. Falkirk and Hamilton drew at Douglas Park when a win for either of them would probably have sufficed. Montrose were rare qualifiers but had done well against Raith Rovers, East Fife and St Mirren. Clydebank beat Cowdenbeath in the supplementary round and were rewarded by a tie against Partick Thistle, while Stenhousemuir faced Celtic, Hibs took on Morton and Rangers were given Queen of the South.

The first legs went as one would have thought with wins for Celtic, Rangers, Hibs and Partick Thistle. It was one of these nights when the argument that the quarter-finals did not have to be two-legged seemed to be a very strong one. But the second legs on 24 September 1975 were very different matters indeed. Celtic, 2-0 up from the first leg at Stenhousemuir, duly qualified in front of a poor crowd at Parkhead in a boring 1-0 win and Partick Thistle suffered their first defeat of the season when they lost 0-1 to Clydebank at Kilbowie Park, but as they had won the first leg 4-0 it did not really matter.

These were the simple ones, the other two games were tense. Rangers were lucky to get away from Palmerston Park on a wild and windy night in front of 7,000 spectators. 'Only in Scotland would people play and people pay to watch football on such an evil night,' wrote Ian Archer in the *Glasgow Herald*, who also talked about *Macbeth*'s witches in this context. Rangers had not played particularly well in the first leg at Ibrox, but they won 1-0 and that goal proved crucial. John Dempster of the Doonhamers was brought down and scored the resultant penalty, Rangers then scored through Derek Johnstone and looked comfortable in the dreadful conditions until the very end when Tommy Bryce squeezed in a low header and took the game to extra time. In such conditions, however, it is always likely that the full-time team will prevail, and so it turned out with Alex MacDonald scrambling a late winner with only six minutes left. Rangers were the victors but Queen of the South were the heroes.

The conditions were no better in Montrose as the wind howled in from the North Sea while Hibs took on Montrose at Links Park. When Arthur Duncan scored in the first minute to make the score 2-0 on aggregate, some of the 4,000 crowd might well have wondered why they had come to see this, but then the amazing happened. No further score until half-time, then Montrose equalised on the night, then equalised the tie, then in extra time won the tie as Hibs, with fine defenders like Schaedler, Stanton and Brownlie, simply had no answer. This gave Montrose their first appearance in the League Cup semi-final and possibly the best night in all their impoverished history.

A man with the name that sounds like it comes from Jane Austen, Dennis D'Arcy, started it all with a long ball that found Bobby Livingstone. Then Les Barr who scored a penalty kick. Montrose won the game with an amazing goal. It was basically a clearance which was sliced into the air and got the benefit of the wind to take the ball over the head of Jim McArthur in the Hibs goal. It was an astonishing goal in an astonishing game, and an unbelievable experience for Hibs and all their talented players to lose like this.

The reward for this was a semi-final date for Montrose against Rangers on Wednesday, 8 October 1975 at Hampden, but before that Celtic took on Partick Thistle on the Monday night in what appeared to be the more competitive of the two games. It is commonly believed that semi-finals do not lend themselves to good entertaining football and this sadly proved to be the case. Partick failed to up their game and the annoying thing was that it would not have taken much to beat Celtic that night. As it was, however, Icelander Johannes Edvaldsson scored the only goal of the game for Celtic, although they were indebted to goalkeeper Peter Latchford for a last-minute save from a Doug Somner header to prevent the game going to extra time.

The other game looked as if it might produce a seismic shock at half-time. The game had been poor, but just on the stroke of half-time Montrose earned a penalty kick which Les Barr duly sank. Rangers left the field at half-time to the boos of their supporters and presumably a rollicking from manager Jock Wallace, but for a long time in the second half Montrose held them. Then Montrose hit the post about halfway through the second half. That was the fateful moment. It was as if someone now pressed a switch, for Rangers then ran up the field and equalised. The floodgates were now open and Rangers finally won 5-1 with goals from Derek Parlane, Alec Miller, Ally Scott, Sandy Jardine and Derek Johnstone.

It was Celtic v Rangers in the Scottish League Cup Final for the sixth time. Celtic had won three and Rangers two, but in 1975 neither team was particularly impressive. Words like 'enigma' and 'unpredictable' were applied to both. A sign of the times was the 1pm kick-off and the closing of all shops in the Mount Florida area of the city to deal with the menace of hooliganism and, to an extent, it was a success. It also, however, contributed to a disappointing crowd of 57,806 which ten years ago would have been doubled.

Last year's talisman for Celtic, Dixie Deans, was out injured, and Rangers reintroduced Colin Stein while playing Derek Johnstone further back, but half-time was reached with the score 0-0 and the standard of football was dire. The game looked like extra time and a replay. Kenny Dalglish was well policed by Tom Forsyth, sometimes none too gently, and Celtic had no one else to get them into the game. But neither had Rangers until Alec MacDonald scored with a diving header late in the game. Celtic, lacking the inspiration of their talismanic manager Jock Stein who was still in hospital, tried to get back into the game but without success.

The teams were:

Rangers: Kennedy, Jardine, Greig, Forsyth, Jackson, MacDonald, McLean, Stein, Parlane, Johnstone, Young

Celtic: Latchford, McGrain, Lynch, McCluskey, MacDonald, Edvaldsson, Hood (McNamara), Dalglish, Wilson (Glavin), Callaghan, Lennox

Referee: W Anderson, East Kilbride

It was Rangers' eighth Scottish League Cup success and possibly one of their least memorable. It was, however, the first step towards their first treble since 1964. For Celtic, without Stein and McNeill and so many other players now near the end of their career, it was a season of transition. They would come back, but Celtic had now lost five League Cup finals out of six. And League Cup Final misery had not yet done with them.

As the football season started in August 1976, Great Britain was enjoying a heatwave. As is the way with the British public, they moaned constantly about not having enough sun and, when they got sun, they moaned about that as well by having to deal with hosepipe bans. When the season started on 14 August, little had changed in the sense that both Celtic and Rangers qualified, Rangers getting the better of Hibs even though Hibs had held them to a draw on the first Wednesday night at Easter Road. Hearts also qualified in a potentially difficult section against Dundee, Partick Thistle and Motherwell, but the team that impressed was Aberdeen.

Aberdeen's history in the early 1970s had not been great. They had never really recovered from the bizarre sale of Martin Buchan in February 1972 when they had a chance of winning the league, and their transfer policy often bewildered their fans. But now they had the ebullient Ally MacLeod as manager who certainly talked a good game and who was apparently able to back up his talk with action. Their section of Kilmarnock, St Mirren and Ally's old team Ayr United was not particularly demanding, but the Dons did well. Aberdeen's record in the Scottish League Cup was nothing to write home about – in fact, it was downright poor, for they had only won the trophy once and had only been in one other final – but Ally soon began to talk up his chances of winning a major trophy.

As was often the case, the most exciting sections were the Second Division ones, in particular the section involving Hamilton Accies and Falkirk. Both teams arrived at Douglas Park on the last Wednesday night with it all to play for. The

4,000 saw an absolute thriller in which Falkirk scored twice early on and looked in command, but Hamilton scored just on the stroke of half-time to set up a great second half in which Falkirk's defence, knowing that even a draw would suffice to qualify on goal difference, took everything that the home side could throw at them and just held out.

It was also close at Annfield where Stirling Albion just got the better of Morton to qualify, but Airdrie and Clydebank had fewer problems. Airdrie and Albion Rovers staged a rare Lanarkshire derby in the supplementary round which Albion Rovers won by the narrowest of margins to earn themselves a tie with Celtic. Rovers were behind from the first leg but managed to persuade 3,000 to attend Cliftonhill (if we ignore the other crowd who had gathered on a hill outside!) to see John Brogan score a hat-trick and take the Second Division side through. Aberdeen got Stirling Albion, Rangers took on Clydebank and, in what looked like the best tie of the round, two feisty old competitors, Hearts and Falkirk, faced each other.

In the event, two games went to replays and one to a second replay. Celtic duly beat Albion Rovers, the wee Rovers being given a great reception when they came out at Parkhead. Coatbridge is generally reckoned to be a Celtic-supporting area, as well as Albion Rovers being the first team that Jock Stein played for. Hearts beat Falkirk, hard though the Bairns fought in the second leg at Brockville to bring it back to 5-7 on aggregate. Aberdeen, however, found Stirling Albion a real handful. The Dons were unimpressive at Pittodrie, winning only 1-0, and the Albion were able to reverse the scoreline at Annfield and take them to a third game at Dens Park which Aberdeen duly won before the minuscule crowd that one gets for play-offs at neutral venues.

Rangers, who would struggle this season, had an even tougher job to get the better of Clydebank. They perhaps should have killed them off at Ibrox but the game finished 3-3, then at Kilbowie, the Bankies came very close to creating a real upset but were held to a 1-1 draw. The toss of a coin then decreed that Ibrox should be the venue for the play-off, but even extra time failed to settle that one, for the game ended 0-0 in a stadium that had all the atmosphere of a public library. And so everyone agreed to go to Firhill the following night and, on this occasion, it was decreed that penalties should be used to determine the winner.

Penalties were not needed, for in front of 12,000 weary spectators Rangers won 2-1 in a somewhat undistinguished (the less kind said 'dreadful') performance. Rangers' scorers were Derek Parlane and Bobby McKean while Clydebank scored through a man called David Cooper, who looked as if he might have a future ahead of him.

The semi-finals were scheduled for Hampden Park on Monday and Wednesday, 25 and 27 October. The first was played in pouring rain before a crowd of 21,000 and saw Celtic scrape through unimpressively with a 2-1 win after Hearts had scored first. Celtic needed a softish penalty and Hearts got a man sent off late in the game to send Tynecastle fans back home feeling that the world was against them. Things would now go from bad to worse for the Maroons for they would end up relegated that season, but Celtic were now in their 13th successive League Cup Final, albeit thanks to one of their poorest displays of the season so far.

It was the other semi-final which made everyone sit up and take notice. Rangers were already in trouble and had suffered bad publicity after their fans rioted in a friendly match in England. They had been compelled to make a public statement to the effect that they would now employ Roman Catholics. This did not go down well with their fans and a poor crowd of 20,990 on a fine dry night reflected that. Aberdeen, on the other hand, went into this game on the back of a 2-1 win over Celtic at Pittodrie in the Scottish League and most people tipped them to win. No one, however, would have predicted a scoreline of Rangers 1 Aberdeen 5. Jocky Scott scored a hat-trick and Hampden Park was deserted long before the end of the game, left to the small knot of Aberdeen fans who had made the journey down. Ally MacLeod purred like a cat that got all the cream and Aberdeen were in their third Scottish League Cup Final.

He was purring in the final too, but he did not get it all his own way against Celtic on 6 November. Far from it. Celtic were the better team and, with a little more sharpness in front of goal, would have won handsomely. Celtic now had lost six League Cup finals out of the last seven, as their fans needed no reminding and yet, on this occasion, they deserved a little more.

Full credit to Aberdeen, however, for taking advantage of Celtic's failure to capitalise and for bringing the first trophy back to Aberdeen since 1970. The attendance was 69,707, reflecting the resurgence of Aberdeen and a slight increase in the Celtic support since Jock Stein had returned to duty. Unfortunately, Jock's two signings, Pat Stanton and Joe Craig, were ineligible for this game because they were cup-tied. The weather was wet and unpleasant and the game, being held in November rather than October, finished in the dark as the game went to extra time. For some strange and unexplained reason, Celtic fans populated the Mount Florida end that day as well as their traditional King's Park end. Perhaps they simply wanted in out of the rain.

Celtic went ahead through a Kenny Dalglish penalty. Most of the Aberdeen persuasion were of the opinion that Dalglish dived and TV replays suggested that they may have had a point. But the lead did not last long and Drew Jarvie headed the Dons back onto level terms. Bobby Clark in the Aberdeen goal and his defence survived a tremendous onslaught for more or less the rest of the 90 minutes with Celtic's frustrations becoming apparent in the number of men being booked by referee Mr Paterson of Bothwell.

Davie Robb scored for Aberdeen early in extra time and, once again, Aberdeen's defence (with Willie Miller outstanding) held out. Full time apparently brought Union Street in Aberdeen to a standstill with cars tooting their horns when their radios told them that the game was over. It was a landmark in the club's history and much was the euphoria and hyperbole about the rebirth of the Dons with the focus very much on the effervescent Ally MacLeod. But the rest of their season failed to deliver, especially after the club was rocked by an apparently groundless story about match fixing. Celtic, on the other hand, bounced back from the League Cup Final disappointment and won a league and cup double. But that too was transient. Trouble hit Celtic in a big way next season.

The teams were:

Aberdeen: Clark, Kennedy, Williamson, Smith, Garner, Miller, Sullivan, Scott, Harper, Jarvie (Robb), Graham

Celtic: Latchford, McGrain, Lynch, Edvaldsson, MacDonald, Aitken, Doyle, Glavin, Dalglish, Burns (Lennox), Wilson

Referee: J Paterson, Bothwell

In some ways, the 1977/78 Scottish League Cup was decided before the season started. The sections were done away with (they would change their minds again a few seasons later) and there would be a straight draw and two-legged ties, usually played on Wednesday nights, apart from the second round – the second leg of which would be allocated a Saturday. The reason was the now-overcrowded season and the perception that the League Cup did not always attract the highest crowds. There was a certain truth in that, but the changes hardly helped.

The other development which determined who the winners would be was the astonishing suicide committed by Celtic who, on the eve of the season, decided to sell Kenny Dalglish to Liverpool. Behind all the cant about 'the player gets to choose for himself' and 'free market' and 'wouldn't you accept advancement if offered it?' lay the undeniable fact that the directors of the club were more interested in money than in having a good football team. The club would never recover in the 1977/78 season and Jock Stein, now older, hunched and bitter as distinct from the confident, assertive and cheerful man of a few years ago, was never the same again.

It was an odd season. It was played against the backdrop of Scotland qualifying for the World Cup in Argentina. They did this in October. The nation was swept away in a tide of jubilation and optimism with even sensible people and revered journalists saying silly things about how well Scotland were going to do in Argentina. There were other factors too like an awful winter and some dreadful domestic football. All in all, season 1977/78 was not one of the best. There was, however, one heroic performance in the League Cup.

There being 38 teams in the three Scottish Divisions in 1977, there were six first-round ties to be played in August so there would be 32 teams in the second round. The six first-round games were all straightforward and predictable, with one exception. Aberdeen, Dundee, Clydebank, Dundee United and Alloa all duly qualified, but Hibs horrified their fans by losing 2-1 to Queen of the South at Easter Road and failed to rectify matters in the pouring rain at Palmerston against a stubborn and well-organised Queens' defence.

The second-round second legs were played on Saturday, 3 September, the first legs having been played the previous midweek, or in the case of Rangers who had European commitments, the Thursday night before that. There were no great shocks. Rangers beat St Johnstone 6-1 on aggregate, Celtic recovered from a poor 0-0 draw at Parkhead to beat Motherwell 4-2 at Fir Park in one of their better performances of the season and Hearts beat Stenhousemuir 6-0. The highest aggregate was Aberdeen's 10-0 demolition of Cowdenbeath. No one really noticed it at the time or thought it in any way significant, but Forfar beat Meadowbank 4-2.

A few eyebrows were raised in the next round when Second Division Forfar Athletic beat Premier League Ayr United. Archie Knox's men lost the first leg at Somerset Park 1-2 but won 3-1 at Station Park. The biggest tie of the round was Aberdeen v Rangers. It was generally agreed that although Rangers were the better team in the Ibrox first leg – indeed, the 6-1 victory was hailed as one of Rangers' best performances in recent years – Aberdeen showed a little promise and resilience in the second at Pittodrie, but the 3-1 win was not enough. Meanwhile, Celtic limped through unconvincingly against Stirling Albion, suffering a further blow to their chances this season when Danny McGrain was injured. Another close encounter came in the game between Hearts and Morton. Hearts, now in the First Division, the victims of awful management – a sadly recurring theme – won the first leg at Tynecastle 3-0 but were mighty glad to hear the final whistle at Cappielow when Morton pulled two back.

The second two midweeks in November were somewhat late dates for the quarter-finals of the Scottish League Cup and, although Rangers and Celtic eased comfortably through with wins over Dunfermline and St Mirren, the other two ties aroused a great deal of attention and interest, not least because Forfar continued their progress with a 1-0 defeat of Queen of the South after a 3-3 draw at Palmerston Park. Billy Gavine became the hero of the town by scoring the only goal of the game in front of a 6,000 crowd. This result persuaded the *Glasgow Herald* to tell its readers that they would have to stop making jokes about Forfar, for they were now in the Scottish League Cup semi-final for the first time.

The greatest excitement of the night was at Tynecastle where Hearts, their side sadly depleted through injury and illness, and 1-3 down to Dundee United from the first leg at Tynecastle, fought back with goals from Walter Kidd and Drew Busby to level the aggregate score at 3-3, and then, after extra time produced no result, the Jambos won the tie 4-2 on a penalty shoot-out.

The semi-final draw paired Rangers with Forfar and Celtic with Hearts. They were scheduled for ridiculous dates in late November, but freezing fog, the harbinger of what would be a very hard winter, compelled the postponement of both games and eventually the wise decision not to try again until late February. Christmas and New Year would be spent in Forfar with everyone talking about the Scottish League Cup semi-final as well as Scotland's chances in the Argentina World Cup. The weather had only marginally improved by Monday, 27 February 1978 when Forfar turned up to play red-shirted Rangers. The pitch was playable but the weather was cold and only 13,000 turned up at a ghostly Hampden. It was the Forfar crowd who made all the noise as well for, with seven minutes to go, they were 2-1 up. Derek Johnstone scored first for Rangers, then Ken Brown equalised and Brian Rankin scored a cracker as he ran 80 yards up the field, totally unmolested, to score. But the part-timers tired and Rangers' full-time training also told as substitute Derek Parlane headed a late equaliser. It was then totally predictable what would happen in extra time, but that game was the start of a long run of Rangers having tremendous problems in beating Forfar.

A total of 18,840 turned up at Hampden a couple of days later to see the other semi-final between Hearts and Celtic, the low crowd bearing evidence of how highly both sets of supporters rated their teams in early 1978. Without being any too impressive, Celtic won 2-0 with first-half goals from Joe Craig and George McCluskey to put them into the Scottish League Cup Final for the 14th year in succession, a world record for any competition. It would be the seventh time they had played Rangers in the Scottish League Cup Final and it stood at three wins for each side. Reaching the League Cup Final, however, was a much-needed boost for Celtic, for the season so far had been an unmitigated disaster.

As two years ago, the game kicked off at 1pm as an anti-hooligan measure on a reasonably bright but still cold spring day. The crowd was 60,618, a rather disappointing turnout in comparison with last year's final between Celtic and

Aberdeen. Rangers were the clear favourites but the Celtic support turned out in reasonable strength in a display of loyalty in spite of a shocking season, caused almost entirely by the sale of Dalglish and its demoralising effect on the team and the support.

In some ways this game was a carbon copy of the game two seasons previously with some very poor football, Celtic arguably being the better team, but Rangers being professional enough to win by the odd goal. The score was 2-1 on this occasion after extra time. Davie Cooper scored first for Rangers, Johannes Edvaldsson equalised for Celtic with only six minutes of normal time to go. Extra time was turgid until, in the 118th minute of the game, Gordon Smith headed the winner. It was Jock Stein's last final as Celtic manager. Now a bitter man, his criticism of the referee did not really convince anyone, although it was generally agreed in the press that Celtic were worth a draw at least.

The teams were:

Rangers: Kennedy, Jardine, Jackson, Forsyth, Greig, Hamilton (Miller), MacDonald, Smith, McLean, Johnstone, Cooper (Parlane)

Celtic: Latchford, Sneddon, Lynch (Wilson), Munro, MacDonald, Dowie, Glavin (Doyle), Edvaldsson, McCluskey, Aitken, Burns

Referee: D Syme, Rutherglen

Rangers went on to win the treble, playing a great deal better in the other two tournaments than they had in this one, but this game finished Celtic's season because they were already out of the Scottish Cup and nowhere in the Scottish League.

And everyone began to turn their attention to Argentina. The horrors of that summer still have their effect over 40 years later!

When domestic football resumed in August 1978, there was a major credibility gap. No amount of glorification of Archie Gemmill and his great goal against Holland could disguise the fact that Scotland had 'blown it big time', as the saying went. It was now difficult to take the international game seriously, and very unfairly, the domestic game suffered as well. All teams, not least Rangers and Celtic, both now under new management of former captains, John Greig and Billy McNeill respectively, faced a future that was uncertain.

The Scottish League Cup opened in August with six games in the first rounds. Celtic and Rangers were both in action on successive Wednesday nights. Rangers won easily enough against Albion Rovers and Celtic did quite well to beat Dundee twice, home and away. Everyone then joined in on the next Wednesday night, and the second round was completed on the following Saturday, 2 September. Celtic continued their success against Tayside teams by removing Dundee United in a couple of tough encounters. Rangers beat Forfar with more ease than they did last year and Aberdeen beat Meadowbank Thistle 9-0 on aggregate. Two games went to penalties: Falkirk beating Partick Thistle and Raith Rovers beating Queen's Park.

For some incomprehensible reason, the month of September was ignored by those who organised the Scottish League Cup in favour of the Anglo-Scottish Cup, which has now been relegated to its deserved obscurity. The third round was played on successive Wednesday nights in early

October. There were some very tight games. Raith Rovers, for example, were 3-0 up from the first leg against Montrose but managed to go out 5-4 on aggregate. Rangers were 3-2 up against St Mirren from the first leg and managed to give their supporters a terrible time until the final whistle at Love Street after a 0-0 draw. Morton were 0-2 down on the first leg against Kilmarnock but managed to fight back to win 5-4 on aggregate in a game that seems to have been a real thriller. Celtic, who had departed Celtic Park a week previously to boos and catcalls after a dreadful (and unpleasant) 0-1 defeat from Motherwell, turned it round at Fir Park with an excellent 4-1 win at Fir Park.

They would fare a great deal worse against Montrose in the quarter-finals. Montrose had flirted with League Cup glory before in 1975 against Hibs. This time they nearly went one better, coming very close to defeating Celtic; 3,872 at Links Park in the first leg saw Montrose take the lead and Celtic needed a penalty to level the tie. Even at Celtic Park, Celtic were none too convincing as they won 3-1. They had a boost in the return of Danny McGrain after more than a year, but the miserable crowd of 10,000 talked volumes about Celtic and their supporters.

By coincidence, Rangers took on Montrose's near-neighbours Arbroath and were similarly unimpressive as they limped to a 3 – 1 aggregate victory (1-0 at Ibrox, 2-1 at Gayfield) before equally low crowds. Hibs, with the benefit of two recently acquired Norwegian players, came from behind on the first leg to beat Morton 2-1 at Easter Road, but the best team of the quarter-finals was Aberdeen. The first leg had been a thrilling affair at Somerset Park, ending 3-3, but the second leg at Pittodrie in front of a respectable crowd of

13,000 on a dirty night saw Aberdeen, now managed by Alex Ferguson, beat Ayr United 3-1.

The two semi-finals were Celtic v Rangers and Aberdeen v Hibs. The Old Firm one was at Hampden and the other at Dens Park, Dundee on the bitterly cold night of 13 December, which was no night for a cup semi-final. Both games did a little to warm up the spectators, although STV managed to alienate them all by advertising highlights from the Glasgow game then failing to deliver for 'operational reasons'. No one was convinced by this and there seemed to indeed a great deal of politics behind it all, but they remained coy about the real reason. Naturally, in Glasgow this was seen as a conspiracy.

Twenty-one thousand were at Dens Park to see a rather disappointing semi-final between Aberdeen and Hibs. Aberdeen were the better team for 90 minutes against a pedestrian but professional Hibs team but the Dons could not score. Extra time was into its second half before they got a strange goal when Aberdeen full-back Stuart Kennedy sent over a hopeful ball which was nowhere near any of his forwards, and seemed to be heading for the goalkeeper, but the ball suddenly went over the goalkeeper's head into the goal. It was bizarre, but enough to put Aberdeen into the League Cup Final for the second time in three years.

A larger crowd of almost 50,000 was at Hampden Park to see the Old Firm game. It also went to extra time and it was one of the more feisty Rangers v Celtic games. Two men were sent off by referee Hugh Alexander, one from each side – Tommy Burns for arguing about a penalty and Alex Miller for persistent fouling, both of them a little harshly, it seemed – and several others were lucky to avoid a similar fate. But the upshot was that Celtic would not be contesting their 15th League Cup Final in a row, for Rangers won a rather ragged game in extra time through an own goal when luckless Jim Casey could not get out of the way of a rebound from his goalkeeper. Celtic pleaded unsuccessfully for offside against a Rangers player, but it was Rangers who went through to play Aberdeen. One would imagine that there would be quite a few Celtic supporters almost relieved by all this, for League Cup finals in the 1970s had been far from happy occasions for those who loved the green and white!

No one in the Scottish League seems to have given any thought to arranging a date for the final, something that says a great deal about those who ran the game in those days. Eventually, it was set for 31 March 1979. It could not really have been any earlier, for football was virtually wiped out in January and February as another hard winter bit hard. But the snow and the frost had cleared by the end of March to allow the playing of one of the most controversial League Cup finals of them all.

The weather was fine, if a little cold, and a crowd of 54,000 attended. They saw an entertaining first half with Rangers perhaps the better side, but Aberdeen came into it near the end. Then, early in the second half, Duncan Davidson scored for the Dons. It followed a good run and cross from Gordon Strachan to find Davidson's head and the ball squirmed out of McCloy's hands and over the line. Aberdeen were energised and Alex Ferguson looked like he was heading for his first trophy as Aberdeen manager, when suddenly everything went wrong.

Only 13 minutes remained when Alex MacDonald equalised for Rangers. It was a fine drive, but the ball seemed to take a deflection on the way in, and there was more bad news for Aberdeen when goalkeeper Bobby Clark injured his hand in his attempts to save. Still, Aberdeen looked good enough for extra time at least, until centre-half Doug Rougvie was sent off. No one seems to have had a good view of it, but Derek Johnstone was seen lying on the ground having been apparently flattened by Rougvie. After some delay, referee Ian Foote pointed to the pavilion and Aberdeen were down to ten men. Whether Mr Foote 'bought it' or whether there was a genuine piece of violence depends on who you support, but the already bad relationship between the two teams deteriorated even further after that. In fairness, it must be said that Rougvie had already been booked, but it must also be pointed out that Johnstone recovered very quickly.

Then, in the very last minute of injury time, Rangers scored a winner which was barely deserved. Tommy McLean sent over a cross which the now-absent Doug Rougvie would have dealt with and Colin Jackson was there to head home. There was no time left for Aberdeen to fight back and Rangers had won the Scottish League Cup for the tenth time.

The teams were:

Rangers: McCloy, Jardine, Dawson, Johnstone, Jackson, MacDonald, McLean, Russell, Urquhart (Miller), Smith (Parlane), Cooper

Aberdeen: Clark, Kennedy, McLelland, McMaster, Rougvie, Miller, Strachan, Archibald, Harper, Jarvie (McLeish), Davidson

Referee: I Foote, Glasgow

CHAPTER SEVEN

A BRIEF TAYSIDE INTERLUDE
1979–1982

IT IS now time to consider the affairs of Dundee United. Until about 1960, when they were promoted to the old First Division, they were looked upon as the poor team of Dundee. One of Scotland's many 'Irish' clubs, they started off life in 1909 as Dundee Hibernian but in 1923, perhaps in an attempt to distance themselves from the Irish troubles of that era, they changed their name to Dundee United. At the same time they changed their strips from green to black and white until, several decades later and to further distance themselves even from Irishness, they changed their strip to orange. Aware, however, of the sensitivities of the issue, they insisted the colour was 'tangerine'!

Their home had tended to be the old Second Division alongside Brechin City, Forfar Athletic, East Stirlingshire and Albion Rovers. However, ambition and finance from a very Taypools lottery allowed them to gain promotion and build a new stand. An odd one it was too, for one end stopped halfway up the field and the other turned a corner. Soon they were permanent fixtures in the First Division, always a challenge for Rangers and Celtic at Tannadice but less successful in Glasgow. Managed since 1971 by a feisty but knowledgeable character in Jim McLean, they had once reached the final of the Scottish Cup, in 1974, but froze on the day. Until the 1979/80 season, they had not yet appeared in a League Cup Final.

The tournament opened again with a first round of six two-legged fixtures in the middle of August on Wednesday nights with only Aberdeen of the big teams (that is potential trophy winners) in action. They beat Arbroath comfortably in the first leg and, although they lost in the second leg at Gayfield, the damage was done and they moved on. St Johnstone, Forfar and Kilmarnock all won through by a narrow margin, but the performance of the round was Stranraer who defeated Dunfermline (a result inconceivable ten years previously) 4-2 at East End Park.

A sign of the times came in the second round when Hearts went out to Ayr United. It wasn't even considered to be a shock, for Hearts were now a yo-yo team, in and out of the Premier League with predictable regularity and paying the price for a succession of incompetent managers and directors. Hibs, on the other hand, squeezed through by the odd goal against Montrose but, apart from Partick Thistle beating Albion Rovers 3-2, all the other games had more than one goal in them on aggregate.

There was little doubt about the game of the third round, the Aberdeen v Rangers clash, a repeat of last year's controversial final, and there was no love lost between them.

Aberdeen played well to beat Rangers 3-1 at Pittodrie, and then at Ibrox, a fortnight later, they won again, 2-0, to defeat Rangers to the tune of 5-1. The result perhaps signified two things: a further indication of the decline of Rangers and the determination of Alex Ferguson not to see Aberdeen bullied or intimidated at places like Ibrox and Parkhead. Elsewhere, Kilmarnock defeated Hibs, Celtic overcame hard-working Stirling Albion and Dundee United got the better of Queen's Park.

The first legs of the quarter-finals were all played on Halloween, a Wednesday night. There were some crackers as well, for in the best game of the night at a packed Pittodrie, Aberdeen edged it over Celtic 3-2, although most neutral observers agreed that Celtic were worthy of a draw at least. Dundee United drew 0-0 with Raith Rovers, Hamilton got the better of Dundee 3-1 and in a splendid tussle at Cappielow, Morton beat Kilmarnock 3-2. Everyone had been impressed by Morton, under Benny Rooney currently at the top of the Scottish Premier League, clearly holding their own with everyone else and having to fight off bids for their talismanic hero Andy Ritchie.

The League Cup was then badly affected by weather. The return legs were scheduled for 14 November but a heavy and early downfall of snow in the west of Scotland knocked out the games scheduled for Celtic Park and Rugby Park. Normally, these games would have been expected to have been played the following midweek but there were international commitments, and they were given a Saturday, 24 November, so determined was the Scottish League to get their tournament finished by 8 December, the date scheduled for the final. Wiser counsel might have suggested a postponement to the spring. However, the two games scheduled in the east of Scotland had been able to go ahead that night of 14 November. Dundee United scored the only goal of the tie through centre-half Paul Hegarty against Raith Rovers at Stark's Park, Kirkcaldy in what was regarded as a poor game in wet, wintry conditions, and Davie McParland's Hamilton Accies survived a late Dundee onslaught to lose only 0-1 and scrape through.

By chance, the two winners were drawn together in the semi-final, and thus they were able to play each other on Saturday, 24 November while the other two quarter-final games were played on the same day. An outbreak of common sense saw the semi-final between Dundee United and Hamilton Accies played at East End Park, Dunfermline. They were rewarded with a crowd which was not particularly large – about 10,000 – but it did create a greater degree of atmosphere in the small Fife ground than it would have in the vast and soulless Hampden. The rain was heavy, but Dundee United turned on one of their best performances to win 6-2 and to reach their first-ever Scottish League Cup Final.

Meanwhile, across in the west, the quarter-finals were being played out. Snow had given way to rain, but it was heavy and miserable. A large crowd at Parkhead was frustrated and angered by Aberdeen's defensive tactics, but the Dons defence was successful and early in the second half Mark McGhee scored for Aberdeen to put the Dons 4-2 up on aggregate and effectively knock Celtic out of the League Cup. It was a far more exciting game at Rugby Park. Kilmarnock fought back to win 3-2 after extra time in the incessant rain that is so typical of Scottish football in November and the game had to go to penalties. Morton managed to score all their penalties, while

Killie missed two and Morton went through after a game in which both teams were deservedly applauded off the park.

One might have thought that the League Cup results would have dominated the sports news on 24 November, but apparently not so, for the newspapers all seemed to think that the appearance of George Best for Hibs at Love Street in a league game against St Mirren was more interesting. It was a gimmick which was full of controversy and did not last long. So it was Morton v Aberdeen on 1 December for a place in the Scottish League Cup Final. Foolishly, Hampden was chosen and they received their just desserts when only 12,000 turned up to watch a dull game in which Aberdeen scored in the first half through Mark McGhee and a penalty from Gordon Strachan. Morton pulled one back late in the game but the competent Aberdeen defence held out to enter their second League Cup Final in the calendar year of 1979.

Clearly unable to learn lessons, the Scottish League went ahead with the final on 8 December at Hampden. The only people who benefitted were the Aberdeen and Dundee bus companies who ferried 27,193 fans to Glasgow to see probably the worst League Cup Final of all. Famously likened to a 'game of chess' by one journalist, the score was 0-0 after extra time. Both teams were grimly proficient at defending and the tough defenders were able to neutralise the goalscoring talent that existed on both sides. Possibly Aberdeen had some territorial advantage, but they couldn't cash in and it was a dark and depressing experience for Scottish football. A penalty shoot-out might have ended the agony, but that did not yet appear to be in the script.

For one horrible moment, we all feared that the Scottish League were to bring them all back to Hampden for more torment, but pressure from the press, radio, TV and the fans themselves convinced them that Dens Park, Dundee should host its first major national cup final on Wednesday, 12 December 1979. The crowd was only 1,000 more than Saturday at 28,933 but the atmosphere was first class, the weather was fine and it was a night that Dundee United fans in particular would never forget.

Jim McLean rightly decided that as his own ground was 100 yards down the road, Dens Park was tantamount to a home game and decided on an attacking formation, telling his men to attack and to take the game to Aberdeen. Willie Pettigrew scored in the first half, simply being in the right place at the right time, his second goal in the second half was a glorious header, before Paul Sturrock with the aid of a deflection killed things off. It was United's first trophy. Everyone had to feel a little happy for them while Aberdeen, whose manager Alex Ferguson was gracious enough to say that he had never seen a better Dundee United team than this one, had the unwelcome distinction of having lost two League Cup finals in the same calendar year. The fast-developing Dons would soon make up for it in other respects, but for many years Alex Ferguson was reputed to have a 'thing' about the Scottish League Cup.

The teams were:

Dundee United: McAlpine, Stark, Kopel, Fleming, Hegarty, Narey, Bannon, Sturrock, Pettigrew, Holt, Kirkwood

Aberdeen: Clark, Kennedy, Rougvie, McLeish, Garner, Miller, Strachan, Archibald, McGhee (Jarvie), McMaster, Scanlon (Hamilton)

Referee: B McGinlay, Balfron

Aberdeen duly won the league in 1980 for the first time since 1955, taking advantage of Celtic's late and unaccountable loss of form. To an extent Celtic redeemed themselves by winning the Scottish Cup, but that cup final will sadly go down in history as the year of the Hampden riot where the thickos on each side showed the world just exactly what was wrong with the Scottish educational system.

Dundee United did well enough that season but, when the 1980/81 season came around, they showed that they had not lost their newly acquired taste for silverware by winning the Scottish League Cup again. Once again, however, the final was at the ground of their rivals – and not only that, but the team that they defeated was none other than Dundee FC!

One might have thought that Dundee United, being the holders, might have been exempt from the first round, but no, they were one of the 12 teams picked to play in the first round, in their case against one of the old heroes of this tournament, East Fife. Not that it gave them any bother, for they won 9-2 on aggregate. In fact, the only game of the first round that one could have said was in any way close would have been the game between Morton and Ayr United, where the Honest Men lost 2-1 in Morton at Somerset Park in the first leg but then won 2-0 at Cappielow in the second.

Most games in the second round were one-sided as well, with some huge aggregate scores: 12-1 for Aberdeen against Berwick Rangers, 8-1 for Dundee United against Cowdenbeath, 7-1 for St Mirren against Albion Rovers and a similar score for Hamilton against Stranraer. There was one tie which gave every impression of being one-sided but was anything but. It was a tie which caused more than a few palpitations down Parkhead way.

Stirling Albion beat Celtic 1-0 at Annfield on Wednesday night but everyone expected a thrashing on the Saturday at Parkhead. So it turned out, but not until very late in the day. Before a paltry and critical crowd at Parkhead, Stirling Albion took the lead to make it 2-0 on aggregate. Celtic quickly pulled one back but Stirling held out brilliantly for the rest of the game until three minutes from time when Tommy Burns spared Celtic blushes with an equaliser to take the game to extra time. Stirling then had a man foolishly sent off for persistent fouling after he had been booked and, in extra time, the roof fell in and Celtic scored four times to reach the next round. Rangers beat Forfar with a little more ease and there were no major shocks at this stage.

The tournament heated up in the next round when two old foes, Aberdeen and Rangers, met. Neither club nor their supporters made the slightest attempt to hide their antagonism to each other. It may have had a lot to do with Alex Ferguson's departure from Ibrox as a player when he was given the blame for the 1969 Scottish Cup Final defeat to Celtic and never played again. Rangers won 1-0 in the first leg at Ibrox but a controversial incident occurred when Willie Johnston came on as a substitute and lasted only a few minutes before being sent off by referee Kenny Hope after 'a boot seemed to swing', as Jim Reynolds in the *Glasgow Herald* rather coyly put it. It was hardly an isolated incident as another eight men were booked!

Three weeks passed, enough time one would have thought for everyone to calm down, before the return leg at Pittodrie. This time George Smith who was the referee and his moment of controversy came in the last minute when, with the scores level on aggregate, he awarded Aberdeen a penalty kick. Colin

Jackson certainly downed John Hewitt but Rangers claimed that it was outside the box. As Mr Smith had already awarded the Dons a penalty earlier in the game, he was certainly not Mr Popular with the travelling support, but Gordon Strachan was not worried. He scored the penalty and won the tie for Aberdeen, making no attempt to hide his feelings about it – to the anger of the Rangers fans. It had been an exciting and thrilling game, and the city of Aberdeen talked about it for months. It takes a great deal to make the douce city of Aberdeen animated and optimistic about football, but Alex Ferguson had managed it!

At Tannadice, in another thrilling game, Dundee United needed extra time to beat Motherwell, and that was after Motherwell had scored first in extra time, but Paul Sturrock and Ralph Milne did the job for Dundee United. Neighbours Dundee needed penalty kicks to beat Kilmarnock after two monumentally dull 0-0 draws, while Celtic and Hibs went through comfortably against Hamilton Accies and Clyde respectively. Hearts crashed out to Ayr United losing 7-2 on aggregate and suffering an embarrassing 0-4 thumping at Somerset Park, collapsing miserably after having a man sent off.

Ayr United continued their success against Edinburgh clubs in the quarter-final when they beat Hibs in bizarre fashion by taking Hibs to extra time and then scoring twice with headers, the first one being a curious back header and the second where one would have thought that the entire Hibs defence had gone on holiday. Dundee United lost the first leg of their game to Clydebank at Kilbowie Park but won through 5-3 at the end. Without being too convincing, Celtic beat Partick Thistle home and away by the odd goal in each case, but the big surprise of the round was provided by Dundee who accounted for Aberdeen.

They did so in dramatic circumstances at Pittodrie late in the second leg. The first leg at Dens Park had been exciting but goalless and the Pittodrie game looked like going the same way, although Aberdeen had more pressure. But then, with four minutes to go in the aftermath of a corner kick, Cammy Fraser picked up a ball on the edge of the box and ran in to score off the post to deprive Aberdeen of their chances of appearing in their third successive League Cup Final. Aberdeen were going out of Europe to Liverpool at about the same time, so autumn 1980 was not a great time for the Dons in spite of their win over Rangers.

The semi-final draw kept the two Dundee teams apart, with United appearing to have drawn the short straw to play Celtic while Dundee played Ayr United. Both first legs at Tannadice and Somerset Park finished up 1-1, but Wednesday, 19 November was a great night for the city of Dundee. Celtic were simply blown apart by Dundee United in the Parkhead rain to lose 0-3, whereas Dundee had to work a lot harder to come from behind to beat Ayr United who were described as 'plucky but unlucky' in the *Evening Times*. It was Dundee, however, who scored the late and vital goal to book themselves a place in the League Cup Final on 6 December 1980.

The Scottish League then made the bold but correct decision to play the final at Dens Park. Although this was the home of one of the finalists, the other finalists were not really all that far away and no one seemed to offer any objections. Dens Park was a great deal bigger than Tannadice in any case. Everyone recalled the dismal atmosphere at Hampden at some previous League Cup finals and agreed that the

Scottish League had, once again, experienced a rare outbreak of common sense.

On 6 December it was cold but dry. One might have hoped that the Scottish League might have utilised their newly found pool of common sense to move the game to the spring, but before 24,466 all-ticket fans, the game went ahead as the city of Discovery and the DC Thomson press basked in the glory of it all. And just to make it even more incestuous, the referee was none other than Dundee's own Bob Valentine. One almost expected guest appearances from Lord Snooty and Desperate Dan, the pitch to be covered in jute and everyone given a free 'peh' (pie) as they entered the turnstiles!

Apart from last year's replay, this was the first time in the 35-year history of the trophy that the final had been scheduled for anywhere other than Hampden. Oddly enough, no one thought of putting the game on television when it would clearly have made sense to do so, as quite a lot of people couldn't get tickets.

The influence of the anti-TV brigade was weakening. The Scottish Cup Final had been shown live since 1977. Why not the League Cup Final as well?

It was a surprisingly one-sided game. Davie Dodds scored late in the first half for United, Paul Sturrock then scored early in the second half and again as time was running out. United were in total command against a Dundee team who had frozen on the day.

The League Cup was presented at the end and taken across the road to Tannadice. Dundee supporters were still able to remind their opponents that they had won the trophy three times as distinct from United's two.

The teams were:

Dundee United: McAlpine, Holt, Kopel, Phillip, Hegarty, Narey, Bannon, Payne, Pettigrew, Sturrock, Dodds

Dundee: R Geddes, Barr, Schaedler, Fraser, Glennie, McGeachie, Mackie, Stephen, Sinclair, Williamson, A Geddes

Referee: R Valentine, Dundee

United continued to have a good season, finishing well up in the Premier League (won by Celtic in an exciting game at Tannadice in April) and reaching the final of the Scottish Cup. Hopes that they could win two trophies in one year, however, sustained a heavy blow when they went down to Rangers in a replay after having the better of the play in the first game. The game was, significantly, played at Hampden and it would be the start of a theme which would almost reach the stage of being a music-hall joke in a few years' time, the League Cup 1981/82 being another manifestation of this phenomenon.

Season 1981/82 started with what seemed to be yet another outbreak of common sense and a resurrection of the old sectional format with every team playing each other twice home and away apart from the six-team section nine, the winners of which would play the winners of another section. It was a formula that had been successful until it was done away with in the early 1970s but would prove less impressive now that the Premier League teams all played each other four times, and the gap between rich and poor had grown to a virtually unmanageable extent.

The new format produced a notable and unexpected casualty in league champions Celtic who got off to a bad start and lost their first two games. They lost their first game to

St Mirren at Celtic Park and then at Muirton Park lost again to St Johnstone, meeting for the first time a man called Ally McCoist, who scored the first goal of a 2-0 victory. Though Celtic recovered well, they could not dislodge St Mirren from the top.

The other sections were less interesting, won without a great deal of bother by Aberdeen, Rangers and Dundee United, and they were joined by Hamilton Accies, Berwick Rangers, Brechin and Forfar Athletic after the Loons had defeated Arbroath in the supplementary round. Some of the lower sections were not without their interest. Although Hamilton qualified with a 100 per cent record, Berwick Rangers beat Queen's Park to qualify but only on goal difference. Berwick needed to win 2-0 in the last game and did so 3-0. Falkirk looked to have earned qualification at Station Park, Forfar until a late winner from Steve Hancock turned the tables on them, and Brechin's 3-1 victory at Boghead was just enough for them to get the better of Queen of the South who could only draw with Cowdenbeath.

The quarter-finals were sadly predictable. Forfar Athletic put up a good performance at Station Park to earn a 1-1 draw against St Mirren but then collapsed woefully at Love Street to lose 6-0 and 7-1 on aggregate, whereas the other aggregates were 9-0 for Dundee United against Hamilton Accies, 8-0 for Aberdeen against Berwick Rangers and 5-0 for Rangers against Brechin City.

The semi-finals were a great deal more interesting. Played on the first and last midweeks in October, Rangers took on St Mirren while the New Firm (as Dundee United and Aberdeen were called increasingly often) faced each other. Games between the two of them were frequently defence obsessed, such was the dour tactical battle between the two managers, Jim McLean and Alex Ferguson, good friends off the park but bitter rivals on it. This game was an exception and Aberdeen finished the first leg at Tannadice 1-0 up after a goal scored by Peter Weir from a Gordon Strachan cross.

The same night saw Rangers lucky to escape from Love Street with a 2-2 draw. Colin McAdam opened the scoring for Rangers with a simple tap-in and young Frank McAvennie scored a wondergoal to equalise. Then, seconds after St Mirren were denied what looked like a clear penalty by referee Douglas Downie, Rangers ran up and took the lead with a fortuitous goal which rebounded off the goalkeeper when a defender tried to clear. But they all count, and Rangers looked likely winners until late in the game when Alan Logan was clearly brought down by Ian Redford. This time the referee did award a penalty kick and Ian Scanlon netted to finish the game at 2-2.

The second legs, played three weeks later, provided a great deal of excitement, although the Pittodrie game was an anti-climax for the home supporters as Dundee United took command, cancelled out the first-leg goal in seven minutes and scored another two. They were not sure whether to play Paul Sturrock, who had been out with an injury, but decided to do so and he rewarded them with the first and the third goals – both crackers – while Ralph Milne scored the second one after the goalkeeper failed to hold a cross. It was a major disappointment for Aberdeen but it meant that Dundee United were now in the Scottish League Cup Final for the third year in a row and were playing well enough to be considered favourites.

Their opponents were to be Rangers, who would be contesting their 15th League Cup final. They did this by edging it over St Mirren 2-1 at Ibrox before a crowd of 25,000 and St Mirren could consider themselves to be unlucky to lose this dramatic and feisty encounter. St Mirren seemed to have a good goal disallowed before both teams scored with penalties. It was looking as if extra time was inevitable until, with only two minutes remaining and immediately after Jimmy Bone of St Mirren had had two shots saved by goalkeeper Jim Stewart, Rangers got the winner when young John MacDonald picked up a free kick from Davie Cooper and scored. It was a welcome win for Rangers, whose league form hitherto had been anything but impressive. But this victory over the Paisley Saints set up a repeat of last season's Scottish Cup Final, won 4-1 by Rangers after a replay.

The game was scheduled for Hampden on Saturday, 28 November and attracted an attendance of 53,777. The day was cold but pleasant enough for the time of year, and the crowd saw an entertaining but controversial game in which the better side clearly lost, a point admitted by supporters of both sides and by journalists and radio and TV commentators alike.

The King's Park or 'Celtic' end had been closed for much-needed repairs and there was a ghostly atmosphere of playing towards nobody at one end of the ground. Whether this caused it or not, Rangers simply could not get going in the first half which was dominated by Dundee United, who nevertheless disappointed the expectations of their fans when they simply could not score.

They did, however, in the second half when, in a fine piece of play early in the half Paul Sturrock released Ralph Milne who scored a fine goal. This was no more than United deserved and then they seemed to have gone two ahead (and this would surely have killed the game) when Paul Sturrock scored from 20 yards only to see the stand-side linesman with his flag up because John Holt was in an offside position. He was indeed technically offside, although hardly interfering with the play. This was hard on United and some of the Rangers fans had already begun to go home before they were alerted to the linesman's flag.

Rangers, reprieved, took full advantage. With nothing to lose, they threw their men forward with reckless abandon, won two free kicks and scored from the pair of them. In both cases, United goalkeeper Hamish McAlpine will not want to be reminded of his part. He got a hand to Davie Cooper's equaliser but the ball still went in, and the winner came when Cooper's free kick found Ian Redford whose lob went over Hamish's head and into the net as the goalkeeper desperately tried to get back to his proper position.

This was cruel on United, who were denied their third consecutive Scottish League Cup. Rangers, on the other hand, had now won the trophy 11 times, three times more than Celtic's eight. More importantly for the psyche of Dundee United, the defeat had been at Hampden. Many more painful Cup Final experiences would have to be endured by their supporters at the national stadium until they won the Scottish Cup there in 1994. It became a standing joke, so much so that their supporters produced a fanzine which they called the *Final Hurdle* on the grounds that that was where they always fell. It was a grim journey home to the city of Discovery that night, all the more so by the knowledge that they really should have finished the game off long before half-time.

The teams were:

Rangers: Stewart, Jardine, Miller, Stevens, Jackson, Bett, Cooper, Johnstone, Russell, MacDonald, Dalziel (Redford)

Dundee United: McAlpine, Holt, Stark, Narey, Hegarty, Phillip, Bannon, Milne, Kirkwood, Sturrock, Dodds

Referee: E Pringle, Edinburgh

The year 1982 saw Scotland in the World Cup in Spain. They had not won the tournament – that goes without saying – but they had not disgraced and embarrassed themselves as they had done so comprehensively four years earlier in Argentina. And the Scottish appetite for football, which had been damaged by Argentina, was now slowly returning. Before the World Cup, Celtic had won the Scottish League, Aberdeen the Scottish Cup and Rangers won the League Cup, so there was no monopoly of honours by any team.

In the League Cup of 1982/83 the sectional format continued, but it was hardly a success with the seeded teams in all the top eight sections doing well. It was no real surprise to see that Celtic, Aberdeen, Rangers, Dundee United, Hearts, Partick Thistle, Kilmarnock and St Mirren all made it through. The only one who had any kind of a struggle was Partick Thistle against whom Brechin City put up a bit of a fight, but Partick's 1-1 draw at Glebe Park was enough to qualify them.

It was section nine with its six teams which provided the interest and the excitement. They all played each other only once and three teams – Cowdenbeath, Meadowbank and Montrose – all finished with seven points, having won three games, drawn one and lost one. Not only that, but Cowdenbeath and Meadowbank had scored seven goals and conceded four. Montrose, who had only scored six (while also conceding four), were eliminated and a play-off was held at Central Park (chosen, presumably, because Cowdenbeath had won the direct match between the two of them earlier) and the Fifers duly won 3-0.

That did not finish the matter, for they now had the supplementary round to negotiate against Kilmarnock. On Monday, 6 September they travelled to Kilmarnock and lost 1-0 but, when Killie came to Central Park two days later, the scoreline was reversed (although Cowdenbeath were indebted to their goalkeeper Jim Allan for twice saving penalties) and the game went to extra time. No further scoring led to a penalty shoot-out, won 4-3 by Kilmarnock. Cowdenbeath had a remarkable journey to *not* qualify and it might have been a lot better for them if they had lost or drawn another game at the sectional stage.

The quarter-finals produced two one-sided ties as Celtic beat Partick Thistle 7-0 and Rangers beat Kilmarnock 12-1 over the two legs, but there was also the meeting yet again of the New Firm. Dundee United beat Aberdeen 3-1 at Pittodrie in an unusually fast and entertaining game on 22 September. The return leg at Tannadice was less wholesome with lots of fouls and bad temper and the only goal of the game coming for Dundee United from a hotly disputed penalty kick. The heroes of the round were perhaps Hearts, now in the First Division, who got the better of Premier Division St Mirren by 2-1 at Tynecastle after a 1-1 draw at Love Street. This was the first appearance of Willie Johnston in a Hearts jersey, and Hearts, who had the reputation in those days of being the Dad's Army team of Scottish football, proved the value of experience.

Nevertheless, when the draw for the semi-final was made, Hearts would have been the team that everyone wanted to meet. In the event, it was Rangers who got Hearts while Celtic faced Dundee United, who were probably the tournament favourites. The first legs on 27 October saw victories for both members of the Old Firm by 2-0. At Ibrox, Hearts, with ex-Ranger Sandy Jardine in immaculate form, held out for one and a quarter hours before conceding two late goals to Davie Cooper and Jim Bett. Across the city at Celtic Park, a penalty from Charlie Nicholas and then a strike from Frank McGarvey put Celtic in apparent control of the tie.

In the second legs on 10 November, Rangers had to struggle at Tynecastle but nevertheless won 2-1 to finish 4-1 on aggregate, while Dundee United were the real heroes at Tannadice, even though they failed in the last minute. They levelled the tie through a Roy Aitken own goal and then a fine Paul Sturrock strike. But then they were reduced to ten men after John Holt was sent off for two yellow cards and, just on the final whistle, Charlie Nicholas scored the winner from a Tommy Burns pass. It was a fine game of football, albeit a little tough on occasion, and it set up an Old Firm League Cup Final – the eighth such event with Celtic having won three and Rangers four.

We have already seen many Scottish League Cup finals held in inappropriate conditions on the wrong day at the wrong time of the year. This one in 1982 was a collector's item. It was played on 4 December 1982, one of the worst days of rain and wind that one could imagine. Fortunately, the wind had abated slightly by the 3pm kick-off time, but there was still the rain which hammered down relentlessly on the exposed Celtic end terracing, although the Rangers fans at the other end had a shelter.

But that was not all. Hampden was in the throes of reconstruction (a process that would take an unconscionable amount of time – about 20 years before it was completed) and we had the incongruous spectacle of the North Terrace being bare apart from a few bulldozers, one or two stewards in yellow oilskins and an advert for a film company that intended one day to show football matches on a big screen. It being December, it was dark before the game started, and one sometimes had to pinch oneself to imagine that this really was a national cup final. If ever there was a case for delaying the final until the spring or moving to a different venue (Ibrox was now more or less complete and Parkhead was still serviceable), this was it. Tossing coins for the choice of venue was not unprecedented nor out of the question but, as it was, this was Hampden at its worst with the approach roads even wetter and muddier than normal. It was another own goal conceded by the Scottish League.

In such circumstances, to counteract the obvious discomfort, a good game between the two Glasgow giants was expected. Fortunately, it was delivered, and although the cliché about making the crowd forget the weather was hardly true, nevertheless they did serve up a great game of football with the better team winning. The result, however, was in doubt until the very end.

Celtic were generally regarded as favourites, and their form had been quite good of late after one or two moments of uncertainty and their usual disappointing exit from Europe. Rangers were struggling to convince their supporters that they had any chance of winning anything this year and were currently fourth in the Scottish League.

Celtic started off playing towards their own supporters and were two goals up by half-time and looking a good bet for a lot more. The first came when Davie Provan intercepted a Rangers throw-in and slipped the ball to young Charlie Nicholas who scored convincingly from the edge of the penalty box. Then Murdo MacLeod scored the second. Provan was again involved, taking a corner kick which found Tom McAdam, and Murdo lashed home from the edge of the box. Half-time at the Celtic end could have done with Gene Kelly among them, for everybody was singing in the rain.

But Rangers were not finished yet. Although outplayed, their tradition demanded that they fight back and they duly did so, scoring a goal early in the second half through Jim Bett from a free kick. It was game on and the 57,000 crowd enjoyed one of the better Old Firm games. Chances were missed at both ends and Celtic were handicapped halfway through the second half when their talisman Paul McStay had to go off injured. It was to the credit of both teams and the referee that not a single player on either side got booked. If anything, Celtic were marginally the better team in that hard-fought second half and got their due reward when referee Kenny Hope blew for time up.

Celtic won 2-1. It was their ninth League Cup Final triumph and their first since 1974/75, since when a great deal of water had flowed underneath quite a few bridges. Rangers were felt to have deserved a draw by their supporters but 1982 was a horrendous year for the Ibrox side. For the Celtic fans in the rain, the lifting of the League Cup was a sight for sore eyes, but a long time would pass before they saw it again.

The teams were:

Celtic: Bonner, McGrain, Sinclair, Aitken, McAdam, MacLeod, Provan, McStay (Reid), McGarvey, Burns, Nicholas

Rangers: Stewart, McKinnon, Redford, McClelland, Paterson, Bett, Cooper, Prytz (Dawson), Johnstone, Russell (MacDonald), Smith

Referee: K Hope, Clarkston

For the authorities, lessons were learned from the awful administration of this League Cup Final. For the foreseeable future the final of the tournament would be played in spring (until they changed their mind again) and even better was the news that the League Cup Final from 1983/84 onwards would be televised live. It was a belated recognition that the Scottish League Cup, for all its inadequacies, was a national competition. National competitions deserve to be seen by the nation!

CHAPTER EIGHT

RANGERS STOP THE ROT
1983–1985

CELTIC DID not hold on to their Scottish League Cup for long and the rest of the 1982/83 season was poor. Charlie Nicholas caused problems by wanting away and mysteriously did not play in the Scottish Cup semi-final when they needed him, the team blew up spectacularly in the League in April and manager Billy McNeill departed in the summer. Rangers were nowhere, Dundee United won the Scottish Premier League for the first and only time and 1983 was distinguished by Aberdeen winning the European Cup Winners' Cup, beating Real Madrid in the final. They then won the Scottish Cup, although manager Alex Ferguson was upset because he felt they did not play well enough!

The Scottish League Cup was tinkered with again for season 1983/84. There was a first round of six games, then a second round (home and home like the first round) of 16 games, and the remaining 16 teams then went into a sectional format. Mercifully, only one team qualified from each, but the major disadvantage was that the six sectional games were played midweek between 31 August and 30 November – possibly too long a period interspersed with European games and international fixtures. Frankly, the format failed to excite the fans and it was only really when the tournament got to the semi-final stage that things got interesting.

The semi-finals and the final were now after the New Year, a welcome change. A major boost was the news that, for the first time ever, the Scottish League Cup Final would be televised live on TV. There was history here. The SFA and the Scottish League had traditionally resisted live television, feeling that it would deter people from going to watch games in person. This bigoted and short-sighted policy often had ridiculous results like the English FA Cup Final being blocked lest it prevent people going to junior games. The English FA Cup Final was, of course, shown in England, so viewers of Border TV who lived in the south of Scotland, or other parts of Scotland where mountains did not get in the way, could still see the game.

Nevertheless, since 1977 (on the insistence of a sponsor) the Scottish Cup Final had been televised live, without any huge effect on the attendance. Attendances had dropped since the halcyon days of the 1960s, but it would be facile to attribute this to television. And the benefit of these games being televised was that everyone could watch them. Now this privilege was extended to the Scottish League Cup, allowing anyone who wanted to see the Scottish League Cup Final as well. You cannot really claim that a tournament is a national one if the nation doesn't get the chance to see the final. And the first televised final was a good game to start with!

The second-round games did not produce any great shocks, although Hearts were lucky to beat Cowdenbeath on penalties and Celtic were booed off the park after a dreadful 0-0 draw against Brechin City at Celtic Park. Fortunately for them, they had won the first leg at Glebe Park 1-0. The New Firm of Aberdeen and Dundee United did better; Aberdeen beating Raith Rovers 12-0 on aggregate and Dundee United getting the better of Dunfermline Athletic 8-1, the same score by which Rangers triumphed over Queen of the South.

The four sections failed to kindle any great interest, for the four seeded teams of Aberdeen, Dundee United, Rangers and Celtic all won through with a degree of ease, the only section in which there was a degree of doubt being Celtic's. They went into the final game at Rugby Park, Kilmarnock on 30 November on level terms. However, a scrappy goal from Jim Melrose and some determined, albeit non-too-skilful, defending saw them win 1-0 and qualify.

The semi-finals threw up Celtic v Aberdeen and Rangers v Dundee United. They were scheduled for early February but bad weather caused delays. The first semi-final to be played was on Valentine's night on 14 February. There was never any love lost between Rangers and Dundee United, but everyone behaved on a foggy night at Tannadice as a late Rangers equaliser earned a 1-1 draw. A week later at Ibrox, before a substantial crowd of 37,000, Dundee United once again obeyed the preordained law of destiny that they must lose in Glasgow. Rangers won comfortably 2-0 with goals from Sandy Clark and Ian Redford. It was one of Rangers' better performances of the season.

The same night at Pittodrie, Aberdeen took on Celtic in their first leg. It was a 0-0 draw, but the scoreline was deceptive. There was some good football played with Celtic unlucky not to win. There were also five bookings. The second leg was arranged for Saturday, 10 March at Celtic Park on the same day that some Scottish Cup quarter-finals were being played, such was the confusion of season 1983/84; 47,000 turned up to see this game at Celtic Park and it was a tight affair with quite a few bookings, a spot of crowd trouble and not a great deal of good football. The only goal of the 180-minute tie came from the penalty spot in the 55th minute when Tommy Burns was brought down by Dougie Bell, and Mark Reid stepped up to slot home.

Celtic organised their defence and held firm to the end, setting up the second Old Firm League Cup Final in a row on Sunday, 25 March. Sunday football was not common in Scotland in 1984 and looked upon as something of a novelty. There was a little tut-tutting from the bigoted Sabbatarian fringe of Christianity but theirs was now a losing cause; 66,369 turned up at Hampden to see the encounter while the rest of the nation settled down in front of their television. Hampden was a great deal different from the last League Cup Final some 15 months before. The North Terrace had been re-done with concrete steps and the weather was far better. It was a typical, still-cool Scottish spring day.

What was immediately apparent in the crowd, though, was that the Celtic section of the North terrace was a great deal less well populated than the Rangers equivalent. The East Terrace was full, as indeed was the West, but there seemed loads of elbow room particularly in the Celtic section at the front of the North Terrace. This did not necessarily reflect any great pessimism about the game on the part of the Celtic supporters. In fact, Celtic were probably the favourites, but there was a general disillusion on the part of the support with the way that Celtic were going. They had made the mistake of selling Charlie Nicholas to Arsenal, a short-sighted piece of money-grubbing which did no one any good, and the supporters felt that he had not been adequately replaced. Jim Melrose, for example, was a good solid player – but he was not Charlie Nicholas. They also missed their great hero Billy McNeill, now reluctantly managing Manchester City and, when interviewed by the media, saying 'we' when he meant Celtic.

It turned out to be a game in which penalties played an important part and in which Ally McCoist scored a hat-trick, two of which were penalties. Celtic, too, got a penalty and all the action took place down at the Celtic end. Referee Bob Valentine of Dundee was much criticised by Celtic players and supporters for the penalties but was possibly right in all cases, even though the challenges were clumsy rather than downright dirty. The first was for Rangers just on half-time, then early in the second half McCoist scored from open play and the game seemed over with Rangers 2-0 up.

But this Celtic team was not without character and pulled one back when Tommy Burns lobbed a free kick over the Rangers defensive wall and Brian McClair ran on to it and scored. That did not seem to be enough until the very last minute when Celtic were awarded a penalty and Mark Reid converted.

This meant extra time and honours were equal until near the end of the first half when Rangers were awarded their second penalty. Ally McCoist took it and the Celtic end cheered when Pat Bonner saved it, but McCoist was first to the rebound and squeezed the ball home. Celtic worked hard in the second half of extra time but ran out of time and were unable to score.

The teams were:

Rangers: McCloy, Nicholl, Dawson, McClelland, Paterson, McPherson, Russell, McCoist, Clark (McAdam), MacDonald (Burns), Cooper

Celtic: Bonner, McGrain, Reid, Aitken, McAdam, MacLeod, Provan (Sinclair), McStay, McGarvey (Melrose), Burns, McClair

Referee: R Valentine, Dundee

It was generally agreed that the idea of putting the final on TV had been a great success. Perhaps it had a slight detrimental effect on the attendance, particularly among the Celtic support. It was regrettable that it had a great deal to do with sponsorship, but nevertheless millions of people in Scotland and all over the world were enabled to watch the game, and that had to be a good thing.

Rangers thus won the Scottish League Cup for the 12th time, but it would be all that Jock Wallace's men were to win this season. Celtic, under the likeable but as yet non-too-successful David Hay, would similarly end up bereft of silverware. Aberdeen won a league and cup double.

Rangers also did well in the following year, but the organisation of the tournament was different again. At long last the penny dropped about home-and-home ties, namely that they did not necessarily excite a lot of interest among spectators. So, this year, there would just be one game, the venue decided on the luck of the draw, and the tie would be decided on the night by extra time and penalties if necessary. Curiously enough, this would be the case in every round apart from the semi-finals which would still be two-legged affairs. There was neither rhyme nor reason in this but it did have a parallel in the English League Cup. It would not be the first or the last time that Scottish authorities, to their detriment, allowed themselves to slavishly follow a bad example from south of the border.

As the 1984/85 season started, the country was in the grip of a miners' strike. It would last a year, and the Government would win handsomely without the country (other than the miners themselves) suffering in the slightest. Both sides had been spoiling for another fight after a series of confrontations in the 1970s and it was sad to see that the dispute had its fair share of violence, something that we would all have liked to think that we had grown out of.

The streamlining of the Scottish League Cup meant that there were no second chances after a bad game. The first major team to find this out was Aberdeen, winners of last year's Scottish League and Scottish Cup, who exited the League Cup at Broomfield, Airdrie. The home team scored first, then, after Aberdeen equalised, scored another two on either side of half-time. Aberdeen's League Cup campaign ended miserably with Alex Ferguson claiming, unconvincingly, that it would give them more time to deal with their other commitments, including the European Cup.

Celtic were not far off sharing a similar fate at East End Park, Dunfermline. Twenty years previously a power in the land, Dunfermline had fallen on bad times and were in the Second Division, but on this night, they gave an indication of what they could do again. Red-haired local hero John Watson scored a goal to put them ahead and then, after Celtic scored twice, he levelled the game. It was beginning to look as if extra time was inevitable before Brian McClair won the game for Celtic. Rangers were never in any real danger against Falkirk but they were hardly impressive in their 1-0 victory.

Everyone agreed that the revamping of the competition was a great success because every game was important. It was a short, snappy tournament and it seemed to be what the people wanted, even though there was no great increase in attendances. The winners of the next round on 29 August were Celtic and Rangers (both 4-0 winners, with Celtic beating Airdrie and Rangers beating Raith Rovers), Hearts, St Johnstone and Dundee United. Dundee FC just got the better of Kilmarnock in a penalty shoot-out, but the major surprise was the defeat of Hibs by comparatively new Meadowbank Thistle. This Edinburgh derby was Meadowbank's best game in their short history so far and it was a major triumph for their manager Terry Christie, a man who doubled as headmaster at Ainslie Park High School, reputed to be the worst in Scotland.

The loss at Easter Road was Hibs' second shock defeat in six months, for East Fife had put them out of last year's Scottish Cup as well. There was no excuse for Hibs, for Meadowbank played as well as they did, scoring in the first minute of extra time and holding on superbly. The press were not slow to point out the irony in the first of Meadowbank's goals being scored by Gordon Smith, the name of arguably Hibs' best-ever player! The other giant-killing of the round was at Cowdenbeath when Lisbon Lion John Clark's young side beat St Mirren 2-0 with goals from Kenny Ward and Dave Armour.

The quarter-finals were played on the first midweek in September. The city of Dundee was the centre of the League Cup again when both local sides were given home draws, Dundee v Hearts and Dundee United v Celtic. Cowdenbeath were rewarded for their efforts in the last round with a home tie against Rangers while Meadowbank entertained St Johnstone.

Logistics and common sense dictated that Dundee's game be played on the Tuesday night to leave the city free for the Wednesday clash between Dundee United and Celtic. The Dens Park clash was a good game marred by dreadful finishing on both sides. Neither team enjoyed the best of luck but Roddy MacDonald of Hearts scored the only goal of the game with a powerful header.

Dundee United had more luck against Celtic the following night before a packed 21,182 crowd. It was a fine game of football with Celtic fighting back to take the game to extra time after United had led for so long but then, in extra time, substitute John Clark got the winner after a Celtic defender miskicked his clearance. Rangers had a bit of a struggle to beat Cowdenbeath at Central Park with the Fifers holding them well for some time before Rangers took control and scored three times. Cowdenbeath netted a consolation but it was a win for the Ibrox men.

The heroes of the round, however, were once again Meadowbank Thistle. The game had been poor in the first half and, when St Johnstone scored at the start of the second half, that seemed to be it. But Meadowbank, in front of a minuscule crowd at their own stadium, earned a penalty. Alan Lawrence carved his name into Meadowbank's as yet not-lengthy history by grabbing a late winner to put them into the semi-final of a national tournament for the first time, to the delight and amazement of their fans.

Those who hoped this run might continue against Rangers at Ibrox on 26 September were given a serious dose of reality when Rangers won 4-0, but this must not disguise the effort put into the game by the Edinburgh men who might have scored first and held Rangers to 1-0 for a long time before full-time training told and 'the roof fell in', as the saying went. The second leg was an honourable 1-1 draw at Tynecastle (rather than Meadowbank Stadium), the only real incident of note being the sending off of Ally Dawson of Rangers.

It was a different story in the other semi-final first leg at Tynecastle where the football seemed almost incidental to the general mayhem that went on. Referee Alan Ferguson of Giffnock was a busy man indeed and the wonder was that only two men, Dave Bowman of Hearts and Dave Narey of Dundee United, were awarded the red card for fighting when it seemed several others on both sides deserved similar treatment and some of the six yellow cards might have been upgraded to red. Hearts actually scored in the first minute from a John Robertson free kick and held on to their lead until half-time before John Clark scored twice with headers in the 50th and the 55th minute. Over half an hour of crunching tackles, yellow cards and uncontrolled muscle followed before Mr Ferguson ended it all, thus giving Dundee United a 2-1 advantage for Tannadice if they were to reach their fourth League Cup Final in six years.

The second leg was well handled by referee Brian McGinlay, who showed a yellow card in the first 20 seconds to Walter Kidd and Davie Dodds soon after that. This showed he meant business and the game settled down. It was well won 3-1 by Dundee United who concentrated on football. Some Hearts fans tried an infantile and incomprehensible pitch invasion – something that proved nothing except the failure of the Edinburgh educational system – but there was little trouble on the field.

It was almost like old times when the Scottish League Cup Final was played on the weekend that the clocks changed, although it was played on Sunday so the clock had already changed. The weather was wet but it was nevertheless disappointing that only 44,698 turned up to see the game. Everyone else could, of course, see it on TV. The build-up was full of the usual clichés with reference to how Dundee United were the better team but tended to get homesick in Glasgow and might freeze at key moments on the big occasion. Dundee United spokesmen repeatedly said that they would not.

You've guessed it, they froze. Rangers worked hard and, after both sides had had one or two half-chances, Iain Ferguson – whom Rangers had signed from United's rivals Dundee – scored in the Mount Florida goal on the half-time whistle. The second half saw Rangers, while not playing with any great flair or panache, nevertheless keep control of the game. Even a mysterious indirect free kick awarded by referee Brian McGinlay for Dundee United inside the Rangers box (apparently for time-wasting) failed to yield a goal for Dundee United and their drookit supporters, whose journey back to Dundee was miserable, albeit familiar and predictable.

One hopes the celebrating Rangers fans made the most of it, for it would be the last honour that Jock Wallace would ever win for them as Aberdeen and Celtic won the remaining honours this season and the next. By the time Rangers were back again in a national final, they would be under new management and the circumstances of the club would be very different indeed. The ante would have been raised significantly.

The teams were:

Rangers: McCloy, Dawson, McClelland, Fraser, Paterson, McPherson, Russell (Prytz), McCoist, Ferguson (Mitchell), Redford, Cooper

Dundee United: McAlpine, Holt (Clark), Malpas, Gough, Hegarty, Narey, Bannon, Milne (Beedie), Kirkwood, Sturrock, Dodds

Referee: B McGinlay, Balfron

The Scottish League Cup reached its 40th birthday in 1985/86. The post-war baby had reached its menopause and midlife crisis and was beginning to look old. But it was certainly part of the scene. A whole new generation or two of football fans had grown up unaware that there had ever been a time when the tournament did not exist. Rangers were ahead in the list of winners, followed by Celtic – no real surprise there. Aberdeen had only won it twice, a shock given the 1980s when they won the Scottish League three times, the Scottish Cup three times and the European Cup Winners' Cup, but not a single success in the Scottish League Cup. Alex Ferguson would laugh it off and Aberdeen supporters would say that it was 'just' the Scottish League Cup, but Alex was hurting. He was grimly determined to do something about it.

The quick-fire snappy format of the tournament was once again deemed a success. After the six games of the first round had been played, it was all in for the second round. No great shocks were recorded, although Morton and Stirling Albion needed extra time and penalties to get the better of Dumbarton and Dunfermline while Dundee were decidedly lucky to win 3-2 at Stranraer.

The third round was in the main predictable – Celtic beat Brechin City 7-0 and Aberdeen beat St Johnstone 2-0, for example – but never did Rangers come closer to a mighty humbling than they did against Forfar Athletic on 27 August. The game had been switched from Station Park, Forfar to Dens Park, Dundee for safety reasons and attracted a reasonable crowd of about 5,000. There had been a little history, with Rangers on several occasions in the past lucky to get past Forfar in both cups, and this time they found themselves two down after 68 minutes. They pulled one back immediately from the penalty spot but it was mighty late before Bobby Williamson got their equaliser. Extra time followed with no addition to the score, then Rangers won 6-5 on penalties in a way that broke the hearts of gallant little Forfar. On the same night Hearts needed extra time to beat Stirling Albion. The next night, in the only other close game of the round, Hamilton beat Dundee 2-1 after extra time.

In the quarter-finals, four close games were played. One went to extra time and penalties, the other three were decided by the odd goal. Arguably, the worst game was at Pittodrie where Aberdeen beat Hearts 1-0 in the rain, the only goal coming from a prod by Eric Black after Henry Smith and his defence had made an awful hash of things. Jock Stein, Scotland's manager, was there for what would be his last-ever visit to Pittodrie; he was fated to die a week later while managing Scotland against Wales. Down the coast at Dundee United, the home side beat St Mirren 2-1, scoring twice in the first half through Ralph Milne although the Buddies put up more of a fight of it in the second half. Rangers continued their struggle to beat lower-league opposition at Douglas Park when they won 2-1 with headers from Bobby Williamson after Hamilton had scored inside the first five minutes.

But the game of the round was undeniably at Easter Road where Hibs took on Celtic. It is commonly believed that for sheer attacking football, the combination of Hibs and Celtic would be hard to beat. Both are built to attack but both are prone to concede soft goals, and so it proved this night; 3-3 at full time, then in extra time Roy Aitken put Celtic ahead until Gordon Durie equalised. Supporters of Celtic often feel that they are not at their best in penalty shoot-outs, and so it proved that night, for Alan Rough saved twice for Hibs and the home team went through 4-3 on penalties.

The semi-final draw paired Hibs with Rangers and Aberdeen with their New Firm rivals Dundee United, with the first legs at Easter Road and Tannadice. At Easter Road, Hibs – 'the team that only comes out on Wednesday nights' as the *Glasgow Herald* described them, for their league form was awful – beat Rangers 2-0 in a competent performance with goals from Gordon Chisholm and Gordon Durie to give them a great chance of reaching the final. The pairing of Dundee United and Aberdeen was often described as 'a game of chess'. This one was more like a boxing bout. Dundee United's Richard Gough was sent off by referee Mike Delaney, several others were lucky to escape the same fate, eight were booked and Eric Black of Aberdeen scored the only goal of a totally unsatisfying and unpleasant game of football.

It was a better game at Pittodrie in a fortnight's time and Aberdeen were again the winners by 1-0, the goal coming from Frank McDougall. Aberdeen had reached the final of the Scottish League Cup without losing a goal, thanks mainly to their excellent central defence pairing of Willie

Miller and Alex McLeish. At Ibrox the same night, Rangers, in front of a large crowd of about 39,000, threw everything at Hibs but their attacks lacked sophistication and seemed to rely on sheer brute force. Davie Cooper scored a free kick in the first half to reduce the leeway but Hibs' defence kept their composure, goalkeeper Alan Rough was in inspirational form and Hibs held out for their fifth Scottish League Cup Final appearance, finishing Rangers' dream of three Scottish League Cup successes in a row. It was also a nail in the coffin of manager Jock Wallace. Changes were coming at Ibrox.

At Hampden on Sunday, 27 October 1985, 40,061 were to see the League Cup final. It was the first time that Aberdeen and Hibs had met in the League Cup Final, although they had contested the Scottish Cup Final in the first competition after World War II in 1947. Aberdeen won on that occasion, and they won this one as well with a degree of ease. The best that anyone could say about Hibs was that they behaved sportingly and referee Mr Valentine did not have to give out a single yellow card. Hibs had played above themselves to beat both Celtic and Rangers to get to Hampden but they were quite simply beaten by a better team. This did little, however, to mitigate the disappointment of their supporters, who turned up in far larger numbers than ever went to Easter Road for league games. As someone said, 'The supporters turned up, but the team didn't.'

The teams were:

Aberdeen: Leighton, McKimmie, Mitchell, Stark, McLeish, Miller, Black (Gray), Simpson, McDougall, Cooper, Hewitt

Hibs: Rough, Sneddon, Munro, Brazil (Harris), Fulton, Hunter, Kane, Chisholm, Cowan, Durie, McBride (Collins)

Referee: R Valentine, Dundee

Aberdeen, playing towards the Mount Florida goal where stood most of their fans, were two up before quarter of an hour had gone. Both goals were made by John Hewitt and finished off by Eric Black and Billy Stark. Hibs made a bit of a fight of it before half-time but could not score and in the second half, long before Eric Black scored the third, it was obvious who were going to be the winners of the League Cup. It was Aberdeen's third Scottish League Cup in what was a remarkable season for Scottish football. Aberdeen won the Scottish Cup as well in May 1986 and the Scottish League would be won by Celtic on 'Albert Kidd' day at Dens Park, Hearts being the losers on both occasions, thus making season 1985/86 yet another heartbreak season for Edinburgh.

The season was marked by several other events. One was the death of Jock Stein on the bench at Ninian Park, Cardiff. Another was Scotland's qualification for the Mexico World Cup (taking them to Australia, of all places, to qualify). Yet another was the fact that the Scottish League and the TV companies fell out and there was no football on television, not even in highlights form. The League Cup Final was an exception, because the sponsors insisted and it was a separate contract, until everyone kissed and made up in April and Scottish League games began to be shown live again. But 1986 was also the year in which Rangers fought back after a gentleman called Graeme Souness appeared at Ibrox towards the end of the season. Things would never quite be the same again.

On the occasion of its 40th birthday the Scottish League Cup had been won by Rangers on 13 occasions, Celtic on nine, Hearts four, Aberdeen three, East Fife three, Dundee three, Dundee United two, and Motherwell, Partick Thistle and Hibs one each.

CHAPTER NINE

RANGERS RAMPANT
1986–1990

THINGS CHANGED totally for Rangers and Scotland in 1986. Rangers had never coped well with Celtic winning the European Cup in 1967 and, after almost 20 further years of bitterness and frustration (with the odd good year like 1976 and 1978), they appointed Graeme Souness as player-manager, a man of proven footballing character and ability to win, even at a European level. Several other things were to happen as well. One would be the engagement of English players (currently frustrated at European level because English teams were banned for the bad behaviour of their supporters, those of Liverpool in particular at the European Cup Final of 1985). The other would be the employment of Roman Catholics, no matter what the supporters felt. They would do this spectacularly in 1989, but for the moment they kept their supporters onside by continuing their policy of bigotry and concentrating, in the first instance, on achieving some domestic success. Other than the two Scottish League Cups of 1983/84 and 1984/85, Rangers had won nothing since 1981 when they won the Scottish Cup. They had not won the League Championship since 1978.

Season 1986/87 was the start of the Souness revolution. It was frightening, deliberately so, as Rangers seemed to set out to intimidate the opposition. Souness was himself sent off in his debut game at Easter Road, and we had the barely believable spectacle of the goalkeeper Chris Woods charging out of his goal and running some considerable distance when a fracas developed; not to calm everyone down, but to join in! The intimidation had its effect. Celtic were immediately and noticeably quietened. Aberdeen might not have been but Alex Ferguson, the man who might have resisted Rangers, was soon on his way to Manchester United. Many supporters, not all of them Aberdeen ones, felt that a more severe test of Fergie's ability would have been to stay on and accept the new challenge.

The Scottish League Cup of 1986/87 must be seen in this context of a ruthlessly determined Rangers, pledged to reassert themselves. The final was an unsavoury spectacle which did Scottish football few favours in the eyes of the world.

The Scottish League had hit on a good format for the competition. There was another beneficial change in that the semi-finals were to be played at neutral venues and there would only be one game. The home-and-home concept which delayed the competition so much had now gone and the final would be played on Sunday, 26 October 1986 in front of TV cameras. The League Cup had taken its time to come up to date but it had now done so and the tournament benefitted as a result, even though this year's final would leave a nasty taste in several mouths.

It all began as normal in August with little untoward happening and all the big clubs duly defeating what was put in front of them, with the exception of Hearts who went down 0-2 to Montrose. Hearts were still struggling to cope with last year's loss of both the Scottish League and the Scottish Cup ('I'm forever blowing doubles!' sang the Hibs fans) and Montrose took advantage of their psychological disarray to record what must be considered among their best-ever results among several fine performances by the couthy and unpretentious Angus club in the Scottish League Cup.

The next round, at the end of August, saw Celtic having to work hard to break down Dumbarton, while Aberdeen and Dundee United did not find it easy to get the better of Clyde and Ayr United. Montrose's fairy tale came to an end as they went down 0-4 to neighbours Dundee at Dens Park and their role of giant killers was taken over by neighbours Forfar, who hammered St Mirren 5-1 at Station Park in what was one of Forfar's many great performances in those days.

But history might have been totally different if East Fife had had better luck in their penalty shoot-out at Bayview. East Fife were one of the leading lights in the early days of the competition and, in front of a packed Bayview, they came close to returning to the great days. They defied Rangers for 90 minutes then extra time with the travelling Rangers support visibly and audibly turning on their team. The game went to the lottery of a penalty shoot-out and Rangers held their nerve better than East Fife to win 5-4, with Rangers indebted to goalkeeper Chris Woods for saving them.

The quarter-finals on 3 September provided close games and some fine football. Three of them went to extra time. The one that finished in 90 minutes was as exciting as any with Hibs going down late to Dundee United at Easter Road, feeling ill-done-by when referee David Syme (who would also make his mark later in the tournament) failed to award what looked like an obvious penalty. Extra time was necessary at Fir Park, Motherwell when the home team had to come from behind to beat a spirited Forfar Athletic side. Forfar, the heroes of the previous round, went ahead before the home side equalised and only six minutes of extra time remained when Fraser Wishart saw Motherwell through.

At Ibrox 33,750 were there to see Rangers v Dundee. The fact that it had to go to extra time was due to a last-minute equaliser for Dundee at a time when quite a lot of the crowd had gone home, convinced that Rangers were in the semi-finals. The triumph was only delayed by half an hour, however, for Ted McMinn and Graeme Souness saw Rangers home. The real tension came at Pittodrie as last year's winners Aberdeen exited to Celtic on a penalty shoot-out. It was a fraught game with loads of bookings and the sending off of Celtic's Tony Shepherd. The game was 1-1 at that point, but Celtic coped with the numerical disadvantage for the remainder of the game and extra time and won 4-3 on penalties, an aspect of the game in which Celtic had not always excelled in the past.

Celtic's skills in this area would be called upon again in the semi-final played at Hampden on 23 September when they went two ahead and looked comfortable, but then Motherwell fought back brilliantly to take the game to extra time and a penalty shoot-out or, as John Greig (commentating on BBC radio in his slightly bucolic style peppered with grammatical solecisms) described it, 'a penalty kick-out'. Young John Philiben was the unlucky man who missed his penalty and Celtic went through in a way which did not exactly reassure their supporters in the 26,541 crowd. Needing two penalty shoot-outs to get to the League Cup Final said quite a lot about the fragility of Celtic in 1986.

A rather larger crowd of 45,249 was there the following night to see Rangers beat Dundee United 2-1 with goals from Ally McCoist and Ted McMinn. Once again, as if by divine decree, Dundee United froze at Hampden and were never really in the game until they scored a consolation goal near the end. It was a fine Rangers performance and their supporters left the ground in fine voice, now confident that, having beaten Dundee United, the current league leaders, they had little to fear from their old rivals Celtic, who were now quite clearly losing the propaganda battle of the Scottish media. Rangers were featured far more often than Celtic in the newspapers and over the airwaves.

The final on Sunday, 26 October was great entertainment for the 74,000 crowd and the vast global TV audience but it was unsavoury, controversial and unpleasant for anyone with the best interests of Scottish football at heart. Ten men were booked, two men were sent off (and one brought back again!) and the feeling of neutrals was that Celtic were ill-done-by and possibly the better team. But they had let themselves down by their behaviour at the end, including a desire expressed by manager David Hay to apply for the English League such was, he claimed, the institutional bias of Scottish referees. It was a bizarre statement, clearly made in the heat of the moment, but it made one wonder whether the idea had been discussed behind the scenes.

Amidst all the bookings there had actually been a lot of good football and two good goals, scored by Ian Durrant for Rangers and Brian McClair for Celtic. Extra time and penalties looked likely when Rangers were awarded a free kick on the right. As the ball came across, Roy Aitken and Terry Butcher both engaged in a spot of arm-wrestling and referee David Syme decided that it was a penalty for Rangers. It was a debatable decision, but Davie Cooper scored for Rangers.

All hell then broke loose. Maurice Johnston (still playing for Celtic in those days), who had already been booked, got himself sent off after an insignificant entanglement with Stuart Munro, who was also harshly booked. Ironically, in view of later events, Johnston blessed himself, making the sign of the cross, as he ran off. Immediately after, another Celt, Tony Shepherd, was sent off. The referee, who gave every sign of having lost the plot completely, had been struck with a missile thrown from the crowd and thought it was Shepherd. Shepherd was called back after the linesman told Mr Syme that the missile had come from the enclosure rather than the field. Manager David Hay then got involved and the only beneficiaries were Rangers, for Celtic lost about five minutes of playing time during which they might have sneaked a deserved equaliser.

The teams were:

Rangers: Woods, Nicholl, Munro, Fraser (McFarlane), Dawson, Butcher, Ferguson, McMinn, McCoist (Fleck), Durrant, Cooper

Celtic: Bonner, Grant, MacLeod, Aitken, Whyte, McGhee (Archdeacon), McClair, McStay, Johnston, Shepherd, McInally

Referee: D Syme, Rutherglen

Souness won his first honour as manager of Rangers. It would lead to more and sustained success – the great years of Souness at Rangers all started at Hampden. Rangers had now won the Scottish League Cup 14 times and other teams would find it very difficult to prise it from their grasp. Celtic, on the other hand, did not take it well. Psyched out, they were ahead in the league race but let it slip, victims of their own mental weakness and inferiority complex as much as anything else.

Thus, Rangers in 1987 won their first Scottish League Championship since 1978, but fell, surprisingly, to Hamilton Accies at Ibrox at the first time of asking in the Scottish Cup, the trophy being eventually won by St Mirren who beat Dundee United in the final. Dundee United are well worth a mention since they reached the final of the UEFA Cup beating no less than Barcelona en route. Celtic had had a trophyless season and brought back Billy McNeill to be their manager for 1987/88 in place of the luckless Davie Hay.

The opening rounds of the 1987/88 Scottish League Cup were unremarkable. Albion Rovers needed penalty kicks to beat East Fife in the second round and Hamilton took Meadowbank Thistle to extra time before yielding, but everything else was as predicted. Montrose, who beat Hearts last year, put up a good show against Hibs but just lost out, and Rangers' 2-1 win over Stirling Albion was not as close as it sounded because Rangers scored first and were always well on top. Celtic duly beat Forfar and Aberdeen beat Brechin City, but perhaps the best performance of the round was Hearts' extremely impressive 6-1 win over Kilmarnock.

The round of the last 16 was played the following week at the end of August and one could honestly say that there was not a single game that was close. The two Glasgow giants, the Edinburgh pair, the Dundee pair, Aberdeen and Motherwell ended up in the quarter-finals to be played at the beginning of

September. The draw paired the two Dundee teams together, sent Celtic to Aberdeen and denied Edinburgh a home tie by putting Hibs to Motherwell and Hearts to Ibrox.

Tuesday, 1 September saw the Aberdeen v Celtic and Motherwell v Hibs games. Both ended in a 1-0 win for the home side. At Pittodrie, a capacity crowd of 23,000 rolled up to see a game that did not really do justice to either team. It was said in some newspapers that Aberdeen had 'fallen asleep' since Alex Ferguson had left and had yet to produce their best form under Ian Porterfield. Ferguson, as it turned out, was there that night watching a few players whom he fancied for Manchester United, and he cannot have been too impressed. Aberdeen at least got the victory with a goal by Jim Bett in the 60th minute and a grim determination to defend. Some 12,000 were at Fir Park to see Motherwell and Hibs, two teams who had so far failed to set the heather on fire. Brian Fairlie scored early in the first half for Motherwell and, try as Hibs might, they could not break down the Motherwell defence.

The following night, Rangers beat Hearts 4-1 in a canter at Ibrox with a magnificent first-half display which had their fans cheering, but the Tayside derby was a totally different story at Dens Park, Dundee before a full crowd of 19,000. United scored first through Iain Ferguson and, with Kevin Gallacher on song, looked more likely to add to their lead. But, crucially, they failed to do that and slowly the outclassed Dundee came more into the game, pulling a goal back. Only four minutes remained when Dundee got their equaliser through Tommy Coyne, enough to take the game to extra time, during which Dundee, without in any way looking likely to do so, grabbed the winner through Keith Wright. United fans gawped in astonishment as to how they had managed to throw away a game which they had seemed to have totally within their grasp.

When Aberdeen were drawn against Dundee in the semi-final, Tannadice Park was the obvious place to play the game and the authorities were rewarded with a crowd of 22,034. This was far more than would have been enticed to Hampden in midweek, but the main thing was that it provided atmosphere in the smart, compact ground that Tannadice Park was. The game was an even one, but Dundee felt aggrieved that it would be Aberdeen at Hampden and not themselves. The outfield, open play of Dundee was on a par with that of Aberdeen, but the Dons were slightly more professional in their clinical finishing. Jim Bett was involved in both goals, one scored by Robert Connor and the other by Brian Irvine, both hitting the net just before half-time. Dundee pressed hard from then on but, as usual in those days, the central defensive pairing of Miller and McLeish was superb. Both men seemed able to read each other's mind with one going back and one going forward as appropriate. The Dons thus returned to Hampden for a major cup final for the first time since the departure of Alex Ferguson.

Even their best friends would have to admit that Rangers were a little fortunate in the two goals which won the other semi-final at Hampden. Paul Smith had put Motherwell ahead after 20 minutes, but before half-time the Steelmen had conceded two goals which were plain daft and which one could not afford against such a sophisticated outfit as Rangers. The first was when Steve Kirk, in trying to clear a ball, simply headed it cleanly into his own net. It would have been a beautiful goal if it had been at the right end! Then, a few minutes later, an intended pass back became more of a pass to a Rangers forward and Robert Fleck made no mistake. Motherwell never recovered from these two self-inflicted blows. Rangers added a third goal close to the end of the game and were into their sixth League Cup Final of the 1980s.

The final on Sunday, 25 October 1987 must go down as one of the best with Rangers emerging as winners after a penalty shoot-out and full credit being owed to Aberdeen for the entertainment that they provided for the worldwide audience. On-form Aberdeen were marginal favourites during the build-up to the game, particularly as Rangers had Graeme Souness, Chris Woods and Terry Butcher suspended; 71, 961 (only just short of Hampden's capacity) turned up to watch the game on a fine autumnal afternoon.

Aberdeen went ahead with a penalty kick in the tenth minute. It looked a soft award and may even have been a dive, but Mr Valentine of Dundee (who, over the piece, had a good game) awarded the penalty which Jim Bett converted. Before half-time Rangers had equalised and gone ahead. A nasty tackle by Willie Miller on the edge of the box allowed Davie Cooper to equalise with the resultant free kick, then a few minutes later Ian Durrant, after a fine move involving a one-two with McCoist, put Rangers in front.

The second half was thrill-a-minute stuff. Less than 20 minutes remained when Peter Weir levelled matters for the Dons with a fine left-foot drive and then, within the last ten minutes, Aberdeen seemed to have won the trophy with a fine header from Willie Falconer. Some teams might have buckled, but not this Rangers side for whom Robert Fleck equalised after being put through by Ian Durrant.

The 90 minutes might have provided enough entertainment and passion for the watching TV audience, but there was more to come. Another 30 minutes followed. Rangers were the better side against a tiring Aberdeen outfit but they missed a few chances and the game had to go to penalties. It was the first time a penalty shoot-out had been used to decide a national cup final and the nation was now enthralled. Even those with no interest in football were drawn in by the excitement of the penalties. They were as transfixed as anyone but asked the logical question, 'Why couldn't they have just done this in the first place?'

The penalties were all taken professionally and well, but there always has to be one who misses, in this case the excellent Welshmen Peter Nicholas whose effort just skimmed the bar on its way to the Rangers crowd behind that goal. When Ian Durrant, who had enjoyed an excellent game, scored the fifth penalty for Rangers, his side had won the Scottish League Cup for the second year in a row and the 15th time overall. Everyone felt a little sorry for Aberdeen, who had contributed so much to the final and the whole tournament, but it was Rangers' day. They would have been well advised to enjoy it, for Celtic went on to lift a league and cup double later that season. But Aberdeen and Rangers would meet again at Hampden in a League Cup Final. The history between these two was far from over.

The teams were:

Rangers: Walker, Nicholl, Munro, Roberts, Ferguson (Francis), Gough, McGregor (Cohen), Fleck, McCoist, Durrant, Cooper

Aberdeen: Leighton, McKimmie, Connor, Simpson (Weir), McLeish, W Miller, Hewitt, Bett, J Miller, Nicholas, Falconer

Referee: R Valentine, Dundee

By the time the 1988/89 season started it was clear that the League Cup format, as it currently stood, was a success. No first leg and second leg which prolonged matters and led to boring football, and the tournament benefitted from finishing before winter started. Some clubs were involved in Europe (and in this era, Scottish clubs often lasted longer than the first round) and although the losers would often be heard to say that it was 'just' the League Cup, the winners would not agree.

The six first-round games passed uneventfully, but a feature of the second round was that all four Lanarkshire teams faced each other, Motherwell beating Airdrie and Hamilton beating Albion Rovers. Elsewhere, there was no great shock but the penalty shoot-out between Falkirk and Raith Rovers reached 9-8 before being decided in the benefit of Falkirk. Kilmarnock were probably rather lucky to beat Forfar, as were Meadowbank against Stirling Albion, but otherwise everything went as planned for the big clubs.

The same could be said about the third round, but Aberdeen had a bit of a scare at Cappielow. They never found Morton easy to deal with – indeed, Cappielow was always a difficult place for anyone to visit – and were indebted to Jim Bett for scoring twice after Morton had scored first. Dunfermline showed a welcome return to better days, as far as the League Cup was concerned, when they beat Motherwell 2-1. They joined the quarter-finals which contained two Glasgow teams, two Edinburgh teams, two Dundee teams and Aberdeen. The tournament once again took off.

Celtic exited the tournament at Tannadice Park. Dundee United were fortunate enough to catch Celtic a few days after their worst result for a long time. The team who had won the league and cup double in May came to a shuddering halt when they lost 1-5 to Rangers at Ibrox. They did not recover for several years and duly lost 0-2 to Dundee United that night. Rangers beat Dundee at Ibrox in a very convincing 4-1 victory; 4-1 was also the scoreline at East End Park, Dunfermline where the home side went down to a fine performance from Hearts, but the best game of the round was the match at Easter Road.

Aberdeen and Hibs served up a great game which went to extra time and it was Aberdeen who edged home through a Brian Grant goal in the 115th minute. This was after Charlie Nicholas, now returned to Scotland from Arsenal, had put the Dons ahead and Paul Kane had equalised. Their reward was a semi-final tie against Dundee United, while Rangers took on Hearts.

The semi-final between Aberdeen and Dundee United was arranged for Tuesday, 20 September at Dens Park and the Dons won comfortably, 2-0. They scored early and late through John Hewitt and Davie Dodds, one time of Dundee United, and their defence kept a stranglehold on the Dundee United forwards. The following night at Hampden, any hopes that Hearts might have entertained of reaching their first League Cup Final for close on 30 years were quickly extinguished in a 4-1 defeat by Rangers in front of a large crowd of 53,000.

Mark Walters was outstanding for Rangers. Mark was a high-profile signing, one of the very few black players to have played in Scottish football. He was, sadly, subject to the cries of the racist ignorant (not least in his own support) and more than once had bananas thrown at him, but he was a fine player and he proved it that night. Once again, the final was between Rangers and Aberdeen.

It would be fair to say that relationships between the two clubs had taken a further dip in the past 12 months. They had never been great in the first place, but there had been one particular tackle a few weeks previously in a league match on Ian Durrant by Neil Simpson which had serious consequences. It almost ended Durrant's career and it, in a way, ruined Simpson's career as well. He was permanently booed by Rangers supporters wherever he went and, to this day, he is recalled not for his very fine career but for that infamous tackle. On 23 October 1988, while Neil Simpson took the field for Aberdeen, Ian Durrant sat at home watching the game on TV with his leg in a plaster cast.

That was only part of the poor relationship between the two teams. Aberdeen supporters sang to Celtic supporters 'We hate Rangers more than you' and there was at least an element of truth in it. The dislike was tangible at both Pittodrie and Ibrox; now at Hampden, when they met for the second League Cup Final in succession, there was pleading from the press and the media that everyone should be on their best behaviour.

They got their wish. The two teams, in a game that was hard but fair and well refereed by George Smith of Edinburgh, served up some great entertainment and the excitement level was on a par with last year's final in the same competition. The point of similarity was that Rangers won. The difference was that they were able to do it without extra time and penalties but in the regulation 90 minutes. Like last year, it was a close-run thing and Aberdeen had every reason to feel let down by providence.

Rangers began attacking the King's Park end and opened the scoring with an Ally McCoist penalty. It had been awarded when Kevin Drinkell was brought down in the penalty box by Aberdeen's Dutch goalkeeper Theo Snelders. It looked soft, at least to the Aberdeen supporters, and Drinkell's dive to make sure that it was inside the penalty box was certainly very impressive. Anyhow, McCoist scored and Rangers were one up. Davie Dodds then equalised when everyone, goalkeeper included, missed a corner and the ball came to him to equalise. That was how it was at half-time – a draw was fair and everyone was behaving.

The second half saw a marvellous goal from Ian Ferguson to put Rangers ahead but, once again, it was Davie Dodds who equalised for the Dons when a looping ball came across the penalty box to him and Dodds headed a similarly looping ball into the net. The goalkeeping did not look too clever, and one might argue that the equaliser was slightly against the run of play, but it set up a grandstand finish.

The winner might have come at either end with Aberdeen, if anything, now in the ascendancy, but it was Rangers who won it. Jim Bett, in a moment that would haunt him the rest of his life, was through on a one-on-one but pulled the ball wide across his body when it might have made more sense to slide it home. But it was Ally McCoist, with an athletic goal that he tended to score so well, who hit the winner after the Aberdeen defence had failed to clear a Rangers corner. Davie Dodds might have reached his hat-trick at the death but had the chagrin to see his shot blocked by a defender getting his body in the way.

It was marvellous entertainment for the 72,000 fans and the massive Sunday afternoon TV audience. Like last year's final, it had not lacked drama, excitement or passion. There were natural feelings of being sorry for Aberdeen, although such feelings tended to diminish when one thought of that tackle a couple of weeks previously, and everyone was glad that both teams had concentrated on playing football, and good football at that.

The teams were:

Rangers: Woods, Steven, Brown, Gough, Wilkins, Butcher, Drinkell, Ferguson, McCoist, Cooper, Walters

Aberdeen: Snelders, McKimmie, Robertson, Simpson (Irvine), McLeish, Miller, Nicholas, Bett, Dodds, Connor, Hewitt

Referee: G Smith, Edinburgh

The bottom line was that Rangers had now won the Scottish League Cup for the third year in a row and the 16th time overall, some distance ahead of Celtic who could only claim nine victories. It was also Graeme Souness's fourth trophy. They would go on and win the Scottish League in 1989, although their attempt at a treble was foiled by Celtic in the Scottish Cup Final. However, as far as the League Cup was concerned, there seemed to be no stopping Rangers. They were not finished yet.

But season 1989/90 put a temporary spoke in their League Cup stride. Rangers started the season with a peculiar problem. They signed a new player by the name of Maurice Johnston, snatching him from under the noses of Celtic after their Glasgow rivals had paraded him in a Celtic shirt before he had actually signed (something that spoke volumes for the lack of business acumen prevailing at Celtic Park in 1989). It was a nifty piece of business by Rangers, but the snag was that Maurice Johnston was a Roman Catholic. Despite threats of boycotts, and words like 'betrayal' and 'Judas' in danger of being overused in both sections of Glasgow, Rangers would win the Scottish League again without a great deal of bother, but both domestic cups would go north to Aberdeen, repeating the success of 1985/86, the last time that they were the possessors of both domestic cup trophies.

The League Cup opened as usual in mid-August. The first round (sometimes referred to as the qualifying round because there were only six games) threw up a couple of remarkable games. One was the tie at Central Park, Cowdenbeath where the final score after 90 minutes was a mundane 0-0 draw between Cowdenbeath and Montrose, the only highlight being a missed penalty by Montrose. But then Gary Murray, one time of Hibs, hit four goals in extra time to win the game for Montrose and earn them a trip to Tynecastle in the next. Another exciting game also in Fife was at Methil where Queen's Park were 0-2 down at half-time but fought back to earn extra time and then won 7-6 on penalties.

The second round a week later had little to recommend it in the shape of shocks or excitement as everything went to plan. It was unusual in that all 16 games were played and settled without a single one having to go to extra time or to penalties. Rangers beat Arbroath, Celtic beat Dumbarton, Aberdeen beat Albion Rovers, both Dundee teams and both Edinburgh teams won at home, and in the Fife derby Dunfermline Athletic comfortably beat Raith Rovers 3-0.

Things were a lot closer in the third round the following week, although in most cases the bigger team won. Aberdeen disposed of Airdrie without much bother and Celtic did likewise with Queen of the South, but Rangers at Cappielow was a different matter altogether. In appalling conditions of wind and rain (bad even for Greenock!) they went one down early on and needed an own goal by the luckless Mark

Pickering to beat Morton. Both Dundee teams fell at this hurdle, Dundee to Dunfermline Athletic and United to Hamilton, and Hibs needed their goalkeeper Andy Goram to score the vital penalty to beat Clydebank in the shoot-out after 120 minutes of distinctly uninspiring football. Hearts, however, beat their old foes Falkirk 4-1 and St Mirren got the better of Motherwell to win 1-0.

Two quarter-final games were scheduled for Edinburgh so the game at Easter Road against Dunfermline had to be played on the Tuesday night to allow Hearts to take on Celtic on the Wednesday. The 16,000 crowd saw a marvellous cup tie which the Pars won 3-1 in extra time, Paul Smith and Ross Jack scoring the vital goals. Even more excitement prevailed at Tynecastle the following night when Celtic beat Hearts on penalties. It was a night that maybe did not have everything, but had most things, and not all of them pleasant: foul weather, a late start to allow more people into the game and an undignified touchline scramble with players and managers pushing and shoving each other but no one actually laying a punch. Eventually, Celtic won on a penalty shoot-out. For a long time, it looked as if Hearts would win, but Dziekanowski scored for Celtic late in the 90 minutes to equalise and both teams scored in extra time, John Robertson's equaliser coming very late indeed, but it was Celtic who had the last laugh.

The other two games were less dramatic with Rangers beating Hamilton Accies with a degree of ease and Aberdeen getting the better of St Mirren at Pittodrie in a game that was lucky to get finished in perpetual torrential rain which made things difficult and dangerous for the players. The draw for the semi-final paired Aberdeen with Celtic and Rangers with

Dunfermline Athletic, both to be played at Hampden, on 20 and 21 September.

Dunfermline disappointed their large travelling support by going down 0-5 to Rangers when recent form might have suggested that they could have done better. It was the other semi-final, though, which attracted a crowd of 45,000 and became a *cause célèbre* of Scottish football. The first half saw Celtic marginally the better side but suffering from frustration in front of goal. Joe Miller was duly brought on at half-time to replace Steve Fulton, but sometime after Ian Cameron scored what turned out to be the only goal of the game, Miller was himself substituted for failing to carry out manager McNeill's instructions. Miller was far from happy and almost threw his Celtic jersey at McNeill in annoyance, then Roy Aitken was sent off after Jim Bett made the most of minimal contact. It was said that Celtic had three Poles playing that night – Dziekanowski, Aitkenoffski and Milleronandoffski!

Thus continued the apparent jinx that Celtic seemed to have in this particular competition – it would go on for another eight years yet – and it was the beginning of the end for Roy Aitken at Celtic as the press and some of the fans turned on him. For the third year in a row the League Cup Final would be contested by Aberdeen and Rangers.

There were 61,190 (some 10,000 fewer than the last two years) at Hampden on 22 October 1989 to see the game; the reason for the smaller attendance was without doubt the heavy rain. It had been on all morning and, although it eased a little just as the game was starting, it was still enough to persuade a lot of supporters to stay in the pub to watch it on TV rather than subject themselves on the uncovered terraces at Hampden. This even included quite a few supporters who had travelled down from Aberdeen that morning and now found the attractions of the Mount Florida and King's Park hostelries irresistible.

It is often said that important games are won by the team which wants to win them more than their opponents. This dynamic may have been in play here. Aberdeen were fed up, having lost the last two finals, and felt that this was their moment, whereas Rangers had temporarily lost their appetite for success. It was also true that Rangers owed a certain amount of their last two successes to luck, that elusive and scarcely definable quality which nevertheless determines so many football matches. This time, it was Alex Smith and Jocky Scott's Aberdeen on whom Lady Luck smiled.

Paul Mason, a Liverpudlian who moved to Aberdeen in a career that seemed to be going nowhere fast, scored the first goal with a looping header. Rangers equalised through a penalty that was the wrong decision and can only really be explained in terms of the referee, George Smith, being badly positioned. If anything, it looked like a free kick for Aberdeen as Ally McCoist backed into Willie Miller, but to the consternation of the TV commentators and the Aberdeen support, the referee gave a penalty kick. Tantrums thrown by Willie Miller and Alex McLeish failed to persuade the referee to change his mind and Mark Walters scored.

It stayed 1-1 until half-time and throughout the second half. Both teams had chances, the weather improved as the sun came out (the clock would not be changed until the following week, so the game finished in daylight) but there was no decision within the 90 minutes. That it was Paul Mason's day in a non-too-distinguished career became apparent when he popped up to score the deciding goal near the end of the first half of extra time, but the real hero for Aberdeen was goalkeeper Theo Snelders, who defied Rangers' attacks time and time again, even when Terry Butcher, with his head swathed in a bandage, joined in. Full time came with the ball in Snelders's hands – appropriately enough – and the whistle indicated that Aberdeen had won the Scottish League Cup for the fourth time. The apparent invincibility of Rangers in the League Cup was broken, albeit temporarily.

The teams were:

Aberdeen: Snelders, McKimmie, Robertson, Grant (Van der Ark), McLeish, Miller, Nicholas, Bett, Mason, Connor, Jess (Irvine)

Rangers: Woods, Stevens, Munro, Gough, Wilkins, Butcher, Steven, Ferguson, McCoist, Johnston, Walters (McCall)

Referee: G Smith, Edinburgh

Rangers regained the trophy the following year. Spring 1990 saw Rangers win the Scottish League while Aberdeen completed a cup double by lifting the Scottish Cup. They did this rather fortuitously in a penalty shoot-out in the final against Celtic. Summer 1990 saw Scotland in the World Cup in Italy, but many of us wished they weren't. The first match saw a shocking defeat to Costa Rica, the result which finally destroyed Scotland's credibility as a footballing power.

When the new season started in August, Queen's Park, that quaint anachronism of amateurism in the sometimes brutal and ruthless professional game, caught the eye. They beat East Fife on penalty kicks and the draw for the next round paired them with Aberdeen at Hampden. Aberdeen were no strangers to Hampden but they would have been taken aback with the crowd of 2,201 and the empty echoing bowl in which you could hear every word said by the players. The Dons won through but it was a struggle; 2-1 with goals from Eoin Jess and Jim Bett.

The rest of the second round contained one or two exciting ties but no real shocks. Rangers beat East Stirlingshire 5-0 and Celtic beat Ayr United 4-0 at Parkhead in the first-ever League Cup game shown live through a television firm called British Satellite Broadcasting. The problem was trying to find someone with a satellite dish in order to watch it. BSB would not last long and amalgamated with Sky TV. Two games in this round went to penalties, Partick Thistle and Queen of the South being the beneficiaries over Falkirk and Dundee, and there were two thrillers: at Motherwell where the home side beat Morton 4-3, and at Kilmarnock, where Killie got the better of Clydebank 3-2. Clydebank, sadly no longer with us, had reached the semi-final of the Scottish Cup last year.

The third round saw four of the eight ties end up 1-0, and they all involved the Glasgow and the Edinburgh teams. Rangers beat a spirited and perhaps unlucky Kilmarnock side at Ibrox and Celtic were indebted to their talismanic and sometimes controversial Pole, 'Jacki' Dziekanowski, to score the goal which beat Hamilton at Douglas Park. Hearts won 1-0 over St Mirren at Love Street after extra time with a goal by Scott Crabbe while Raith Rovers, hinting perhaps at future League Cup glory, pulled off a surprise by beating an admittedly very poor Hibs side 1-0 at Stark's Park with George McGeachie scoring the only goal of the game. The heroes of the round were Queen of the South who defeated Dunfermline Athletic 2-1 at East End Park, while the other three qualifiers were Dundee United, Motherwell and Aberdeen.

Three of the four quarter-finals were won easily by the favourites. Darren Jackson and Jim McInally scored the goals for Dundee United to beat Motherwell at Tannadice, Rangers crushed Raith Rovers 6-2 at Ibrox, while Aberdeen beat Hearts with a considerable degree of ease 3-0 at Pittodrie.

Nothing surprising there, but Queen of the South put up a great deal of resistance before eventually succumbing to Celtic in heavy rain at Parkhead. Queen of the South's manager was Frank McGarvey, ex-Celtic hero, and he and his team were given a great reception. In the second half, when Celtic were failing to impress, there were signs that the disappointing and disappointed Celtic crowd of 18,000 were beginning to turn against their own team. Dziekanowski had scored early on but Celtic failed to add to their advantage and, halfway through the second half, young Andy Thomson equalised for Queens. In the end it was Joe Miller, brought on as a substitute by Billy McNeill, who scored the winning goal. Last year's villain became this year's hero as he grabbed a place for Celtic in the League Cup semi-final.

Celtic's semi-final was played at Hampden on Tuesday, 25 September against Dundee United. Had the game been at Tannadice it might have been a different story, but Dundee United chose to obey the immutable law that they must lose at Hampden. Perhaps this is doing less than justice to Celtic, however, who turned on one of their better performances this season to win 2-0 with goals from Paul McStay and Gerry Creaney before an appreciative crowd of 49,975.

There were 40,855 at the other semi-final the following night to see Aberdeen take on Rangers. At least with the two of them meeting in the semi-final, they couldn't meet in the final as they had done for the previous three seasons. Once again the game was close, but it was Rangers who scored the only goal of the game through Trever Steven, and a great individual goal it was. Aberdeen supporters claimed that a few refereeing decisions did not go their way, but Rangers had done enough to win.

And so we had another Old Firm League Cup Final, the tenth between them. Rangers had won in 1964/65, 1970/71, 1975/76, 1977/78 and 1986/87 whereas Celtic had been triumphant in 1957/58, 1965/66, 1966/67 and 1982/83. This year it ought to have been Celtic who wanted it more, for 1990 had been a dreadful year for them so far. Their fans yearned for silver, which the team seemed unable to deliver. Celtic were without diehard Roy Aitken, had been defeated in a heartbreaking penalty shoot-out by Aberdeen in the Scottish Cup Final and were struggling to keep pace with Rangers in the league. Their board was showing every sign of not being able to cope.

Rangers, on the other hand, were ruthlessly professional. They had a better team than Celtic, although it was probably true that Celtic had one or two players like Dziekanowski and McStay who had more flair and could win a game on their own. Nevertheless, most pundits were tipping a Rangers win in the competition which they seemed to be making their own.

The game was played at Hampden on 28 October 1990 and it attracted an all-ticket crowd of 62,817 on a bleak day, the traditional League Cup Final time from the early years of the tournament, namely the day that the clocks went back. Winter began that day, and for the losers there was thus always a feeling of more than the average depression. Yet the two teams produced a good game. Rangers were slightly hampered by injuries but the replacements were more than adequate.

The Celtic end seethed with rumours about referee Mr Jim McCluskey of Stewarton. He had been fined £25, it was said, for being drunk and incapable in Ayrshire on the day of an Orange Walk in July! Glasgow being the place that it was, gossip tended to centre on the fact that it was the same day as an Orange Walk rather than on the simple fact that he had been drunk, something that perhaps raised a more legitimate question about whether he was a suitable man to take charge of the game. He did not have a good game, it would have to be said, but there was no evidence or suggestion that he favoured Rangers, nor indeed that he had been influenced by strong drink. On one occasion he might have given a penalty kick and sent goalkeeper Pat Bonner off after he collided with Ally McCoist, but he wisely left things well alone. In fact, the late Jim McCluskey, who died in 2013, was usually one of Scotland's better referees.

Half-time saw no score with Celtic playing the better football, particularly Paul McStay. And after about eight minutes of the second half, Celtic, attacking the goal behind which were congregated their own supporters, went ahead. A John Collins corner found Joe Miller who sent it back into the penalty area and found the head of Paul Elliott to put Celtic ahead. The lead lasted about quarter of an hour as Rangers tried ever more desperately to get back into the game. A long ball from Richard Gough found Mark Hateley who headed on to Ally McCoist. McCoist then slipped the ball to Mark Walters, who scored from the edge of the box. It was a good goal, but by the time 90 minutes came, neither side could claim to have had any significant advantage over the other.

Then we come to the moment that defines the tragic career of Dariusz Dziekanowski. A good player is only good if he performs well when his team needs him to. Dziekanowski was put through in the first minute of extra time and, to the chagrin of his worshippers behind the King's Park end goal, fired straight at the goalkeeper. Neither he nor Celtic recovered and, when a chance presented itself to Richard Gough, he had no inhibitions about scoring to give Rangers their fourth League Cup in five years and their 17th overall. Out of 45 years, that was not a bad record.

They would also win the Scottish League that year, but not the Scottish Cup which went to Motherwell. Celtic beat Rangers in the quarter-final of the Scottish Cup on a day that Rangers chose to show the unacceptable side of their nature by having three men sent off, but it ended up a bad season for Celtic, whose supporters were about to suffer even more.

The teams were:

Rangers: Woods, Steven, Munro, Gough, Spackman, Brown, Steven, Hurlock (Huistra), McCoist (Ferguson), Hateley, Walters

Celtic: Bonner, Grant, Wdowczyk, Fulton (Hewitt), Elliott, Rogan, Miller (Morris), McStay, Dziekanowski, Creaney, Collins

Referee: J McCluskey, Stewarton

CHAPTER TEN

TAINTED GLORY
1991–1998

IT IS sad that, as we move to the end of the 20th century and record the sustained success of Rangers, we must reflect that so much of the success – they won the League Cup five times in the 1990s – was achieved by dubious means including dodgy deals, spending money they did not have and refusing to pay income tax. Opponents will add the bribing of referees to this tally, but that is difficult to prove! Nevertheless, Rangers came to spectacular grief in 2012 and have duly suffered for what they had done. The verdict of history has been delivered, but we must at least acknowledge their successes in this tournament, however they were achieved.

Before Rangers won the Scottish League Cup again, there was a remarkable year in which Hibs were to reach the pinnacle. They did so in October 1991 and it was a particular cause of joy for their supporters who had been to hell and back – and for a while it looked as if they might not come back. The history of Hibs in the 1980s was nothing short of woeful. No strangers to relegation, frequent changes of management, the buying of inferior players, the selling of talented ones – all were inflicted on the Easter Road support. Granted, there had been no great success on the other side of the city at Tynecastle either, but at least there had been one or two near things, notably in 1986, and Hearts were being noticed and reaching the headlines on the back pages of *The Scotsman*. But Edinburgh and football success did not really go together and it was with this in mind that Hearts' chairman, Wallace Mercer, proposed a merger of the two clubs in summer 1990. The proposal, to an outsider at least, was not without merit. An Edinburgh United or an Edinburgh Rovers with a strong fanbase and the support of a wealthy city should really do well, at least in theory. The example of Aberdeen was pointed to, in contrast to that of Dundee where there existed a similar situation of two mediocre clubs cursed with feckless directors and unable to make any great sustained impact on the Scottish scene.

However sensible the proposal might have seemed to those outside the city and to some of the Hearts persuasion within it, all hell broke loose in Leith. Long-forgotten passions were aroused. There were undeniably the religious passions of long ago, not helped by Hearts supporters waving Union flags and imitating Rangers, but there was, more pronouncedly, the geographical factor. For anyone born east and north of Princes Street, Hibs were looked upon as their team. Their dander was up! How dare the chairman of Hearts, not always the most blameless of individuals (however suave and plausible on the surface), try to take over Hibs?

The writer recalls two uncles by marriage. Two worthy gentlemen, sadly no longer with us, neither of whom one would have immediately identified as a football fan. But they had been born in Leith and suddenly, thanks to Mr Mercer, became rabid Hibs fans arousing in themselves childhood memories of Easter Road and Lawrie Reilly!

The issue ran throughout the 1990/91 season and was only finally put to bed in 1991/92 when Hibs won the League Cup. Their success must be seen in this context. The passion of players and supporters had been inflamed. It was now up to the players, under manager Alex Miller, to produce the goods.

Even without the Hibs factor, the early rounds of the League Cup were interesting. A lot of interest centred on Airdrieonians. They shocked the Scottish footballing world by beating Aberdeen 1-0 at Pittodrie, adding to the misery of Aberdeen supporters who had watched their team blow up rather badly last spring by failing to draw with Rangers at Ibrox and win the league. Airdrie then compounded the felony by putting Celtic out in the quarter-final. Admittedly, it was only on a penalty shoot-out, but it was after this game that Liam Brady, Celtic's new manager to replace the luckless Billy McNeill, said that it was no huge disaster for Celtic to lose to Airdrie since 'they had beaten Aberdeen as well'. It showed how little the man understood Scottish football and Celtic and he never recovered his credibility. He had not realised what a colossal disaster it is to Celtic fans to lose in any context!

Airdrie remained the centre of controversy in the semi-final against Dunfermline Athletic at Tynecastle. Before a crowd of 10,662, they were leading 1-0 late in extra time when referee David Syme awarded Dunfermline a penalty when Jimmy Sandison of Airdrie seemed to have been hit with the ball on his chest and was outside the box anyway. Dunfermline scored the penalty and then won on the shoot-out. Airdrie did not take the decision graciously and, on future occasions when Mr Syme was refereeing them, they refused to shake his hand before the start!

Dunfermline had just sacked their manager Ian Munro and replaced him with Jocky Scott. They had reached this stage not without a little luck, for they needed a penalty shoot-out to beat St Mirren, but their 3-1 defeat of Dundee United in the quarter-finals was a very creditable victory. Their appearance in the League Cup Final was their first since 1949 and was much anticipated by their fans, who had a taste of glory in the 1960s but very little since.

Hibs reached the final by beating Stirling Albion 3-0 in a game played at McDiarmid Park, Perth because Stirling Albion had an artificial pitch and clubs were not compelled to play on such a surface if they did not want to. Hibs then travelled to Ayrshire for their next two games, beating Kilmarnock 3-2 in a thriller at Rugby Park and Ayr United 2-0 with a little more ease at Somerset Park, before their big triumph of the campaign when they beat Rangers in the semi-final at Hampden on 25 September before a crowd of 40,901. New signing Keith Wright headed the only goal of the game after a bad clearance by Andy Goram (a Hibs player until recently) and, with veteran goalkeeper John Burridge in good form, Hibs held out against a determined Rangers side for whom Mo Johnston hit the post.

So it was that Hibs took on Dunfermline for the Scottish League Cup on 27 October 1991. It was Hibs' sixth League Cup Final, for they had won it in 1972/73 and lost it in 1950/51, 1968/69, 1974/75 and 1985/6. Dunfermline had been there only once before, in 1949/50. Most people fancied Hibs and 40,377 turned up to see the game on this damp but not too cold Sunday afternoon on the day after the clock had changed. One wonders where the 40,377 came from and, although it was nice to see so many fans in their green-and-white and black-and-white regalia, one cannot refrain from making the waspish comment that it would have been nice if they all attended their home games as well. The first half had a few exciting moments but remained goalless. Pundits often remark at half-time that 'the game needs a goal'. The implication then is that the game isn't very good at all. Certainly there was a feeling that both teams had been overwhelmed by the occasion, but if that were so, things immediately perked up after the interval when Hibs went ahead with a penalty. This came about when Mickey Weir (in a Hibs shirt that looked several sizes too big for him) was wrestled to the ground by a Dunfermline defender and referee Brian McGinlay had no hesitation in pointing to the spot. Tommy McIntyre made no mistake.

Dunfermline fought valiantly to get back into the game but Hibs were in command for the rest of the 90 minutes and the win was confirmed when Keith Wright was put through in the 86th minute and effectively killed the game. Hibs even had time to hit the post before the full-time whistle with a fierce drive from Brian Hamilton.

The teams were:

Hibs: Burridge, Miller, Mitchell, Hunter, McIntyre, MacLeod, Weir, Hamilton, Wright, Evans, McGinlay

Dunfermline: Rhodes, Wilson, Sharp (Cunningham), McCathie, Moyes, Robertson, McWilliams, Kozma, Leitch, Davies, Sinclair (McCall)

Referee: B McGinlay, Balfron

Hibs had succeeded in their aim of silencing Wallace Mercer and, from that day to this, we have heard a great deal less about merging the Edinburgh teams. The pity was that Hibs' success was not maintained and a predictable relapse to mediocrity became the order of the day as Rangers took the Scottish League and the Scottish Cup. The return to Edinburgh that October night, however, was a memorable one as the team changed from their team bus to an open-top one for a triumphal celebration through the streets, remarkably undisrupted by Hearts fans. It was not, after all, that Edinburgh triumphs were an everyday occurrence; the last one for Hibs was 19 years before in December 1972. For Hearts, one had to go back a further decade to October 1962 when the world was in the throes of the Cuban Missile Crisis.

It was one of the more interesting League Cup campaigns, not least because the main contenders were not the usual ones and the political issue in Edinburgh which, however much one denies it, had a great influence on the outcome of the 46th Scottish League Cup.

It was back to 'auld claes and porritch' the following year as Rangers once again took over, beating Aberdeen once again in the final, but by season 1992/93 things were changing radically in football. And it all had to do with TV. Throughout the 1980s, there had been live football matches regularly every weekend on TV – but not in Scotland. Incredible as it may seem, the Scottish authorities were able to stop TV games coming to Scotland from England or Europe under the guise of such clichés as 'protecting the game' and 'looking after the interests of the fan', even though depending on one's geographical location, one could be lucky now and again. Occasionally there was a live game – and the Scottish

League Cup Final since 1984 had been one of them. It was much looked forward to and relished by everyone.

But the early 1990s saw the rise of satellite TV with loads of money. The SFA and the Scottish League quivered and buckled, then in summer 1992 came the big breakthrough for terrestrial TV when Channel 4 started to show Serie A games from Italy on a Sunday afternoon. The dam burst. One hundred years ago, it was said that trying to stop professionalism was like trying to stop Niagara Falls with a kitchen chair. A century later, for 'professionalism' read 'live TV'. And how the fans loved it!

This was in the background as the 1992/93 season started and there can be little doubt that Scottish football suffered. The national team went from bad to worse and the travails of some clubs, Celtic in particular, showed how much harm an autocratic, paternalistic and distant form of direction could do to the club. The Celtic revolution was still some time away but, like the train in the film *The Bridge on the River Kwai*, it could be heard in the distance and was fast approaching.

In the meantime, neither Celtic nor anyone else could stop Rangers. Hibs started the defence of their trophy with an impressive 4-1 win over Raith Rovers but then lost 1-3 to Kilmarnock at Rugby Park. It was almost as if Hibs supporters had enjoyed their ration of happiness and would now have to wait another 15 years for some more!

While Rangers marched on, beating Dumbarton and Stranraer with few problems, a feature of the third round in the middle of August was that three other big teams were extremely lucky to get through. Hearts struggled to beat gallant Brechin City at Glebe Park. At Pittodrie, Aberdeen had to dig deep to win 1-0 over a Dunfermline side who fancied another taste of Hampden. The Dons needed extra time before Mixu Paatelainen scored, and also needed the benefit of Dunfermline being reduced to ten men. Celtic beat Dundee by a similar score at Parkhead, and here again Celtic got the benefit of a Dundee player – Ian Gilzean, son of the illustrious Alan of 30 years prior – sent off for an offence not immediately apparent to the 30,000 crowd.

The quarter-finals, played in the last midweek of August, showed once again the ability of the Old Firm to win games by the odd goal when they had to. Duncan Shearer scored an impressive hat-trick for Aberdeen as the Dons beat Falkirk 4-1 at Brockville and St Johnstone impressed their supporters with a 3-1 win at Kilmarnock, but the Old Firm struggled, Rangers getting the better of Dundee United at Tannadice, a ground that had always proved difficult for them, and Celtic at Tynecastle. Rangers won 3-2 and Celtic 2-1. Things might have been a lot different if chances had been taken by the home sides at key points of the game.

The semi-final draw paired Celtic with Aberdeen and Rangers with St Johnstone. The Rangers v St Johnstone game was played at Hampden on Tuesday, 22 September and the other game a day later. Rangers, playing in an unfamiliar white strip to avoid a clash with St Johnstone, won 3-1 with a hat-trick scored by Ally McCoist. It was in some way a typical McCoist hat-trick with Ally showing the striker's knack of quite simply being in the right place at the right time. None of his goals were particularly spectacular but they all hit the back of the net, and that is what counted. They did not call him Super Ally for nothing. Paul Wright scored a penalty for St Johnstone. The attendance was a little disappointing at 30,062.

The following night saw a rather larger attendance of 40,618 to see the Celtic v Aberdeen game. This was a close-fought game (as was often the case between these two teams) but it was Aberdeen who scored the only goal. It came just as half-time was approaching. Paul Mason took a corner kick on the stand side of the field and found the head of Mixu Paatelainen. The ball was stopped on the line, but not cleared, and eventually Eoin Jess was able to scramble it over. It was a long second half for the stalwart band of Aberdeen fans who had made the journey as Celtic came close once or twice through Gerry Creaney and Stuart Slater. The full-time whistle meant that Aberdeen would now play Rangers in the League Cup Final for the fourth time since 1987. It also meant that the travails of Celtic, particularly in this competition, continued.

The final was played on Sunday, 25 October 1992. Rangers were going for their 18th success in the tournament, while Aberdeen were pursuing their fourth. Rangers were the favourites on league form, having lost only once to Dundee and drawn with Celtic, and they were also going strong in Europe. On the Wednesday night immediately before this game they had beaten Leeds United 2-1 in the first leg of their European tie and hopes were high that this could be the year that would see them emulate, at last, Celtic's success in 1967, the event that had haunted them ever since that date and had dominated so much of their thinking.

It was a fine autumn afternoon as 45,298 watched referee Dougie Hope give the signal for battle to commence. Aberdeen were, as always on such occasions, well supported but their fans saw another of their cup-final horror stories, something that does not make the long journey home any easier. Willie Miller, for many years their centre-half and captain, was now manager, having replaced Alec Smith the previous February.

A recent change in the laws of the game played its part. The pass-back rule, something that had the best of intentions to eliminate negative play, was amended. Maurice Malpas of Dundee United, for example, was nicknamed Maurice Backpass for his inclination to stifle the game. On this occasion, a Rangers attack by Ian Durrant saw the ball come to David Winnie who stuck out his foot and diverted the ball towards Theo Snelders. Had Snelders caught the ball, the referee would have awarded an indirect free kick, so Snelders decided to let the ball hit him. Unfortunately, it bounced off the Dutchman to Stuart McCall, who gave Rangers an early and somewhat fortuitous lead. The Aberdeen defenders shouted at Snelders but he quite clearly stated that he couldn't do anything about it other than expose Aberdeen to the danger of an indirect free kick well inside the box.

So it stayed to half-time, but then Aberdeen's equaliser was in stark contrast to Rangers' goal. It was a magnificent swivel and shot from Duncan Shearer and was well deserved on the balance of play. The rest of the 90 minutes saw chances at both ends but everyone agreed that extra time was deserved by both teams who provided, in the tradition of all Rangers v Aberdeen League Cup finals of the recent past, magnificent entertainment for the crowd and the TV audience.

It would have to be something special to separate these teams – and it was certainly different! Unfortunately, it was a horror story for Aberdeen's young centre-half Gary Smith. A cross from David Robertson, who once played for Aberdeen but had now joined Rangers, got round the back of the Aberdeen defence and Smith dived with the intention of heading the ball past for a corner kick. The luckless Smith headed the corner into his own net.

Only six minutes of extra time remained and Rangers were able to ride out the storm and win the Scottish League Cup for the seventh time in ten years. Aberdeen fans could, with a certain amount of justice, feel that fate was against them, for neither of the Rangers goals were clear cut, but no one could deny Rangers their glory. Anyone with any goodness in his heart, however, would have to spare a thought for Gary Smith. Football can be a very cruel game.

The teams were:

Rangers: Goram, McCall, Robertson, Gough (Mikhailichenko), McPherson, Brown, Steven (Gordon), Ferguson, McCoist, Hateley, Durrant

Aberdeen: Snelders, Wright, Winnie, Grant, McLeish, Smith, Aitken (Richardson), Bett (Booth), Jess, Shearer, Paatelainen

Referee: DD Hope, Erskine

Rangers won the treble in 1992/93, the Scottish Cup Final against Aberdeen being played this year at Celtic Park as Hampden was being refurbished. The League Cup Final on 24 October was also arranged for Celtic Park and Hampden's unavailability caused a problem for the semi-final, but what must be recorded in favour of the Scottish League was that the tournament's format of one-off games and everything finished by the end of October was voted a success with many good games of football. Inevitably, there were a few mismatches as well. Giant-killing occurred now and again, although never with any great frequency.

This season, 1993/94 saw two grand old teams of Scottish football receive their worst-ever defeats. Albion Rovers were compelled to play their second-round game against Partick Thistle at Fir Park, Motherwell and lost 1-11, while in the third round, Arbroath, who had recorded a creditable win against Premier Division Raith Rovers in the previous round, lost 1-9 to Celtic at Gayfield. What added insult to injury, that Arbroath's current manager was Celtic hero Danny McGrain!

On only one occasion were penalties required in the first three rounds – Dundee beating Meadowbank – but on several occasions extra time was required; Dundee United, for example, being very lucky to get the better of Hamilton Accies and Dunfermline Athletic similarly over East Stirlingshire. Playing with a slightly weakened team, Rangers appalled their fans with a lacklustre performance against Dumbarton at Ibrox in the second round, winning only 1-0, although in the third round they put up a better display at East End Park to remove Dunfermline Athletic.

The best performance of the third round was Aberdeen's 5-2 win over Motherwell at Pittodrie, yet it was not as impressive as it seemed, for the score was 2-2 after 90 minutes and only in extra time did the Dons turn it on. Hibs beat Dundee 2-1, while three games in that round ended 1-0 to the away team, Dundee United beating St Mirren, Hearts beating Falkirk and Partick Thistle getting the better of Morton.

The quarter-finals held on 31 August and 1 September caught the attention with three of them going to extra time and two of them going to penalties. The only one that finished within the 90 minutes was Celtic's 1-0 win over Airdrie, a rather pedestrian performance over which the Parkhead crowd of 25,378 had a great deal to say. They would very soon erupt in open rebellion against their board. On the same night at Firhill and Tannadice, thrills abounded. Dundee United were two up against Falkirk, but Richard Cadette pulled Falkirk back into the game to take it to extra time. Then, in extra time, Cadette scored again with Falkirk looking good for the semi-finals until John Clark equalised for Dundee United at the death. Dundee United then won the shoot-out. Falkirk's manager Jim Jefferies was unhappy at the penalties being taken in front of the Dundee United fans at the Shed end of the ground, rather than the other Arklay Street end which was bare due to renovations. It was hardly a convincing excuse. Things were similarly tight at Firhill, but Hibs won 3-2 on penalties after a 2-2 draw.

The following night, in a feisty encounter at Ibrox which did little to dilute the bad blood that existed between the two clubs, Aberdeen's wretched luck against Rangers at Ibrox continued. Our old friend David Syme was the referee, penalties were awarded or should have been awarded, tackles were rough, but the bottom line was that with the game 1-1 at 90 minutes, Ian Ferguson scored for Rangers early in extra time and Rangers' defence was good enough to keep it that way.

The semi-final draw threw up Dundee United v Hibs and Celtic v Rangers. There was no problem about the venue for the Dundee United v Hibs game, arranged for Tynecastle, but, with Hampden not available, it was agreed that the toss of a coin would decide whether it was to be Celtic Park or Ibrox. Walter Smith (Rangers' manager) and Joe Jordan (Celtic's assistant manager) met. A coin was duly tossed and Joe Jordan won. The tie seemed to be heading for Celtic Park, but then it emerged that that toss of the coin was merely to decide who was going to toss the coin for the real thing! Joe Jordan then called wrongly and the tie went to Ibrox. It did the Celtic paranoia complex no harm at all, but all it really proved was that the Scottish League had not yet lost its innate propensity for making a fool of itself.

In no way was this a normal home tie for Rangers. Celtic were given the Govan stand and the Broomloan End of the ground. Mischievously, one wonders whether they tossed a coin for the home dressing-room or not – did they have a pre-toss first? – and it was maybe a blessing that the game did not go to penalties, for which end would have been chosen or tossed for? Maybe the vulgar got it right when they described the Scottish League as a bunch of t*****s!

In the event, Rangers won a good game 1-0 with a goal from Mark Hateley. Most neutral opinion was that Rangers were the better side, even though they were reduced to ten men for a considerable part of the game after Peter Huistra received his marching orders. In retrospect, it was the last chance for Liam Brady and the old Celtic board to save themselves. A victory here would have bought them some time, but a couple of weeks later, after a defeat at St Johnstone with fisticuffs, apparently, in the Celtic dressing room, Brady was sacked. Revolution followed in the spring.

The previous night at Tynecastle, 19,024 had seen a close game between Hibs and Dundee United. Darren Jackson, who had played previously with United but was now with Hibs, scored the only goal of the game in the tenth minute. So it was Hibs who took on Rangers in the final of the 48th Scottish League Cup Final at Celtic Park on 24 October 1993.

Hibs were a team who inflicted dreadful things on their supporters. With yo-yo performances varying between brilliant and awful, they now seemed to have settled down under the guidance of Alex Miller. They were doing well in the Scottish League and still had their triumph in the League Cup of two years ago to remind them that they could win things. But this time it was not Dunfermline; it was the juggernaut Rangers who radiated invincibility, at least in Scotland.

The final attracted a crowd of 47,632 to Celtic Park on a fine autumnal afternoon after some recent rain. Celtic Park, itself about to be totally refurbished (although no one knew that at the time), was hosting its first-ever League Cup Final. It was only the third time that the final had not been held at Hampden. The crowd and the TV audience saw a game worthy of the occasion, with something of a fairy-tale ending for Rangers supporters and their hero Ally McCoist. The first half was interesting but goalless. Keith Wright, one of the heroes of 1991, became a villain when he became one of the first players ever to be booked for diving and trying to win a penalty by fraudulent means.

The second half saw Rangers gradually take command, particularly after they went ahead following a nice one-two involving Ian Durrant. But Hibs came back and Dave McPherson of Rangers realised what Gary Smith in last year's League Cup Final must have felt like when he did exactly the same – heading the ball into his own net following a cross which one could only describe as hopeful, as there was no Hibs man in sight. Fortunately for McPherson, his mistake was not fatal for, to loud cheers, Ally McCoist was brought on. He had been out for a prolonged spell with a broken leg which seemed to threaten his whole career, but now he was back. Fortune decided that it would be he who would win the trophy for Rangers, which he did with a nice move and an overhead scissors kick after the Hibs defence gave him too much space. No one, even Ally's worst enemies, could grudge him the moment of glory.

Hibs tried desperately but Mr McCluskey's full-time whistle indicated that Rangers had now won the Scottish League Cup for the 18th time. Since 1982/83, when they lost to Celtic, they had only failed to win the trophy in 1985/86, 1989/90 and 1991/92. It was near-total domination, but Rangers fans did not complain. In fact, as they had won the Scottish Cup there in May as well, they were beginning to like Celtic Park!

The teams were:

Rangers: Maxwell, Stevens, Robertson, Gough, McPherson, McCall, Steven, Ferguson, Durrant, Hateley, Huistra (McCoist)

Hibs: Leighton, Miller, Mitchell, Farrell, Tweed, Hunter, McAllister, Hamilton, Wright, Jackson (Evans), O'Neill

Referee: J McCluskey, Stewarton

Rangers won the Scottish League again in 1994 and were only denied back-to-back trebles when Dundee United beat them at Hampden in the Scottish Cup Final, but by then changes were happening at Celtic Park. Not, specifically, on the pitch at Celtic Park. Part of the Celtic revolution of March 1994 involved the redevelopment of Celtic Park. Therefore, for season 1994/95 they moved to Hampden. This would be significant in the Scottish League Cup.

Summer 1994 saw two new teams admitted to the Scottish League, and therefore to the Scottish League Cup. At last, the Scottish League acknowledged that football was played in the Highlands and admitted two teams from that area. One was Ross County of Dingwall, and the other was an amalgamation of two Inverness teams, Caledonian and Thistle. Some supporters of both Caledonian and Thistle shouted 'never' to this amalgamation and sulked, refusing to attend. It was their loss, for Inverness Caledonian Thistle soon became one of Scottish football's success stories.

There were now eight ties in the first round and both Highland teams passed their first test with flying colours, beating Queen's Park and East Stirlingshire. More stern opposition was forthcoming in the second round and they bowed the knee to Dundee and Raith Rovers, but everyone has to start somewhere and both Highland outfits would have their moments in future years.

The rest of the second round saw no real surprises but several lucky scrapes for a few of the larger teams. Celtic, Aberdeen and Dundee United all won 1-0, against Ayr United, Stranraer and St Mirren. Rangers thumped Arbroath 4-1 at Gayfield. Falkirk and Airdrie both needed penalties to beat Montrose and Airdrie.

Falkirk's win over Montrose may well have been fortuitous but, in the next round, they became the talk of the country after going to Ibrox and winning 2-1, courtesy of two goals by Richard Cadette. Very few teams defeated Rangers at Ibrox in those days but Falkirk proved they could upset an apple cart or two. At Dens Park, Celtic were lucky to get the better of Dundee in a game which saw the normally placid Paul McStay receive a red card after a clash with Dundee's Dusan Vrto before Andy Walker notched the winner. The League Cup of 1994/95 would be an unfortunate one for Paul McStay. Elsewhere, Hearts exited to St Johnstone but

Hibs and Aberdeen both won. Raith Rovers beat Kilmarnock 3-2, Airdrieonians won the Lanarkshire derby at Fir Park, Motherwell, while also in Lanarkshire, Dundee United defeated Hamilton Accies in a penalty shoot-out.

Rangers being out of the competition, the Scottish League Cup now offered an exciting opportunity to quite a few teams like Celtic and Aberdeen, both of whom had endured a few disappointing seasons and were looking for ways to get themselves back among the honours. The quarter-final draw for 20/21 September threw up some exciting ties.

One game was played on the Tuesday night, the game at McDiarmid Park, Perth where St Johnstone disappointed their fans in the 6,287 crowd by losing 1-3 to Raith Rovers. Raith, who had been relegated from the Premier League, were doing well in the First Division (the second tier) and won the game well with goals from Ally Graham, Shaun Dennis and Danny Lennon. Celtic had a very poor game against Dundee United at Hampden but scraped home through a late John Collins goal. Falkirk might have expected to do better against Aberdeen at Brockville but were well beaten 4-1; Hibs were booed off the field by their own fans after a dismal 1-2 defeat to Airdrie.

The semi-finals were held at the end of October, something that delayed the final until 27 November. Quite why this happened, only the authorities could explain, for it certainly was always a good idea to finish the tournament in October. The unusual venue of McDiarmid Park, Perth was nevertheless a logical choice for the first semi-final on Tuesday, 25 October between Raith Rovers and Airdrie and 7,260 turned up to see a hard-fought tie which went to a penalty shoot-out. Raith had a problem in that their goalkeeper Scott Thomson had been sent off thanks to a piece of overzealous refereeing when the stand-side linesman noticed Thomson had overstepped the line with the ball in his hands. The silly rule meant that teenager Brian Potter had to be brought on to guard the goal. He performed competently and had a brilliant save in the penalty shoot-out to see Raith Rovers into their first Scottish League Cup Final since 1949.

The following night saw two current underperformers, Celtic and Aberdeen, play at Ibrox. Neither deserved to win and the game went to extra time. It was only rescued from a penalty shoot-out by the one piece of good football on the night, namely a headed goal from Brian O'Neil which saw Celtic into their first League Cup final (indeed, their first cup final of any description) since 1990. The Celtic fans in the 45,384 crowd fancied their chances of the return of silverware to Celtic Park. After all, Raith Rovers were only a First Division team.

But excitement raged in the town of Kirkcaldy, whose miserable footballing history since 1883 had seen not one single major honour and only one appearance in the final in each of the two national tournaments – defeat to Falkirk in the Scottish Cup Final of 1913 and to Rangers in the League Cup Final of 1948/49. They had produced some great teams and some great players, notably Alex James and Dave Morris in the 1920s and the mighty 'burglar proof' half-back line of Young, McNaught and Leigh of the 1950s, but not one piece of major silverware had as yet made its way to Stark's Park.

Now with enthusiastic Jimmy Nicholl as manager, they had assembled a fine young side who had won the First Division by some distance in 1993 and only just been relegated in 1993/94. Their supporters were upbeat and optimistic after some encouraging performances – but this was Celtic they were facing.

Celtic seemed to have turned the corner. The Kelly regime had been deposed and new chairman Fergus McCann was pouring money into the club, starting with the rebuilding of Parkhead, partly financed by a new share issue. For this reason, Celtic were playing their home games at Hampden, and therefore the Scottish League Cup Final had to be at Ibrox for the first time because Hampden was not considered neutral enough. Tommy Burns was the Celtic manager but results had not been great with a tendency to draw games rather than win them. Many Celtic supporters were honest enough to admit that this Celtic team contained many players who were simply not Celtic class. The joke was: 'What was the difference between Celtic and Cardinal Winning? Well, the Cardinal is winning!' Celtic supporters desperately needed this League Cup. They were aspiring to their first honour since 1989.

The game at Ibrox on 27 November was played in virtually perfect conditions in front of a sellout crowd of 45,384. It would produce one of the most dramatic League Cup Final moments of all. Steve Crawford scored first for Raith Rovers but Andy Walker, with a fine diving header, pulled it back before half-time. Late in the second half, Charlie Nicholas scored for Celtic and seemed to have won the game until Jason Dair shot from a distance, goalkeeper Gordon Marshall could not hold the ball, and Gordon Dalziel was on hand to head home a late equaliser.

Extra time followed but no goal came from two exhausted teams and we had a penalty shoot-out. The penalties were all taken excellently and we moved to sudden death. After

Raith had scored their sixth penalty, it fell to Paul McStay to attempt to equalise. This time goalkeeper Scott Thomson guessed correctly and Raith Rovers won their one and only trophy. It was totally deserved and they made much of their rare honour in the town for days and weeks afterwards. Civic receptions and goodness knows what else followed in Kirkcaldy.

But football can be a cruel game and even the hardest-hearted had to feel sorry for Paul McStay, by some distance Scotland's best player at the time. How awful it was to hear him the butt of jokes and songs of the ignorant, with even some of his own supporters in their anger and unhappiness turning on him. For Celtic supporters, there seemed to be no end to their distress and it was as if the gods were playing a vicious game on them. Sad faces, however, would turn happier by the end of the season when they won the Scottish Cup. But, as far as the Scottish League Cup was concerned, there seemed to be no end to their misery.

The teams were:

Raith Rovers: Thomson, McAnespie, Broddle (Rowbotham), Narey, Dennis, Sinclair, Crawford, Dalziel (Redford), Graham, Cameron, Dair

Celtic: Marshall, Galloway, Boyd, McNally, Mowbray, O'Neil, Donnelly (Falconer), McStay, Nicholas (Byrne), Walker, Collins

Referee: J McCluskey, Stewarton

The season of 1994/95 having been a very exciting League Cup, the following season was something of an anti-climax, but this was the season in which the tournament reached its 50th birthday. The infant which quite a few people reckoned would not survive had not only done so but was almost reaching the venerable stage. There were those who asked questions about its future and wondered if it would last for much longer, given the amount of other football, particularly in Europe, that was played on autumnal midweeks, but the guardians and trustees of the tournament need not have worried, for now seldom was there a Scottish team in Europe for very long. The Scottish League Cup Final had now become as important an occasion for television and all its worldwide implications as the Scottish Cup Final was.

The early rounds of the 50th Scottish League Cup provided no great surprise although Motherwell needed penalty kicks to get the better of Clydebank. In the third round, Celtic had their revenge on Raith Rovers for last season's cup-final defeat. It was a bizarre game with an even more bizarre allegation by Jimmy Nicholl of Raith Rovers. The game was played on a Thursday night, 31 August, at Celtic Park, which did not have stands at either end as they had not yet been built. It was a windy night and the pitch was perpetually strewn with litter. In this surreal atmosphere, Celtic scored the winner at the end through Simon Donnelly.

What upset Jimmy Nicholl was that it came about after an injury to a player. Raith put the ball out and, after the injury was dealt with, Celtic took a throw-in and a Celtic player promptly headed the ball out again so Raith would have a throw-in. It looked fair to most people, but not to Mr Nicholl who felt that the ball should have been kept in open play. It was an odd sour-grapes way of looking at things, but it was a sign of how far Raith had come that Celtic treated this game as a huge victory. Rangers (although they only scraped through 3-2 v Stirling Albion) and Aberdeen won as well, but Premier League teams Hibs and Kilmarnock fell to First Division opposition in Airdrie and Kilmarnock. Motherwell, Hearts and Partick Thistle made up the last eight.

The quarter-final draw produced an Old Firm clash, played at Celtic Park on Tuesday, 19 September 1995. It was generally agreed to have been one of the better clashes between these two and was enjoyed by the watching millions on Sky TV, but it was also clear that Celtic, although having now broken their trophy famine the previous May, had still not rid themselves of their inferiority complex and death wish about Rangers. They dominated most of the time but it was Ally McCoist who scored the only goal of the game, heading home a Paul Gascoigne cross. They were also indebted to some good (Celtic supporters said 'lucky') goalkeeping from Andy Goram. There seemed to be no end to Celtic's woes in the Scottish League Cup.

The three games played on Wednesday, 20 September all went to extra time and two of them went to penalties. A crowd of 9,137 were at Fir Park to see the visit of Aberdeen, a team who were infuriating their supporters with inconsistent play. Dougie Arnott scored first for Motherwell and for a long time it looked as if that would be enough until Billy Dodds scored for the Dons, then in extra time John Inglis notched what turned out to be the winner. Most neutrals were sorry for Motherwell but it was Aberdeen who went through.

Only 4,311 turned up to see Airdrie v Partick Thistle, a big shame because those who stayed away missed a cracker which finished 1-1 after extra time (McIntyre and Forster being the goalscorers) and then Airdrie won 3-2 in the nerve-wracking penalty shoot-out. But that was as nothing compared to the game at Dens Park, Dundee against Hearts, both of whom were once giants of the Scottish game but had fallen on bad times thanks to improvident and incompetent management. The home side, then in the First Division, were 2-0 up at half-time against their Premier opponents before being pegged back. After extra time the score, with the crowd in a constant ferment, was 4-4. Dundee won 5-4 on penalty kicks. Hearts supporters who had watched their team blow up against Albert Kidd on that very ground to lose the league almost a decade ago were never likely to consider Dens Park to be their favourite ground.

The semi-final draw threw up one all-Premier League game and one all-First Division game as Rangers played Aberdeen at Hampden on Tuesday, 25 October, and Dundee faced Airdrieonians the following night at McDiarmid Park, which had done such a great job hosting last season's semi between Raith Rovers and Airdrie. A slightly disappointing crowd of 26,191 saw Aberdeen beat Rangers 2-1 at Hampden. The first half was rather dull, something that did not happen very often when these two met, but after the turnaround Billy Dodds scored twice, once taking advantage of a defensive mix-up to score from an angle, the other with a powerful header. This knocked the stuffing out of a poor Rangers team. Oleg Salenko scored a late consolation goal but it was just too late for Rangers to mount a challenge. The game is famous for a keepie-uppie routine by Eoin Jess which delighted Aberdeen fans, but that was secondary to the fact that, at long last, their team had stood up to Rangers.

Then came Dundee v Airdrie at McDiarmid Park; 8, 930 were there – a fine crowd for the compact stadium – and they saw a great game remembered for the late goal scored by Neil McCann. The game was tied at 1-1 with goals having come from Paul Tosh for Dundee and Peter Duffield for Airdrie. Minutes remained when the ball rebounded off an Airdrie defender and was slipped through to McCann on the left. He made ground and, from a difficult angle at the edge of the box, lobbed the ball over the goalkeeper's head and in off the post. It was a brilliant piece of individualism and earned Dundee their first big game for many years, since they were defeated at Dens Park in the 1980/81 League Cup Final. It was their first trip to Hampden on League Cup business since they won the trophy on a dreadful day of sleet and ice in December 1973.

Both teams, Dundee and Aberdeen, had put their supporters through the mill in recent years. Dundee had been relegated more than once and Aberdeen flirted with it on occasion, not least at the end of the 1994/95 season where they came close to losing their cherished position of never having been relegated. They had also gone out of the Scottish Cup to Stenhousemuir. Their supporters found that difficult to accept and, although manager Roy Aitken had strengthened their squad over the summer, it was clear that this was a hard-working and competent Aberdeen side but by no means a vintage one. Dundee, under the likeable and ebullient Jim Duffy, still playing as player-manager, were little more than a journeyman outfit. The only real crumb of comfort was that their city rivals down the road, Dundee United, were also in the same boat.

A total of 33,096 turned up to see a rather low-key League Cup Final on 26 November 1995. It would be the last final to be played at Hampden for some time (the next three would vary between Celtic Park and Ibrox) and last to be played in front of the old stand, which would be demolished and replaced in another phase of Hampden's ongoing, prolonged and somewhat tedious renovations.

The Dons were hot favourites and the bookies are seldom wrong. The game was one-sided and goals were scored on either side of half-time. Billy Dodds scored first, then there was a header from Duncan Shearer who was only playing because Scott Booth was injured. Aberdeen simply took control of the tie and, with Stephen Glass and captain Stewart McKimmie outstanding, barely gave Dundee a kick of the ball.

It was a fine win, Aberdeen's fifth. Had it been on a Saturday there would have been a parade through the city on the Sunday but, the game having been played on the Sunday, there was not enough time to get everyone to Aberdeen on time for such an event. It was postponed until the following Sunday when the weather was foul. Possibly the elements were warning everyone that it would be a long, long time before the city of Aberdeen could enjoy itself again.

The teams were:

Aberdeen: Watt, McKimmie, Glass, Grant, Inglis, Smith, Miller (Robertson), Shearer, Bernard, Dodds, Jess (Hetherston)

Dundee: Pageaud, J Duffy, McQueen, Manley, Wieghorst, C Duffy, Shaw, Vrto (Farningham), Tosh (Britton), Hamilton, McCann (Anderson)

Referee: L Mottram, Forth

The League Cup was 50 years old and had been won as follows – Rangers 19, Celtic nine, Aberdeen five, Hearts four, East Fife and Dundee three, Dundee United and Hibs two, and once each by Motherwell, Partick Thistle and Raith Rovers. It had been a glorious half-century. The same half-century had also seen almost unbelievable changes in the social life of the country. The League Cup started in an atmosphere of austerity, rationing and recovery from a dreadful war. The world had changed. So had football, with the scale of the World Cup and number of European cups virtually unimaginable to those who had been around to see the first season of the Scottish League Cup.

If the previous year's competition lacked its usual sparkle, the same could not have been said about 1996/97. It was a thriller of a competition with a thrilling final and controversy throughout. Much of the excitement centred on Jim Jefferies's Hearts and how different things could have been if the Jambos had not won a penalty shoot-out at Tynecastle against lowly Stenhousemuir in the second round on the early date of 14 August. Adrian Sprott, who once in his Hamilton incarnation had put Rangers out of the Scottish Cup, looked like doing the same to Hearts in this competition. It was only when Neil McCann equalised in the 72nd minute that Hearts got back in. Stenny then had a man sent off for two yellow cards which did not help the cause and Hearts eventually calmed the shattered nerves of their 9,303 fans by winning 5-4 on penalties.

Albion Rovers, too, earned one of their sparse moments of glory in the League Cup (or indeed any other cup, though they reached the final of the Scottish Cup in 1920). Thumping Arbroath 4-0 in the first round was good enough, then they went to Brockville to beat Falkirk, a team two divisions above them and who would later that season beat Celtic to reach the final of the Scottish Cup. Albion Rovers put up a good show in the next round before losing 0-2 to Hibs.

There were no other major casualties in the second round other than Motherwell who exited to Alloa on penalties, but

Alfredo Morelos misses a crucial penalty in the Scottish League Cup Final of 8 December 2019

Celtic have just won the League Cup against Aberdeen on 2 December 2018, and Scott Brown and Mikael Lustig lift the trophy

Jim McIntyre, manager of Ross County with the trophy in 2016

Partick Thistle v Celtic 23 October 1971 and celebrations in the Partick Thistle dressing room

Alex Smith of Rangers scores against Celtic in 1966's League Cup Final but the goal is chalked off

Callum Davidson with St Johnstone's first-ever League Cup in 2021

Action from the League Cup Final between St Mirren and Hearts in 2013 as Esmael Goncalves charges through the Hearts defence. St Mirren won 3-2.

George Niven saves against Celtic in the famous League Cup Final of 1957 which Celtic won 7-1

Rangers v East Fife in the League Cup on 7 August 2012. This was the 'new' Rangers' first game at Ibrox

Dixie Deans scores for Celtic in the League Cup Final of 1974/75 against Hibs. Celtic won 6-3

Jim McLean, manager of Dundee United

Ally MacLeod, who won the League Cup with Aberdeen in 1976/77

Paul Gascoigne and Ally McCoist with the League Cup

Aberdeen with the League Cup which they won on a penalty shoot-out against Inverness at Celtic Park in March 2014

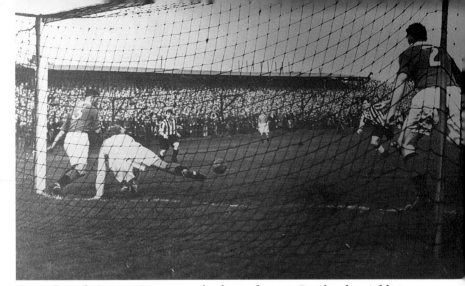

Action from the League Cup quarter-final game between Dunfermline Athletic and Rangers in September 1951

Programme cover of East Fife v Dunfermline Athletic League Cup Final of 1949

Tommy Walker, manager of Hearts who won the League Cup four times between 1954 and 1962

Bobby Evans, captain of Celtic who have just beaten Partick Thistle in the Scottish Cup Final replay of 31 October 1956

Celtic with the Scottish League Cup on 23 October 1965

Gordon Dalziel turns away after scoring the equaliser for Raith Rovers in the Scottish League Cup Final of 27 November 1994

Celtic, winners of the 2021/22 Scottish League Cup, beating Hibernain 2-1 in the Final.

the next round threw up a Dundee derby at Tannadice and 11,389 (a disappointing crowd, but then again, the form of both teams in recent years had been nothing to write home about) saw a great game on a warm humid night which, perhaps predictably, went to penalties after a 2-2 draw. Dundee won 4-1 with ex-United goalkeeper Billy Thomson, now playing for Dundee, being the hero of the hour both in the penalty shoot-out and open play. Hearts once again needed extra time at McDiarmid Park to beat St Johnstone 3-1 and Aberdeen hit the highlights by scoring seven at Cappielow. Celtic, Rangers and Hibs all won comfortably.

The quarter-finals had some great ties, the pick being the game at Tynecastle between Hearts and Celtic on 17 September. Both teams approached the game suffering self-inflicted wounds. On the Saturday before, Hearts had managed to get four players sent off in a game at Ibrox (another one would have compelled the referee to abandon the game) so they had four absentees through suspension, whereas the Celtic players had seen fit to pick a fight with their management about more money. They managed to do this quite a lot in the era of emotionally unstable players and it was something that their fans had little sympathy for. Manager Tommy Burns used the word 'greed' and quite correctly pointed out that they would have earned a lot more money in any case if they had won more games and reached more finals! In addition, Paul McStay was injured and they missed his calming influence in the Tynecastle cauldron. Both teams had a man sent off, Salvatori of Hearts and Grant of Celtic, but it was John Robertson who got the only goal of the game for Hearts.

There was a major shock for Aberdeen who lost to their old rivals Dundee as the Dens Parkers gained revenge for last season's League Cup Final; 8,670 were at Dens and were reconciled to extra time and penalties (Paul Tosh having opened the scoring for Dundee and Billy Dodds equalising for Aberdeen) when up popped Jim Hamilton to grab the winner in the 89th minute and to put his side into the semi-final to meet Hearts. The other semi-final was between Rangers and Dunfermline, both of whom qualified comfortably. Dunfermline impressed with a 2-0 win over Partick Thistle at East End Park, whereas Rangers beat a very disappointing Hibs side 4-0 at Ibrox.

A feature of the Scottish League Cup in those days was the poor crowds that it attracted. The Dundee derby was poorly attended and the Hearts v Celtic game only attracted 14,442. One wonders why this was the case, for there was certainly no lack of entertainment. But the Hearts v Celtic game was on satellite TV and this probably played a part. Not everyone found it easy or cheap to get to a game in midweek and the TV in the pub was quite an attraction.

Nevertheless, the 16,791 who appeared at Parkhead to see Rangers v Dunfermline semi-final was very disappointing indeed inside the huge and rapidly developing ground. One cannot really believe that the poor crowd was because Rangers fans did not like to go to Celtic Park. Those who were there saw a mismatch with Rangers winning 6-1. The other semi at Easter Road between Hearts and Dundee saw a crowd of 15,653 and a better match, although Hearts were always on top and won 3-1 with Dundee's consolation goal coming too late to make any real difference.

It was Rangers v Hearts in the League Cup Final at Celtic Park on Sunday, 24 November 1996. Those Rangers fans who might have had ethical scruples about attending Parkhead managed to overcome them and 48,559 were in the ground, now completed on three sides and with temporary seating on the other. Glasgow had seen some snow in the previous 24 hours but nothing to threaten the game. Nevertheless, it was still a bitterly cold day and snow was seen at the side of the pitch.

The two teams had met before in finals. In 1961/62, Rangers had needed a replay to beat Hearts in the League Cup Final; they had also met in the Scottish Cup finals of 1903, 1976 and 1996, Rangers winning all three. The two teams also had a little history – the game at Ibrox where Hearts had four red cards was still a raw memory – and Hearts and their fans nursed a certain grievance about Rangers, something that makes it hard to understand why their fans sing the same offensive, sectarian songs.

This game is surrounded by legends involving Paul Gascoigne. It is said that he had a couple of snifters out of a bottle at half-time, that he nearly punched Ally McCoist and that he did something awful in the bath at Celtic Park and left it there. How much of this is true we do not know, but the irrepressible and not always likeable Gazza did little to deny it.

This must not blind us to the fact that this was one of the best games of football seen in a League Cup Final for many years and that both teams emerged with great credit for their part in the seven-goal thriller which could have yielded even more goals. McCoist scored twice for Rangers in the first half with well-taken goals but his excessive and emotional celebrations did little to enhance his popularity with anyone other than Rangers fans. Just on half-time, Steve Fulton kept Hearts alive with a goal at the other end. John Robertson equalised for Hearts on the hour mark, but scarcely had the celebrations died down than Paul Gascoigne scored twice for Rangers to apparently kill the game at 4-2. But this Hearts team did not lie down and Davie Weir managed to score in the 88th minute to set up a great finish. The TV audience would not have grudged Hearts extra time for their efforts, but when referee Hugh Dallas blew for time, Rangers had won the Scottish League Cup for the 20th time.

The teams were:

Rangers: Goram, Cleland (Robertson), Moore, Gough, Petric, Bjorklund, Miller, Gascoigne, McCoist, Albertz, Laudrup

Hearts: Rousset, Weir, Pointon, Mackay, Ritchie, Bruno, Paille (Beckford), Fulton, Robertson, Cameron, McCann

Referee: H Dallas, Motherwell

Hearts fans were left wondering yet again whether they would ever win anything. Their trophy famine had lasted since October 1962 and they had come close on so many occasions. There was nothing new about a Hearts trophy famine; they had gone from 1906 until 1954 without winning anything in the past. They were not to know that their famine would end against the same opponents at the same ground in 18 months' time. As it was, it was a miserable trudge back to the buses for a depressing journey along the M8.

Hearts would, however, finish a respectable fourth in the Premier League, while Rangers simply went from strength to strength, winning the Premier League for the ninth season in a row and equalling Celtic's record from 1966 to 1974. The Scottish Cup went to Kilmarnock who beat Falkirk at Ibrox in a good final.

And where were Celtic in the middle of all this? They had last won the Scottish League Cup some 15 years ago in December 1982 and since then their record had been deplorable. They had some moments (but not all that many) in other competitions, but since 1982 they had lost four League Cup finals (three to Rangers and one to Raith Rovers) and had often not even reached the semi-final stage. One always notices the sour-grapes phenomenon whereby supporters whose team are not doing well often ridicule the tournament or mock Scottish football generally. Celtic supporters did this quite a lot in the 1990s and yet the Scottish League Cup had given them their single-best domestic result, the 7-1 win over Rangers in October 1957. And they had also, in the Jock Stein era, won the League Cup five years in a row, something that no one else had done.

Tommy Burns had been axed and their manager now was a curly-headed Dutchman by the name of Wim Jansen. His primary task was to win the league championship and prevent Rangers winning it ten years in a row. Success in the League Cup, however, would give them something tangible, an earnest of further success. The campaign opened with a 7-0 defeat of Berwick Rangers in a game played at Tynecastle since Shielfield Park was not considered suitable for the large crowd. Rangers were fortunate to beat Hamilton 1-0, although Aberdeen won comfortably enough 5-1 against Dumbarton. Dunfermline and Motherwell both needed penalty kicks to get the better of Ayr United and Inverness Caledonian Thistle, but Dundee, Dundee United, Hearts and Hibs all got through against lesser opposition.

In the next round, Celtic were very lucky indeed. They eventually got through against St Johnstone at McDiarmid

Park thanks to a debatable penalty kick in extra time, but the performance was woeful and attracted all sorts of adverse criticism. Elsewhere, Rangers had few problems in defeating Falkirk and Aberdeen beat Dundee 3-0 at Dens Park, beating opponents whom they tended to encounter quite often in those days. The Edinburgh teams had mixed fortunes. Hearts got the better of Raith Rovers in a tight game at Stark's Park, whereas at Tannadice, Hibs lost 2-1 to Dundee United in a similarly close game which went to extra time. Dunfermline Athletic and Motherwell (for whom Owen Coyle scored a hat-trick) both got the better of the Renfrewshire duo of St Mirren and Morton, but possibly the best result of the night was Stirling Albion's 6-2 beating of Kilmarnock.

The quarter-finals, with one exception, were decided by scores of 1-0. The exception was at Forthbank, Stirling where the Binos were sadly unable to reproduce the six goals they had put past Kilmarnock, and a competent Aberdeen with goals from Joe Miller and Stephen Glass were able to go through without any great bother. At Parkhead, Celtic, who now seemed to have turned the corner following their dreadful start to the season, beat Motherwell 1-0 with a goal from Henrik Larsson in a performance that should really have seen more goals.

The other two games which had been played on Tuesday, 9 September both went to extra time. Dunfermline put in one of their better performances when they beat Hearts 1-0 at East End Park while, at Ibrox, Dundee United rocked Rangers with a goal scored in the 98th minute by ex-Ibrox man Gary McSwegan. It was a great performance from the Tannadice men whose league performances hitherto had been none too impressive, and it was the beginning of a run, in which Dundee United tended to do well in cup ties against Rangers.

Tuesday, 14 October saw the first semi-final. Hampden being out of commission, Ibrox had to be deployed. It was a typical Glasgow night of unrelenting rain but Celtic were well on top, and the wonder was that they did not score more than they did. As it was, the goal was a peach, a Larsson lay-off back to Craig Burley who hammered home from the edge of the box. This was in the 69th minute and was enough to guarantee Celtic victory, although right at the very end, goalkeeper Craig Gould had to do very well to save a shot from Hamish French.

The weather had kept the crowd down to 27,796. The following night, 10,459 were at Tynecastle to see the game between Aberdeen and Dundee United. Aberdeen were bottom of the Premier League, and it showed. Several players were simply not up to scratch. Andy McLaren released Robbie Winters to put Dundee United ahead and, although Dean Windass equalised for Aberdeen just after half-time, United soon regained control and Craig Easton put them ahead before Robbie Winters added a third with a wonderful strike in the 70th minute. Aberdeen's manager Roy Aitken would not last long after this and Aberdeen's supporters, pessimistic and critical as always, braced themselves for a few years of gross underachievement in which their foreign players let them down.

So it was Celtic v Dundee United in the League Cup Final of 30 November. Much has been written about Dundee United's death wish in Glasgow and this seemed to be very much in play here. They had won the League Cup twice, both times at Dens Park. They had never faced Celtic in a League

Cup Final, although they had now done so three times in the Scottish Cup and Celtic had won them all. Celtic and their supporters, now desperate for a trophy, were clear favourites. Not only were they challenging for the league, they had also performed creditably and been very unlucky against Liverpool in Europe and the week before had beaten United 4-0 in a league fixture at Parkhead. Celtic had won the trophy nine times, Dundee United only twice. For historical reasons and on current form the green and whites were clear favourites to lift the trophy.

Yet Celtic can't have been totally confident either. At the back of their minds (or even perhaps the front) was the day three years ago in that same stadium when they went down to Raith Rovers in a penalty shoot-out. It had been a dreadful experience for their supporters.

There were 49,305 at Ibrox that crisp November day to see Celtic play one of the best games they played during their dreadful decade of the 1990s. It wasn't as if Dundee United played badly, it was just that they were overwhelmed by Celtic, for whom Regi Blinker played one of his rare good games. The first goal came in the 20th minute from a header from Danish centre-half Marc Rieper, a few minutes after that Henrik Larsson scored from the edge of the penalty box with a wicked deflection that totally deceived Sieb Dijkstra in the United goal. One could argue that it was lucky, but then again if you don't shoot, you can't get deflections.

That was how it stayed at half-time but then, just before the hour mark, a good run and cross from Regi Blinker saw Craig Burley score Celtic's third. The Dundee United supporters in the Govan stand could have started the car and gone home, for the game was over. To their credit, they didn't do that. They stayed and watched what must have been painful for them. Celtic could have scored again through Andreas Thom, but 3-0 was enough to give Celtic their tenth League Cup win (still only half of Rangers' tally of wins, however) and left Dundee United wondering why the Glasgow curse was still evident when they thought that they had laid it after winning the Scottish Cup in 1994.

The teams were:

Celtic: Gould, Boyd, Mahe, McNamara (Annoni), Rieper, Stubbs, Larsson, Burley, Thom (Donnelly), Wieghorst, Blinker (Lambert)

Dundee United: Dijkstra, Skoldmark (McSwegan), Malpas, Pressley, Perry, Pederson, Olofsson, Zetterlund, Winters, Easton, Bowman

Referee: J McCluskey, Stewarton

Celtic supporters thus spent a happier Christmas than they had done for a while, with the Scottish League Cup on the sideboard for the first time since 1982. Truly a 'stranger in paradise' as the words of the song went. It was not, however, their main target. That came in May when they won the Scottish League, but who is to say that things might not have been the same for them if they had not won the League Cup that day? Amazingly, it was only their second trophy of the 1990s.

Spring 1998 also saw the welcome return of Hearts to the honours board when they beat Rangers in the Scottish Cup Final at Celtic Park. Many were delighted for Hearts, whose supporters had suffered the horrors of hell since 1962. For Rangers, 1998 was a temporary fall from grace. They would be determined to fight back in 1998/99.

The last Scottish League Cup of the century was held in autumn 1998 because the next League Cup would finish in March 2000. Thus the final at Celtic Park on 29 November 1998 brought down the curtain on the 20th century as far as Scottish League Cup finals were concerned. It would also be the last Scottish League Cup Final not to be played at Hampden Park for, by 2000, Hampden's redevelopment, for good or bad, had been completed.

There must be some doubt about the legality (and certainly the morality) of some of Rangers' wins, given what we now know about the goings-on at Ibrox in that era, but it must also be stressed that it was a fine achievement by Rangers to finish the 20th century with 21 wins out of 53 League Cup tournaments. It was a good era for the Ibrox side but it must also be stressed that the organisation of some of the other clubs had a long way to go to reach even acceptable standards. The 1980s and the 1990s (the decades of Thatcher and Major) were greedy, grasping decades with TV companies now muscling in and dictating kick-off times – sometimes ridiculous times like 6.05pm on a Sunday night. The truth was that Rangers were simply more able to deal with the pressures of the 1990s than other less-ruthless organisations were. They would be held to account, but not for a long time.

The Scottish League Cup was rearranged to allow for the fact that there were 40 senior teams. There was no return to the sectional format, nor were there any home-and-home fixtures, for which everyone heaved a sigh of relief, but there were now 12 games in the first round, then the 12 winners joined another 12, and the top four (the teams who were likely to be involved in Europe) joined in at the last-16 stage. It was a reasonable format and it lasted 16 years until someone decided to interfere with it again. This year saw quite a few cup upsets. Dundee and Dunfermline Athletic (both of whom could have done with a cup run) fell at the first hurdle, Dundee going out to Alloa at an angry Dens Park, the mood of their supporters hardly improved by the news that Dundee United had defeated Stirling Albion on penalties. Dunfermline went down to the very impressive Livingston whose manager was the Pars' old boss Jim Leishman. The round of the last 16 also saw the demise of Aberdeen and Celtic. Aberdeen at least lost respectably to Hibs 1-0, but Celtic's downfall was a disgrace and there were feelings of déjà vu among the supporters.

Celtic had cut their own throats in 1996 with a pay dispute. They did the same thing in 1998 with a demand for an increase in bonus money. However, Fergus McCann, the new owner, did not become a millionaire by giving in to blackmail. His background was shaped by his grim determination to rise from his background in the Celtic heartland of Croy. There were two winners in this stand-off. One was the Yorkhill Hospital who received donations from both sides as each tried to capture the moral high ground and to outdo the other side in goodness and piety, the other winner was Airdrie who beat Celtic 1-0. Words like 'greed' were freely bandied about and the lesson was: if you want bonus money, you have to produce the goods on the field and one of the best ways of producing the goods on the field is by not moaning about money. Teams who are divided among themselves seldom do well.

Dundee United fell to Ross County, who were then very unlucky not to beat Hearts in a penalty shoot-out in the quarter-final, but the team that was beginning to catch the eye, apart from Rangers, was St Johnstone, in some ways a sleeping giant of Scottish football whom manager Sandy Clark was doing his best to arouse. They beat Falkirk 1-0 and handed out a very impressive 4-0 thumping to Hibs to reach the semi-final, there to join Rangers who had defeated Alloa and Ayr United, Airdrieonians who aside from knocking out Celtic had also beaten Kilmarnock 1-0, and Hearts.

The semi-finals, at the end of October, were as one-sided as they sounded; 21,171 turned up at Celtic Park to see Rangers thrash hapless Airdrie 5-0, but the result that really made everyone sit up and take notice was at Easter Road when St Johnstone scored twice before half-time and once before full time to hammer Hearts 3-0, a performance which had Hearts supporters streaming out of Easter Road in their droves long before the final whistle while Hibs' stewards found it very difficult to keep the smiles off their faces.

Success and St Johnstone had hardly gone hand in hand since St Johnstone were formed in 1884. As often in the lower reaches, the club struggled in the Fair City, far from a typical Scottish footballing hotbed. Curling, cricket and golf seemed to be as popular as football in a predominantly middle-class part of the world. Only once before had they reached the final of the Scottish League Cup, in 1969/70 under Willie Ormond, when they lost narrowly and unluckily 0-1 to Celtic. Even their name caused problems. For a while they were confused in the minds of Englishmen with Jimmy Johnstone, and there is a twin in Renfrewshire called Johnstone. However, another name for Perth used to be St John's Town, hence the name of the club, which in 1998 Sandy Clark was hoping to propel to great heights. But, three weeks before the final, they went down 7-0 to their cup-final opponents, Rangers.

Perhaps it was with this in mind that only 45,533 turned up at Celtic Park that dull day of Sunday, 29 November 1998. St Johnstone were not a well-supported club but the occasion did give the opportunity for parents to take children to a big game. One normally hates the phrase 'family centred' in the context of a football club because it implies that everyone else lives in children's homes and orphanages, but one would have to say that the St Johnstone support contains a large number of ladies and children. Foul language is not common.

Sadly, however, Celtic Park did not look at its best with rows of empty seats, something that looks bad when the game is televised throughout the world. Cup finals really need teams that have a big support and, as some Rangers fans seem to go into a sulk when asked to turn up at Celtic Park to see their team, Celtic Park had plenty of elbow room. There would have been room for another 15,000 fans.

Rangers' manager was now a Dutchman by the name of Dick Advocaat, in his first season at the club. This would be his first trophy on the way to a treble in a controversial and unpleasant season, but the League Cup Final saw a fine game of football played by both teams. Any thoughts that there would be a repeat of the 7-0 scoreline were dispelled by a fighting St Johnstone performance which earned them many paeans of praise from the media, but the simple fact was that Rangers, without being brilliant, were simply too good and too professional.

It was a sign of the growing internationalism of the game that the starting XIs contained only nine Scotsmen between the two teams and Rangers had only two. And it was Frenchman Stephane Giuvarc'h (one of the few participants in Scottish football with an apostrophe in the middle of his name) who scored first for Rangers before Canadian Nick

Dasovic scored a fine goal to equalise for the Perth Saints. This all happened in the first ten minutes, but it was German Jorg Albertz who scored the decisive goal in the 37th minute after St Johnstone had given as good as they got.

The second half yielded no further goals. Hard though Sandy Clark's men tried, they could not get through a stout Rangers team who appreciated the value of not defending too deep. Once or twice near the end, St Johnstone might have scored to take the game to extra time, but similarly Rangers might have added to their lead. When referee Hugh Dallas blew for time up, Rangers had won their 21st Scottish League Cup and St Johnstone had won the admiration of their support and the respect of the rest of the footballing world. Success would eventually come for St Johnstone in the Scottish Cup in 2014, but that was a long way away.

The teams were:

Rangers: Niemi, Porrini, Numan, Amoruso, Hendry, Albertz (I Ferguson), B Ferguson, van Bronckhorst, Kanchelskis, Wallace, Guivarc'h (Durie)

St Johnstone: Main, McQuillan, Dods, Kernaghan, Bollan, Scott, O'Neil (Preston), Kane, O'Boyle (Lowndes), Dasovic, Simao (Grant)

Referee: H Dallas, Motherwell

Rangers' celebrations were a little muted. They were still involved in Europe (they would fall to Parma in early December) and were also aware that the league would be difficult. But it was at least a piece of silverware for Mr Advocaat, something that had evaded the clutches of Rangers the previous season.

CHAPTER ELEVEN

INTO THE NEW CENTURY
1999–2003

ONE OF the unfortunate by-products of Rangers' sustained success in the Scottish League Cup (and the other two tournaments as well) throughout the 1990s was the effect that it had on other teams. There seems to be a dynamic that whenever your rivals do well, you must become worse, make the wrong decisions, choose the wrong man as manager and alienate your supporters further. This happened to both Celtic and Aberdeen, both of whose supporters look back on the 1990s with more than the occasional frisson of horror. Good moments existed but they were few and far between. These two teams found themselves in opposition in the first Scottish League Cup Final of the 21st century on 19 March 2000 but they were hardly at a high point of their existence. They were likened to two old enemies who had been badly injured in the same earthquake and found themselves in adjacent hospital beds!

The decision was taken that the Scottish League Cup Final would be played in March (usually the third Sunday) at the revamped Hampden. Some hankered after the original idea of the final being played at the end of October, but playing the game in March had certain advantages, mainly that days were getting longer and there would be loads of daylight in reasonably good weather. It must be said that the finals played in March did enjoy a fair amount of spring sunshine, albeit with a nip in the air. Indeed, this particular decision lasted a little longer than most. It lasted until 2016, when someone else came along and decided to play once more with the Scottish League Cup.

Little of note happened in the first two rounds of 1999/2000, although East Fife punched above their weight against Stirling Albion and Airdrie before succumbing, after a brave fight, to Hearts in the third round, now played in the second week in October. Aberdeen, who had limped through against Livingston in the previous round, needed an own goal from Falkirk before eventually winning on penalty kicks. The 8,166 Pittodrie crowd were not slow to let their team know their opinion of that performance! Rangers were similarly less than their best when they beat Dunfermline 1-0 at Ibrox, but there were two crackers: at Rugby Park where Kilmarnock beat Hibs 3-2 and at McDiarmid Park, Perth where Dundee United needed a last-gasp winner to beat St Johnstone. Motherwell, too, had a tough game in the Highlands, winning 1-0 over fast-developing Inverness Caledonian Thistle, who were now in the First Division and on the brink of rocking Scottish football. Celtic won comfortably enough 4-0 at Ayr United.

The quarter-finals were when the tournament really came alive with one major shock, one postponement and every game settled on the odd goal. The postponed game was at

Kilmarnock where Hearts were the visitors. All the other games were played on 1 December; this one was put off until 2 February! A winter shutdown, one of the curses of the modern game, had been introduced and the game went ahead two months after its original date. The game was eventually settled by a fortuitous deflected goal by Mike Jeffrey in favour of Kilmarnock.

Two months earlier on 1 December 1999, the major shock was Aberdeen's defeat of Rangers at Pittodrie. In normal circumstances this would hardly have been rated a seismic shock, but Aberdeen's league form had been appalling with only one win and hammerings from both Celtic and Rangers. The crowd of 12,108 told its own story and cannot be entirely explained away by the reluctance of Rangers fans to travel in wintry conditions. Rangers pressed and pressed but were denied by veteran goalkeeper Jim Leighton and, with Aberdeen having hardly been in the game at all, late in extra time Andy Dow wrote his small part in Aberdeen history. He slammed a ball into the roof of the net from short range before an incredulous but nevertheless delighted Pittodrie who thought that Santa Claus had come early.

One hundred and fifty miles further south at Celtic Park, 38,922 fans saw a dreadful game of football when Celtic took on Dundee. Passions were inflamed when referee Hugh Dallas rightly sent off Stephane Mahe for the second time in seven months, but the game lacked any sparkle until the last minute of the 90 when Morten Wieghorst headed the only goal of the game to give Celtic a victory which they just about deserved. The best game of the night was at Tannadice and it was a shame that it attracted the lowest crowd, with only

5,086 seeing a thriller as Dundee United beat Motherwell 3-2 and Motherwell unfortunate not to earn extra time.

The semi-final draw paired Dundee United with Aberdeen and Celtic with Kilmarnock, none of the four teams setting the heather on fire. The first game between Dundee United and Aberdeen was played on Sunday, 13 February 2000 at Dens Park. The game was on satellite TV and the standard of play was not high in front of a small and becalmed crowd of 9,500. Games between these two were never great (the old comparison to a game of chess was trotted out once again) and this one was made worse by the fact that real talent was not in great supply and no one had the tactical nous to deliver a checkmate. As the commentators tried manfully to cheer everyone up with the prospect of extra time, Arild Stavrum of Aberdeen scored the goal which proved to be the winner in the 78th minute. It put Aberdeen into the League Cup Final and raised the interesting idea of a League Cup win and relegation in the same year.

Their adversaries would be Celtic. They were hardly the most intimidating of opponents. The day of 8 February 2000 had been their greatest disaster in modern times when they went down to First Division Inverness Caledonian Thistle in the Scottish Cup, leading to the departure of manager John Barnes and his replacement (on a temporary basis) by Kenny Dalglish. On a cold night on 16 February, with snow at the side of the pitch, a miserable crowd of 22,926 came to Hampden to see an equally miserable game between Celtic and Kilmarnock, the teams being separated only by a Lubo Moravcik header late in the game to put Celtic into the final.

As Rangers were winning the Scottish League by some considerable distance, all that Celtic had left was the Scottish

League Cup if they wanted any self-respect from a desperately bad season. It had gone from bad to worse when their talismanic striker Henrik Larsson broke his leg in a European tie in France. The form of Celtic and Aberdeen gave little for the fans of either team to be confident, but in an impressive expression of loyalty and love, both ends of Hampden were filled on Sunday, 19 March 2000, a bright, pleasant spring day but still cold enough to remind everyone that winter had not yet gone entirely.

Celtic started off attacking the Mount Florida end where the Aberdeen fans were congregated and after 15 minutes of undistinguished play took the lead. Following a break down the left and some good work from Morten Wieghorst, the ball came to Norwegian Vidar Riseth who scored with a slight miskick. That was how it was at half-time, then Aberdeen suffered three blows. First Hicham Zerouali was stretchered off, then Celtic scored a second goal when Tommy Johnson, a likeable but hitherto underperforming Geordie, was put through and scored, running back to the centre circle pretending he was smoking a Groucho Marx cigar. Finally, Thomas Solberg of Aberdeen was sent off by a rather overzealous Kenny Clark for two bookable offences, neither of which looked particularly bad.

These three occurrences meant that there was no comeback for the Dons but there might not have been anyway because, as Dons supporters themselves quite happily admitted, this was a dire Aberdeen team. Celtic were not a great deal better but were good enough to remain on top, and indeed might have scored more if Mark Viduka, the villain of the piece as far as their Inverness fiasco went, had not missed several chances. The game finished with Celtic still 2-0 up, and the Celtic fans were charitable to Aberdeen as they received their losers' medals. They knew exactly what they were going through.

The teams were:

Celtic: Gould, Boyd, Riseth, Mjallby, Mahe, McNamara, Wieghorst, Petrov, Moravcik (Stubbs), Johnson (Berkovic), Viduka

Aberdeen: Leighton, Perry, McAllister, Solberg, Anderson, Dow, Bernard, Jess (Mayer), Guntweit (Belabed), Zerouali (Winters), Stavrum

Referee: K Clark, Paisley

Celtic won their 11th Scottish League Cup and their season fizzled out. They played Rangers the following week in the league and went down by the embarrassing scoreline of 0-4, even though Kenny Dalglish held his pre-match press conference in Baird's Bar in the Gallowgate before some bewildered Friday lunchtime drinkers!

Aberdeen finished bottom of the league and were only saved from relegation by league reconstruction. Cynics were not slow to point out that their old pals rallied round them and made sure that a team with a big support was not relegated. They also completed a remarkable season by reaching the final of the Scottish Cup where they went down to Rangers in a one-sided game.

Despite Celtic's League Cup triumph, 2000 was still dominated by Rangers, but the summer was the time when Celtic eventually struck back, appointing the right man in Martin O'Neill. The new manager made some shrewd (and expensive) purchases and Henrik Larsson came back from his broken leg. Not only that, but Celtic Park was now completely redeveloped, and the feelgood factor was immediately obvious in the demolition derby of late August 2000 when Celtic beat Rangers 6-2 in the Scottish Premier League, as it was now called.

There were now 42 teams in the Scottish League, Elgin City and Peterhead having joined the party in a welcome move to make the league more geographically inclusive. Naturally they joined the League Cup as well, the only problem being that some clubs might find it difficult to reach these distant and remote spots on a midweek night. The logistical nightmare of Peterhead v Stranraer on a wet Tuesday in November was always a possibility.

Elgin City lost to Cowdenbeath and Peterhead lost to Inverness in what was almost a derby in the first round, which now contained 14 matches. The 14 winners then were joined by another ten teams in the second round, making 12 winners, who were then joined by the teams who would be playing in Europe. The draw was not yet seeded, meaning that Rangers played Aberdeen at the first time of asking in the third round. Interestingly, two former winners of the League Cup failed to make it past the first round – East Fife losing to Raith Rovers (another former winner) and Partick Thistle to Airdrieonians.

The third round was held in the first week in September and produced one or two close ties, the best one being at Falkirk when Russell Latapy scored twice, once in extra time, for Hibs. It was a good night for Edinburgh because Hearts also won at Livingston beating the home side 2-0. Kilmarnock, for whom Ally McCoist was now playing, defeated St Johnstone 1-0 at McDiarmid, McCoist scoring the only goal of the game. At the venerable old Love Street ground, St Mirren beat an aimless Dundee side 3-0 in Paisley, and after a shocking 0-0 after extra time, Dundee United and Airdrie at last managed to produce some excitement in a penalty shoot-out won 4-3 by the home side at Tannadice. Dunfermline beat Motherwell 2-0 at East End Park but the other Fife side, Raith Rovers, went down 0-4 at Celtic Park in a fixture which, a few years ago in this competition, might have been a great deal closer.

The big game was at Ibrox, and Aberdeen, who started the new season not a great deal better than they had finished the previous one, raised a few hopes in the travelling support in the 37,026 crowd by taking a 2-1 lead early in the second half before being overwhelmed by a late onslaught from Rangers who ran out 4-2 winners.

Three of the quarter-finals were played on Halloween and the other on 1 November. Dundee United continued their unfortunate trait of freezing in Glasgow, losing two first-half goals to Rangers at Ibrox and failing to recover in the second half. The other two games were closer with both deserving a bigger attendance; 7,879 were at Rugby Park to see Hibs take an early lead through the prodigious Russell Latapy, but Andy McLaren and Craig Dargo scored in the second half for Bobby Williamson's side. At Love Street, St Mirren beat Dunfermline 2-1 with all the goals coming in the first half and Dunfermline feeling unlucky not to get extra time.

The following night, the TV audience saw a great game at Tynecastle when Celtic called. Hearts had been going through a bad patch including some fan protests (a by no means unusual occurrence at Tynecastle) and Celtic felt justified in resting some of their players and giving men like Colin Healy,

Barry Smith and Stephen Crainey a game – and all three of them scored, as it turned out. The match is remembered for a horrible clash of heads which resulted in two Hearts players, Gary Locke and Thomas Flogel, being carried off, and also a spirited Hearts performance which took the game to extra time, albeit with the help of two silly penalties conceded by the Celtic defence. In extra time, however, Celtic scored three times through Colin Healy, Lubo Moravcik and Jackie McNamara to win by the flattering margin of 5-2.

The semi-finals were scheduled for the midweek of 6/7 February 2001. There was little doubt that the Celtic v Rangers game had to be at Hampden, but the decision to make Hampden the venue for the Kilmarnock v St Mirren game came in for a little criticism when less than 10,000 turned up on a wet and windy night to watch it. The original, more sensible decision had been to play the game at the more compact and atmospheric Fir Park, Motherwell, but both clubs wanted to play at the national stadium for a reason that baffled the press. Not that it bothered Kilmarnock, for they turned on one of their best performances in years to beat the Buddies 3-0 with goals from Andy McLaren, Craig Dargo and Peter Canero.

The next night saw the Old Firm semi-final. Celtic won 3-1 in a game eccentrically refereed by Willie Young, who awarded a soft penalty to each side and rightly sent off Claudio Reyna for persistent fouling. In the aftermath of the red card, when everyone started pushing and jostling, Young also sent off Lubo Moravcik of Celtic and Michael Mols of Rangers, possibly the two mildest-tempered men on the pitch. There was nothing biased about Willie Young, although his judgement could be questioned! Before all that,

Celtic had scored two early goals through Chris Sutton and Henrik Larsson and were comfortably the better side.

And so Celtic had a chance to defend their League Cup against Kilmarnock on 18 March 2001. Kilmarnock had appeared in three Scottish League Cup finals but had never won the trophy whereas Celtic had now won the cup 11 times. Kilmarnock were going well, respectably placed in the league, but they had suffered a bad blow the week before when they went out of the Scottish Cup to a last-minute Hibs goal. Celtic, unbeaten since November, were now struggling with player availability. Two were ineligible, another two were suspended and, the Wednesday before the game, the influential Stilyan Petrov suffered a bad injury at St Johnstone.

Fortunately for Celtic, they had good reserve cover and, even more fortunately, they still had Henrik Larsson. This was his season and he was freely compared to Jimmy McGrory – an astonishing height of adulation in Celtic circles – because of his goalscoring ability. He would prove his quality that day.

The teams were:

Celtic: Gould, Mjallby, Valgaeren, Vega, Petta (Crainey) (Boyd), Healy, Lennon, Lambert, Moravcik (Smith), Larsson, Sutton

Kilmarnock: Marshall, McPherson, McGowne, Dindeleux (Canero), Innes, Hay, Holt, Durrant (Reilly), Mahood, Cocard (McLaren), Dargo

Referee: H Dallas, Motherwell

It was a nice, bright spring day at Hampden (although there had been some frost in the morning) with Celtic wearing yellow and Kilmarnock wearing black. The first half was anodyne and flat, although the understrength Celtic team looked marginally better and it was clear that the reserves were not letting anyone down. They did suffer another injury blow in the early departure of Bobby Petta, the victim of a rather robust tackle, to put it euphemistically.

Early in the second half, Celtic took the lead through Larsson with a trademark swivel, turn and shot through a packed Killie defence. There followed a moment which might have rocked a lesser team than Celtic when Chris Sutton was rather harshly sent off for a high challenge on Gary Holt, who had fouled him once or twice. Celtic fans were already preparing their 'Hugh Dallas is a puppet of Rangers' excuses when events proved them unnecessary. First Larsson earned a second goal from a deflection. If there was a bit of luck about that, his third goal was a collector's item. Picking up a ball on the halfway line and ignoring several foul challenges, he ran the length of the Killie half before rounding the goalkeeper, even at one point changing foot to do so. It was a wonderful goal and there was now no way back for Kilmarnock.

Celtic won their 12th Scottish League Cup, still some distance (as they themselves were all too uncomfortably aware) behind the tally of Rangers. This victory was one of their best, given their problems of player availability and one or two debatable refereeing decisions. It was also the first stepping stone on the way to their first treble since 1969. Three weeks later they would clinch the Scottish League, in May they would be back at Hampden to win the Scottish Cup.

The first full season of the new century meant that the Scottish League Cup had been competed for 55 times. Although attendances in some of the earlier rounds remained poor, there was little doubt that it was now beginning to challenge even the venerable Scottish Cup as a tournament of prestige. Occasionally one heard moaning that the League Cup was a waste of time, but it was noticeable that such moans came from the supporters, not the management of the clubs – and even then, it was usually only after their team had been eliminated. The tournament made some money, or at least it could, if clubs reached the later stages.

Now and again, ideas emerged in the press about an amalgamation of the Scottish and the English League Cups to make a British Cup. It was an idea not without merit, but the thought of Torquay v Inverness on a Wednesday night was absurd. It might have worked at a later stage with the four semi-finalists going into the quarter-final of the British League Cup, but nothing ever came of it. Curiously, something similar would happen some 15 years down the line with the Scottish League Challenge Cup, but that competition did not contain the Scottish Premier League teams.

The Scottish League Cup kicked off as usual in August 2001 and three-time winners East Fife delighted sentimental historians by beating Arbroath to get to the second round, although they were compelled to bow the knee to Livingston. Airdrie put out Motherwell and Aberdeen were lucky to get the better of Queen of the South, but the big shock of the round was Ross County beating Hearts on penalties. Fifteen years later such a result would have been less of a shock but, in 2001, it made everyone sit up and take notice of Ross County. Fellow Highlanders, Inverness Caledonian Thistle, beat the other Thistle, the Glasgow one called Partick, on penalties after a thrilling 3-3 draw watched by a crowd of only 1,038 at the new Tennent Caledonian Stadium. Stirling Albion, before a crowd of even smaller than that, beat St Mirren, a team which had a great history in the Scottish Cup but were not quite so good in the League Cup.

The third round was played on the midweek of 9/10 October apart from the game containing Celtic who were involved in the European Champions League, a tournament which had had its schedule knocked on its head following the destruction of the Twin Towers on 11 September. Celtic eventually beat Stirling Albion 8-0 in early November. In the other seven games, there was one major shock and one minor one. Aberdeen's woes continued (a shame because their league form improved considerably and they were the only team to beat Celtic all season) when they went down 1-6 to Livingston before 9,049 shell shocked-spectators at Pittodrie. Admittedly, Livingston were a Premier League team, but it was a dreadful defeat for a team of Aberdeen's standing to sustain at home.

A lesser shock was the removal of Dundee by Ross County, while three games went to extra time and two of them to penalties. Dundee United beat St Johnstone in extra time while Ayr United won the Ayrshire derby against Kilmarnock on penalty kicks and Inverness did likewise against Dunfermline Athletic at East End Park. In the other two games, Hibs beat Raith Rovers 2-0 at Stark's Park and Rangers beat Airdrie 3-0 at Ibrox.

The quarter-finals again saw Celtic playing at a different time from anyone else. This time it was a major embarrassment for Livingston, whose floodlights failed on the scheduled night of 28 November. The game did not get started but TV cameras were there, the players were ready and Tommy Burns, now acting as a TV pundit, had to ask the question of what was going to happen to all the pies? The pies could hardly have lasted until the game was played the week before Christmas, three weeks later. Celtic won 2-0 with goals from Bobo Balde and John Hartson.

They joined Rangers, Ayr United and Hibs in the semi-finals. They had all played at the end of November. It was Rangers' turn to face Ross County in this round and they had to make the long trip to Dingwall to do so. The 2-1 scoreline in favour of Rangers flattered Ross County, for the Dingwall men only scored in the 90th minute after Shota Arveladze and Claudio Reina had scored for Rangers in the first half. Ayr United impressively beat Inverness Caledonian Thistle 5-1 at Somerset Park after Inverness had scored first and, in the best-attended game of the round, Hibs beat Dundee United 2-0 at Easter Road. The draw paired Celtic with Rangers and Hibs with First Division Ayr United. It was the second year in a row that Celtic and Rangers had crossed swords at the semi-final stage, thereby putting an end to the suggestion that they are kept apart for the final.

The Old Firm game on Tuesday, 5 February 2002 was a classic and 43,457 were there (part of the East Terrace was closed for repair) to see a game which was feisty, to put it mildly, although there were no red cards. It was also full of good football with the result in doubt until the very end, and the goal that won the game in extra time was a spectacular one. Celtic had made a habit of beating Rangers of late and were already far ahead in the league, so far that it would have been unrealistic to expect Rangers to catch them, but this was the night that Rangers struck back.

Alex McLeish had recently been appointed manager of Rangers after the departure of Dick Advocaat, and his arrival seemed to make a difference. The game ebbed to and fro.

Peter Lovenkrands scored just on the point of half-time, Bobo Balde equalised in the second half, Rangers missed a penalty kick, before, in extra time, Bert Konterman, hitherto the butt of jokes from Celtic supporters and occasionally from his own fans as well for his perceived inability, struck from a distance to settle the tie.

It had been a great advert for the Scottish game, well refereed by Kenny Clark, and much enjoyed by the vast TV audience. Celtic felt that they had been the better side – they certainly missed a few chances, but then so too did Rangers – but it was Rangers who went through to the League Cup Final.

One could not have said that the game the following night was anything like as good. The crowd was a woeful 11,799 and the atmosphere in Hampden was non-existent. Hibs, a middle of the table Premier League team, really should have done a great deal better against a First Division team called the Honest Men by the commentators because there was no lack of honest effort but a lack of talent. Ninety painful minutes came and went and eventually, some ten minutes into extra time, referee Mike McCurry awarded Ayr a penalty kick. It was converted by Eddie Annand, a man who already knew that he would be ineligible for the final because he had picked up another yellow card!

Hibs rallied but simply lacked the technical ability to break through a confident Ayr defence. Ayr manager Gordon Dalziel was delighted but Hibs' manager, likeable Frenchman Franck Sauzee, slated his players for a shocker of a performance. Poor Franck was not destined to last long for Hibs were truly awful, and yet one has to feel that poor Sauzee (who had been a good player for Hibs) deserved more than the 69 days he got!

St Patrick's Day, 17 March saw Ayr United face Rangers in the League Cup Final. It was looked upon as a mismatch, although that does not credit the Somerset Park men who were enjoying a good run in the Scottish Cup. In fact, Ayr United did themselves proud until almost half-time. It was their first national cup final since they were formed in an amalgamation between Ayr and Ayr Parkhouse in 1910 (thereby justifying the nomenclature of 'united') and, most unusually for the times, their team consisted entirely of Scotsmen.

The teams were:

Rangers: Klos, Vidmar, Ricksen (Hughes), Amoruso, Numan, Konterman, Ferguson, Latapy (Dodds), Caniggia, Flo, Lovenkrands (McCann)

Ayr United: Nelson, Robertson, Lovering, Duffy, Hughes, Craig, Wilson (Chaplain), McGinlay, McLaughlin (Kean), Grady, Sheerin

Referee: H Dallas, Motherwell

Ayr United had a good first half, twice making Stefan Klos bring off saves, and anxiety began to permeate the sectarian songs on the West Terrace. But then, in the 43rd minute, Torre Andre Flo, who had hitherto disappointed and failed to convince anyone that he was worth the £12 million that Rangers had shelled out for him, scored. A softish penalty followed early in the second half, awarded by referee Hugh Dallas and sunk by Barry Ferguson, and the game was over long before Argentinian Claudio Caniggia scored another two at the end. Caniggia's presence in the team, incidentally, allowed the good people of Argentina the opportunity of a rare treat, a Scottish football match on TV. This had been arranged so that Argentinians back home could see how well their hero performed. It was almost certainly the first time that a Scottish domestic game had been shown live on Argentinian TV!

Everyone was sorry for Ayr United, who had captured the hearts of the public, but the bottom line was that Rangers had now won their 22nd Scottish League Cup out of 56 starts. That was some performance and their joy was not yet complete, for although they lost the Scottish League by 18 points to Celtic, they still managed to beat them in the Scottish Cup Final thanks to a late winner from Peter Lovenkrands.

The year of 2003 was an odd one in Scottish football. It was the year in which a Scottish team achieved something that no other Scottish team had done for 16 years, and which quite a lot of people felt would never happen again: get to the final of a European trophy, in this case the UEFA Cup, a feat achieved by Celtic. They could be considered unlucky not to win against Jose Mourinho's Porto, but they reached the final with many fine victories, not least over English teams Blackburn Rovers and Liverpool.

At a time when the fortunes of the Scottish national side continued to slide from moderately poor to downright terrible, it was a welcome boost to the national ego, and the Celtic fans did the nation proud by their enthusiasm and exemplary behaviour.

But Celtic paid for it by maybe overstretching themselves and not doing so well in the domestic trophies, although they came close in two of the three. No one else stood up to the plate, and therefore Rangers won a treble, including the League Cup which they won for the 23rd time. And once again the tournament provided plenty of material for fans to gossip and argue about.

There were two new teams in the Scottish League Cup. One was Gretna, who would have a brief and scarcely believable few years in Scottish football, scaling the heights before vanishing almost as quickly as they appeared. There was also a new team called Airdrie United who, to the punter at least, bore an astonishing resemblance to Airdrieonians deceased. Airdrieonians were replaced by Gretna, but when Clydebank also went bust and died, Airdrie United's owners were able to convince the Scottish Football League that they were worth a go using the same ground as Airdrieonians. Confusing, yes, and possibly even a little underhand, but in the League Cup, Gretna at least failed to trouble the scorers for long, going out 2-1 to East Fife. Airdrie United on the other hand lasted until the third round before going out to Dundee United, having beaten Kilmarnock on penalties on the way.

For various reasons, the ties in the third round were scattered over a period of three weeks, the final one Aberdeen v Motherwell being played on the same night as one of the ties in the next round was being played. This sort of fixture congestion did the tournament little good – the footballing public are usually very easily confused! The best tie of the round was at Easter Road where Hibs put up a brave fight but eventually lost 2-3 to Rangers, their cause not helped by one of their substitutes being sent off! The substitute had been brought on to replace an unfortunate Hibs player, Austrian Alen Orman, who suffered what seemed to be an epileptic fit on the field.

Celtic had endured a fair amount of trouble with Inverness in the recent past but they beat them 4-2 at Parkhead. Dundee

United beat Airdrie United but their neighbours Dundee went down to Partick Thistle and Livingston continued to impress with a 1-0 win over St Johnstone. Aberdeen beat Motherwell at Pittodrie before a small and unhappy crowd of only 6,557, Hearts beat Ross County and Dunfermline got the better of Falkirk.

The quarter-finals were played over two weeks and on four separate nights: Celtic v Partick Thistle and Dunfermline v Rangers in the first week in November; Aberdeen v Hearts and Livingston v Dundee United the second week. Neither Celtic nor Rangers looked very impressive in their ties. Some fringe players were given a game so Celtic could rest some first-teamers for European excursions, but that was no excuse for a poor show against Partick Thistle at Parkhead. The game finished 1-1 at 90 minutes with Thistle perhaps unlucky not to grab a winner; it was still 1-1 after extra time, then Celtic won 5-4 on penalties after both teams had taken nine penalties each. It was a woeful display of penalty taking; the players were as poor at that skill as they were converting chances in open play.

Rangers were held by a determined Dunfermline team at East End Park until Claudio Caniggia scored the only goal of the game. At Pittodrie, a desperately poor crowd (reflecting more poor performances on the field in the Scottish Premier League) saw Hearts scrape through to the semi-final with a Kevin McKenna goal on a night when the stadium was said to have all the atmosphere of a public library or undertaker's parlour. Finally, on 13 November, the semi-final line-up was completed when Dundee United won with two goals from Derek Lilley against Livingston at Almondvale.

The past two seasons had seen Celtic and Rangers clash in the semi-final. Not this time. The draw placed Hearts against Rangers and Celtic against Dundee United, both games to be played at Hampden in the first week of February; 31,609 were at Hampden on Tuesday, 4 February to see a good game between Hearts and Rangers, but one in which Rangers always had the upper hand and, although Rangers only scored once through Ronald de Boer in the first half, the result was seldom in doubt.

Two days later, before a disappointing crowd of only 18,856 in the incessant Glasgow rain, Dundee United, currently struggling at the bottom of the Premier League, suffered their normal bout of travel sickness in Glasgow and went down 0-3 to a fairly ordinary Celtic side. Bobo Balde scored twice for Celtic, Henrik Larsson once, but United's cause was not helped by the sending off of Jim Lauchlan for a scything tackle on Henrik Larsson, a sending off all the more stupid because Larsson, admittedly a permanent menace, was hardly in a threatening position at that point.

So it was Celtic v Rangers yet again in the Scottish League Cup Final on Sunday, 16 March 2003. It was the 12th meeting between the two of them in a League Cup Final, with Rangers having the lion's share of the victories 7-4 so far. It was a shame that this particular League Cup Final was overshadowed by other events. On the world stage, the Second Iraqi War was about to begin, if one could use the word 'war' to describe an international cosmic extension of playground bullying with two big boys against a small one with the idea of robbing him of his pocket money. Even in football itself, Celtic at least were more than a little preoccupied with their UEFA Cup campaign in which they were in the middle of an ultimately successful struggle with Liverpool. Not only that, but Celtic and Rangers were embroiled in a tremendous fight for the Scottish League in which a Celtic win at Parkhead the week before had seemed to give them the upper hand.

But this was the Scottish League Cup, Rangers' favourite tournament, and although the bookmakers gave Celtic a slight edge, there was not very much in it. It would turn out to be one of the most exciting and controversial cup finals of them all. This time the game was televised on Channel Five and much enjoyed throughout the world, including the troops on standby in the Middle East.

And yet at half-time it looked all over. Rangers dealt with Celtic's early pressure and Peter Lovenkrands and Claudio Caniggia put them two up, leaving everyone wondering whether the pressure was getting to Martin O'Neill and his Celtic side, who were beginning to look stale and uninterested. But this Celtic team knew how to fight back and Henrik Larsson brought them back into the game with a header.

It was then that Celtic suffered four blows, two of them self-inflicted. John Hartson equalised from a clearly onside position and yet was flagged by the stand-side linesman. Chris Sutton was carried off with a broken wrist after an accidental collision with one of his own men. One had less sympathy, however, with the sending off of Neil Lennon for two yellow cards, neither of which was all that bad but Neil should have known better and then, to cap it all, the luckless John Hartson fired a last-minute penalty past the post and Rangers had won their 23rd Scottish League Cup.

The teams were:

Rangers: Klos, Ricksen, Moore, Amoruso, Bonnissel (Ross), Arteta (Konterman), Ferguson, Caniggia, de Boer (Arveladze), Lols, Lovenkrands

Celtic: Douglas, Mjallby (Petrov), Valgaeren, Balde, Thompson, Lennon, Smith (Sylla), Lambert, Sutton (Maloney), Larsson, Hartson

Referee: K Clark, Paisley

Although Celtic beat Liverpool the following Thursday night, thereby raising the prestige of Scottish football to a great degree, their domestic woes continued. O'Neill picked the wrong team for a Scottish Cup tie at Inverness, underestimating the opposition and paying the penalty. Then a draw at Dundee and a defeat at Hearts was enough to knock them off the top of the league, which they finally lost a few days after coming back from their UEFA Cup Final in Seville by scoring fewer goals at Kilmarnock than Rangers did against Dunfermline.

Rangers won a treble when they beat Dundee in the Scottish Cup Final at the end of May. They had benefitted from the break of the ball once or twice that season, not least in the League Cup Final, but you do not win a treble purely by luck. Arguably, had Celtic not been involved in Europe, it might not have happened, but next year would prove to be a different matter.

The 2003/04 Scottish League Cup was a fairy tale of the sort that one would not have believed even a season previously. Soon after the Second World War (not long after the Scottish League Cup itself was founded), a team called Ferranti Thistle emerged in Edinburgh. They grew ambitious and, in the mid-1970s moved to Meadowbank Stadium (which had been built for the 1970 Commonwealth Games) and called themselves Meadowbank Thistle, gaining entry to the Scottish League at the same time. In 1995, not without a little opposition from their supporters in Edinburgh, they moved to Livingston and from then on they prospered, so much so that they were promoted to the Premier League in 2001 and became a permanent fixture. They had not won a major tournament, but 2004 would change all that and allow Davie Hay, who had achieved some success in this competition as a player but never as manager of Celtic, to claim that he had won the Scottish League Cup as a manager as well.

But they were not the first fairy tale of this year's Scottish League Cup. That honour must belong to Forfar Athletic, a team who had enjoyed one or two moments in the League Cup, notably in 1978 when they reached the semi-final. On 23 September they put out Motherwell, a team two divisions above them, in a penalty shoot-out after they had been 3-1 up at one point. Motherwell had equalised but could not score the winner and paid the penalty – and how the 1,110 fans at Station Park enjoyed it!

Their neighbours Brechin City also had a good night. Less spectacular but equally worthy of praise, they beat Kilmarnock 1-0 at Glebe Park. It was only a couple of seasons before that Killie had been in the final. Still in Angus, Arbroath fought bravely against Falkirk but lost 3-4 in extra time at Gayfield. The other Angus team, Montrose, were less fortunate. They went down 0-9 to Hibs at Easter Road. There might have been another surprise at Balmoor, the home of Peterhead, but Partick Thistle struggled to a win on penalties, earning a few corny newspaper headlines to the fact that 'they got out of jail'.

When Livingston won at Hampden, beating Queen's Park 3-1, little did anyone realise that they would be back to the same ground very soon!

Forfar were rewarded (if that is the appropriate word) with a trip to Ibrox where they were on the wrong end of a 6-0 thrashing, the pain more than a little mitigated by a share in the 26,330 gate. Brechin lost only 0-5 at Aberdeen and did not have the compensation of a large gate, the pitiful 3,631 being an eloquent testimony to how well Aberdonians thought their team were doing. There were even fewer at Dundee United, only 2,899, to see Livingston ease through in an undistinguished match. Possibly the best game of the round was at St Johnstone where Dunfermline's late rally was not enough to save the game and the Saints won 3-2. Dundee had a good win 5-2 over Clyde and Hibs, Hearts and Celtic all won through as well without anyone being too impressed by their performances, Falkirk putting up their usual battling performance against Hearts, but this time in vain.

The quarter-finals were held in the first week in December, although the Hibs v Celtic clash at Easter Road had to be postponed until the week before Christmas because Celtic, heavily involved in Europe, were still playing their previous round's tie against Partick Thistle. The ties, ill-attended as often in the League Cup those days, nevertheless provided some great entertainment with both Celtic and Aberdeen biting the dust when they might have been expected to win. At Pittodrie, the depression which gathered round the city was not dispelled when Livingston twice went ahead but were twice pulled back by goals from Steve Tosh to take the game to extra time. It was Lee Makel of Livingston, however, who scored the vital goal.

There was another tense game at Dens Park with no goals scored during the 90 minutes and Dundee were indebted to Bobby Linn for the only goal of the game in extra time. St

Johnstone disappointed their fans in a tame 3-0 surrender to Rangers at Ibrox and, at Easter Road a couple of weeks later, Hibs got the better of Celtic in the Parkhead side's only reverse of the season so far. Celtic had a slightly weakened side out, but only slightly, and Hibs' Kevin Thomson was the man who scored the vital goal in a 2-1 win.

There was a slightly comic (if it hadn't been so tragic) aspect to one of the semi-finals in February 2004. Dundee were already in administration and, the day after the semi-final, Livingston joined them. It was dubbed by the press as the 'all-administration semi-final'! Livi had overreached themselves in recent years and Dundee had repeatedly alienated their support through crazy dealings in the transfer market. Fortunately, both teams survived, but it was a close-run thing.

There were those who felt these two teams should have been removed from the tournament as some sort of punishment (in Dickensian times, they would have been put in a debtors' prison) but it was sensibly agreed that they should have a chance to make some money. Not that they would get a great deal of cash from the 7,231 who came to Easter Road to see them, but there was TV money and a chance to appear in the League Cup Final. The semi-final was a dreadful game played in an atmosphere of impending doom with neither team likely to score a goal until, in the very last minute, Dundee brought down Fernando Pasquinelli in the box and Derek Lilley converted the penalty kick, bringing relief to the small knot of Livingston fans and sending the Dundee fans home more convinced that the end had come for their club.

The other semi-final at Hampden between Hibs and Rangers (another two teams who would soon become no strangers to penury) was at Hampden a couple of days later. The crowd was a disappointing 27,954 on a dreadfully wet night but the TV audience saw a spirited 1-1 draw which required extra time and penalties to settle the winners. All the penalty shoot-out proved was that the standard of penalty taking on both sides was dreadful. Three players from each side missed their penalties and, when Frank de Boer of Rangers missed his by hitting the post, Hibs were into the final. Poor Frank! His Christian name, with its unfortunate rhyme, became part of a song for Hibs and Celtic supporters to commemorate his miss. Yet he was a fine player and, on this occasion, not the only player to miss a penalty.

It was Hibs v Livingston in the final on Sunday, 14 March. It was Livingston's first appearance, and the eighth time that Hibs had appeared in a League Cup final. On two occasions they had been victorious, but Hibs supporters were uncomfortably aware and did not need to be reminded by the press and supporters of other teams that their side had an unfortunate tendency to blow up on big occasions at Hampden. The form of both teams was mediocre and unpredictable but most people were of the opinion that Bobby Williamson's Hibs had a little more than the paupers of Livingston.

Both clubs made a major effort to sell the final to their fans. Hibs fans didn't always turn out in great numbers to support their team but they did on this occasion, and in the new town of Livingston, it was difficult to find a bus that was not commandeered to take fans to Hampden. Strangely, Celtic were allowed to play Motherwell at Celtic Park in the league that day, but nevertheless a crowd of 45,443 appeared at Hampden on a fine sunny day (proving, yet again, the value of playing the final in March) to see the 58th Scottish League Cup Final.

The first half began in a lively fashion with Hibs looking the more likely of the two teams, but no goals came and the score remained 0-0 at half-time. Then came Livingston's golden patch. First Derek Lilley scored from 12 yards, a few minutes later (Livi having made the decision to twist rather than stick) Jamie McAllister broke through to score again.

The silence of the Hibs fans was almost tangible. They knew in their heart of hearts (to use some unfortunate imagery for Edinburgh fans) that they had blown it again and, although their players rallied, the departing trickle of fans became a flood, telling its own depressing story. The shoals of silent buses heading back along the M8 was an eloquent testimony to the support for the club – but how long could this perpetual heartbreak last? For Livingston, however, one could not exaggerate the sense of triumph. A new club in a new town with a major financial problem and battling for survival, they had nevertheless managed to win one of Scotland's major trophies. Davie Hay deserved his moment in the sun – even though it would be little more than a moment.

The teams were:

Livingston: McKenzie, McNamee (McLaughlin), McAllister, Rubio, Andrews, Dorado, Makel, O'Brien (McGovern), Lovell, Fernandez (Pasquinelli), Lilley

Hibs: Anderson, Murdock, Smith (McManus), Edge, Doumbe, Caldwell, Thomson, Reid (Dobbie), Riordan, O'Connor, Brown

Referee: W Young, Clarkston

CHAPTER TWELVE

SAME OLD FIRM
2004–2010

WHEN THE 2004/05 season opened in August, there were quite a few people in England who looked north and wondered about the sanity of the organisation calling itself the Scottish Premier League, an organisation founded on exclusiveness and selfishness yet making pompous statements about how what they were doing was for the good of the Scottish game. One of their more outrageous decisions was when they compelled Inverness Caledonian Thistle, a hard-working and thoroughly deserving outfit, to play their home games at Pittodrie, a ground more than 100 miles away! The specious reason for this nonsense was that their stadium did not come up to Premier League standards, but fortunately the Scottish *Football* League, who still administered the Scottish League Cup, had no such problems. On Wednesday, 22 September, Inverness played their first real home game of the season in the League Cup. Sadly, they lost to Motherwell and had to wait until the Scottish Cup came around for another home game. The opening round of the Scottish League Cup in early August brought bad news for both Saints. St Johnstone went down 2-3 to Alloa at McDiarmid Park despite a late fightback after most of their supporters had gone home. St Mirren at Love Street had the bad luck to meet Forfar Athletic on one of their better nights and went down 2-5 to the Loons. Raith Rovers made the long trip to Stranraer to lose 2-1 but the other Rovers, Albion Rovers, had better luck down south when they beat Queen of the South 2-1 with two late goals.

The heroes of the first round were poor in the second. Forfar were hammered 0-4 by neighbours Dundee and Alloa suffered by a similar score at Easter Road, although Albion Rovers won a penalty shoot-out at Glebe Park. A Highland derby at Victoria Park, Dingwall saw Ross County lose to the peripatetic Inverness, while last year's winners Livingston won through at Stirling Albion. Dundee United extinguished the hopes of Stranraer, while Aberdeen, Kilmarnock, Motherwell and Partick Thistle all won by three-goal margins over teams from lower down the scale.

The third round brought in the big guns again. Celtic swept Falkirk aside 8-1 and Dundee United had few problems in disposing of Clyde 4-0. There was a close call for holders Livingston, however, at Almondvale. They were losing 1-0 to Dundee in what was charitably described as a 'drab' game but then earned extra time through a penalty converted by Jim Hamilton, who also scored the winner in the 111th minute. These were the games played on the Tuesday, but on the Wednesday, the game of the round appeared to be Aberdeen v Rangers at Pittodrie and was chosen by the BBC to be televised. It turned out to be more disappointment for Aberdeen supporters. Rangers won 2-0 with goals from

Fernando Ricksen and Steven Thompson, and they were always on top. Hibs and Dunfermline marched on beating Albion Rovers and Partick Thistle, while there was a far closer game at Tynecastle where Paul Hartley's two goals for Hearts were just enough to beat Kilmarnock 2-1.

Inverness's long-awaited first home game of the season was a massive disappointment. In the first place, only 1,494 turned up at their ground to see Motherwell, and they were ill-rewarded. Motherwell won comfortably 3-1 with goals from Richie Foran, Phil O'Donnell and Kevin McBride as against one from Ross Tokely.

The draw for the quarter-final, to be played on the second week in November, brought together the Old Firm at Ibrox but kept apart the two Edinburgh teams, sending Hibs to Dundee United and Hearts to Dunfermline, while Motherwell were paired with holders Livingston. Livingston's hopes of retaining the trophy for another year were spectacularly demolished in a 5-0 beating from a Motherwell side who were on a bad run of league form. Hearts went to East End Park where they beat Dunfermline 3-1. The other two games went to extra time. Hibs were looking good for the semi-finals at Tannadice, where a Derek Riordan goal scored in the first half looked as if it would do the trick for them, until Jim McIntyre equalised for United with only three minutes remaining and the same player scored the winner in injury time.

Celtic would have been similarly optimistic at Ibrox, but it was Rangers who triumphed. It had been a long time since Rangers had beaten Celtic – Celtic had won the last seven games – and when John Hartson scored with his head halfway through the second half, it began to look as if it might be eight. But, after a mix-up in the Celtic defence, it was Dado

Prso with his head wrapped in a bandage who equalised as time was running out, and in extra time Shota Arveladze, called Mr Bean by some supporters because of his slight facial resemblance to Rowan Atkinson, scored the winner for Rangers. It was generally agreed to have been one of the better Old Firm games, an agreeable feature being the lack of red or yellow cards dished out by referee Stuart Dougal.

The semi-finals were once again played in the first midweek of February. One was an embarrassingly one-sided affair on Thursday, 3 February as Rangers hammered Dundee United 7-1, Dundee United's traditional lack of love with Hampden being confirmed and carried on to a ridiculous extent. Rangers scored first and at half-time it was only 2-0, and when Jason Scotland pulled one back for United, it looked as if there might be a fightback. Rangers scored the next goal, however, and a flurry of goals at the end confirmed their victory as the roof fell in on United.

Two days earlier, Easter Road had seen a real cracker between Hearts and Motherwell. Terry Butcher's Motherwell side had opened the scoring through Stephen Craigan with a great header, and when Richie Foran slotted home a penalty in the 78th minute, it looked all over. But Hearts fought back and two substitutes, Mark Burchill and Hjalmar Thorarinsson, scored within the last five minutes to give their side a lifeline.

The drama continued into extra time with two exhausted teams giving of their best until another substitute, Marc Fitzpatrick of Motherwell, settled the issue as a penalty shoot-out loomed. It was one of the best games ever seen at this stage of the League Cup with the issue in doubt until the very end. Hearts had cause to be unhappy but they had nothing to reproach themselves for after having come back so brilliantly. But it was Motherwell who went through to meet Rangers.

Astonishingly, this was only Motherwell's third Scottish League Cup Final. They had won the trophy in 1950/51, beating Hibs 3-0, and they had reached the final exactly 50 years ago when they lost 4-2 to Hearts, but since then their record in the tournament had been woeful. Nevertheless, well managed by Terry Butcher and his assistant Maurice Malpas and with good players like Stephen Craigan, Phil O'Donnell and Scott McDonald, it was felt that they had a chance. They were a workmanlike, hard-to-beat, middle-of-the-table sort of a side rather than one which sparkled with talent. The important thing was not to freeze on the day.

Rangers, on the other hand, were in their 30th League Cup Final, full of internationals and were involved in a grim battle for the Scottish League against Celtic, who had put them out of the Scottish Cup in early January. There had been better Rangers sides in the past, but just about everyone fancied them to beat Motherwell in the League Cup Final at Hampden on 20 March. Some people called it the David Cooper Final in honour of the man who had played with distinction for both clubs and had died ten years previously.

The final turned out to be Motherwell's worst nightmare. They never really got going. Two goals conceded in the first ten minutes to Sotirios Kyrgiakos and Maurice Ross meant it was always an uphill struggle and, although David Partridge pulled one back, Fernando Ricksen scored again before half-time and Nacho Novo and Sotirios Kyrgiakos put the game out of Motherwell's reach in the second half. The game fizzled out disappointingly and it was as one-sided a League Cup Final as there had been for some time. Provincial Motherwell had indeed frozen. Rangers won 5-1 and had won the Scottish League Cup for the 24th time.

The teams were:

Rangers: Waterreus, Ross, Malcolm, Kyrgiakos, Ball, Ricksen, Ferguson, Vignal (Rae), Buffel, Novo (Thompson), Prso

Motherwell: Marshall, Corrigan, Partridge, Hammell, Craigan, McBride (Quinn), O'Donnell, Leitch, Paterson (Fitzpatrick), Foran (Clarkson), McDonald

Referee: M McCurry, Glasgow

The season was not yet over for Motherwell. By a supreme irony, it would be Motherwell who would win the Scottish League for Rangers on the last day of the league season, a day that Celtic supporters would dub 'Black Sunday'. Rangers needed to beat Hibs in Edinburgh and Motherwell to beat Celtic at Fir Park. Rangers duly beat Hibs but Celtic were 1-0 up over Motherwell. Crucially, however, Celtic failed to score a second goal and Scott McDonald scored twice for Motherwell to win the league for Rangers. Even more ironically, sometime later McDonald joined Celtic whom he said he had always loved! Celtic did have the consolation of the Scottish Cup.

Season 2005/06 saw the League Cup reach its 60th birthday. It was also a remarkable season in Scottish football, for the Scottish Cup that year was contested by Hearts and Gretna and it went to a penalty shoot-out. Celtic won the other two trophies in Gordon Strachan's first year of management at the club, despite two awful giant-killings they were on the wrong end of – Artmedia Bratislava in Europe and Clyde in the Scottish Cup. Rangers had a poor season, Aberdeen still showed few signs of recovery, and in some way the team of the season was Hearts despite some strange, even bizarre, management decisions, a theme which would continue for several years.

In the first round of the Scottish League Cup, Albion Rovers, who had done well last year, went out to Gretna, and Forfar did likewise to the fast-emerging Ross County while, if we had not known it before, the great days of East Fife in this competition were now long gone as they lost to Stranraer. The second round saw last year's beaten finalists Motherwell struggle at local rivals Hamilton, needing a late goal to win and only then after two Hamilton men had been red-carded. Years ago a defeat of Dundee by Stranraer would have been a shock of seismic dimensions, but in 2005 it was less so. Stranraer won comfortably 3-1, Livingston beat Raith Rovers 2-1 while, in the battle of the Saints, the Paisley ones emerged triumphant over the Perth ones. Gretna lost at home to Dunfermline, and Ayr United beat Ross County 2-1.

Stranraer's reward for their progress was a home tie in the third round against Aberdeen, a club going through one of its recurrent crises and now seriously pushing its luck about losing its hitherto-loyal support. The Dons, without impressing anyone too much, managed to get through 2-0. Celtic, too, put in a rather uninspired performance to beat Falkirk 2-1 at Parkhead in front of 20,000 frustrated spectators and Rangers needed extra time to beat Clyde at Ibrox after Clyde had been ahead very briefly in the second half. Extra time killed off gallant Clyde, who lost 5-2.

The best performance of the round was possibly that of Dunfermline who beat Kilmarnock 4-3 at Rugby Park even though the tie was not quite as close as it seemed because the Pars were 4-1 up at one point. Hibs beat Ayr United 2-1 but their city neighbours were less successful at Livingston, going down 0-1, while Motherwell won at St Mirren only in extra time after a great performance from the home side. In the Highlands, Inverness Caledonian Thistle beat Dundee United 2-0.

Once again, the quarter-final draw brought the Old Firm together, this time at Celtic Park, and this time it was Celtic who won very comfortably 2-0 to put the holders out of the League Cup, their goals coming from Shaun Maloney (a superb strike from 30 yards) and a late, scrappy one from Bobo Balde which some sources give as an own goal. Kyrgiakos of Rangers was sent off for making sarcastic comments and gestures to the referee.

The previous night had seen wins for Motherwell, Dunfermline Athletic and Livingston. At Fir Park, Motherwell beat Aberdeen 1-0 with an early goal from Brian Kerr, but this time the Dons deserved better, their cause not being helped when centre-half Zander Diamond was harshly sent off for handball. There was a good game at the poorly attended Almondvale when Livingston, despite losing a goal to Inverness in the first minute, fought back to win 2-1 in extra time, while Hibs once again managed to break the hearts of their supporters by losing 3-0 to a competent Dunfermline side.

The semi-finals were played on two separate Wednesday nights at the end of January and the beginning of February. Dunfermline took on Livingston, now managed by Paul Lambert, at Easter Road before a pitiful crowd of 4,360, generally agreed to have been the poorest attendance at a semi-final in modern times. It was also agreed to have been one of the worst games ever seen on live television. Darren

Young scored the only goal of the game with a penalty kick towards the end of the first half for Dunfermline and this was enough to see them into their third League Cup Final, to the delight of manager Jim Leishman. It was a trophy they had never won, although they had enjoyed two successes in the Scottish Cup in 1961 and 1968.

The following week saw a larger attendance (but still a poor one when one considers the teams involved and that it was a semi-final) of 32,595 at Hampden to see the other game between Celtic and Motherwell. It was not a great game and Motherwell might have taken better advantage of some slack Celtic defending on occasion, but Celtic won 2-1 in a game with a remarkable ending. Celtic needed that victory for there would be no Scottish Cup for them this year as they had managed to lose to Clyde at Broadwood in early January.

Motherwell scored first through a header from Richie Foran with Celtic's goalkeeper Artur Boruc claiming unconvincingly that he had been impeded. Before half-time, however, Celtic equalised with a fine strike from Maciej Zurawski after he had been put through by Shaun Maloney. Extra time and penalties looked inevitable such was the feeble finishing of both sides until, in virtually the last minute of the 90, Motherwell conceded an indirect free kick from the pass-back rule when goalkeeper Graeme Smith was compelled to save what might have been an own goal from Martyn Corrigan. Hampden and the TV audience were now treated to the remarkable sight of every Motherwell player starting on his goal line and running to block an indirect free kick, although John Hartson tapped to Shaun Maloney who drove the ball high into the net. It was one of the more unusual ways of winning a game, but it did little to disguise Celtic's inadequacies on the night. Celtic would face the Pars in the final, a repeat of the Scottish Cup Final of 2004.

But Celtic improved during the month of February and a significant event took place at East End Park on 19 February, exactly one month before the League Cup Final. Celtic came to Dunfermline in the SPL and won 8-1, rightly not letting up for propaganda and psychological reasons. Maciej Zurawski scored four and even Neil Lennon got one of his rare goals. From then on, it was clear that something remarkable would have to happen before Celtic lost to Dunfermline in the Scottish League Cup Final on 19 March.

The great Jimmy Johnstone died the week before and some Celtic supporters called it the Jimmy Johnstone Final. He was much mourned and Celtic's victory was a fitting tribute to the memory of one of their greatest talents, with every player wearing the number 7 on their pants in honour of Jimmy. Celtic were without the suspended John Hartson but had Roy Keane, once of Manchester United and Republic of Ireland, on board. The Pars were well supported, as always on such occasions, but approached the game fearing the worst, however much Jim Leishman tried to cheer everyone up.

The teams were:

Celtic: Boruc, Telfer, Balde, McManus, Wallace, Nakamura, Keane (Dublin), Lennon, Maloney, Zurawski, Petrov

Dunfermline Athletic: McGregor, Shields, Wilson, Ross (Donnelly), Campbell (Derek Young), Mason, Thomson, Daquin (Tarachulski), Labonte, Makel, Burchill

Referee: S Dougal, Burnside

The weather was a bit cooler than some Scottish League Cup finals had been in the past but it was still not a bad day.

The game was not as one-sided as the league game a month previously had been, but it was hardly competitive. Maciej Zurawski scored just before half-time, cleverly getting on to a ball which looked as if it were going past, then Shaun Maloney, who was having a good season for Celtic, scored from a free kick just outside the box in the 76th minute. This effectively killed the game but there was still time for a little piece of history when Dion Dublin, a man who had played for many clubs in England but never won a single honour, carved out a wee niche in Celtic history for himself when he scored the third goal on the final whistle.

Thus ended the 60th Scottish League Cup Final, Celtic having now won 13 of them but still a good distance behind Rangers in this tournament. It was Gordon Strachan's first trophy for the club, although he would win the Scottish League as well in a few weeks' time. Dunfermline finished second from bottom and were lucky they had Livingston underneath them and that only one team was relegated from the SPL. And, once again, a World Cup took place in the summer, in Germany, without any Scottish representation.

But we were all back again for more punishment at the start of the 2006/07 season. Between the years of 2005 and 2011, the League Cup was won by a member of the Old Firm with the welcome exception of 2007, when Hibs were the winners. The sound of the triumphant Hibs crowd singing 'Sunshine on Leith' at the end of that final will long live in the memory, quite a moving experience for the worldwide TV audience even for those not of the Hibs persuasion. Possibly, the cynics might add, it was more moving because it was heard so seldom. Indeed, some of the singers did not seem to be any too familiar with the words!

There are few clubs who treat their fans quite as badly as Hibs do in terms of leading them up the garden path and then blowing up spectacularly. It had happened so often at Hampden in semi-finals and finals of both national tournaments that, for a spell, there was a danger that the phrase 'to Hibs it' might come into the English language, meaning to lose something that did not seem possible. In addition, their dismal record of selling their best players is second to none. Like most selling clubs, Dundee springing to mind, they usually pay for their folly in terms of poor results, relegations and flirtations with bankruptcy – and Hibs had been no strangers to all that. Their support, large but alienated, generally well behaved (give or take a few pathetic attempts at yobbery), really did deserve something better.

And yet they had had some great moments too. Their great days were the early 1950s and their Famous Five forward line, but the League Cup was never one of their favourites any more than the Scottish Cup was. They won it in 1972/73, at last beating Celtic about whom they were in danger of having a complex; and in 1991/92, in the wake of the proposed hostile takeover by Wallace Mercer of Hearts, they also made their point.

Three former League Cup winners bit the dust in the first round of the 2006/07 competition in Raith Rovers, East Fife and Dundee who lost to Airdrie, St Johnstone and Partick Thistle respectively. The second round produced several very close ties and two major talking points. One was that last year's finalists Dunfermline Athletic only scraped through at Somerset Park on a penalty shoot-out, 7-6, after a 0-0 draw in 90 minutes and extra time. A press report, in a masterly piece of journalistic understatement, claimed that no one would ever say that 'the standard of play reached the lower reaches of the Himalayas, let alone Everest'.

The other awful game (and this one resulted in the downfall of a giant) was at Firhill (because Hampden was being used for a Rolling Stones concert) between Queen's Park and Aberdeen. Mercifully for Aberdeen, very few fans (1,588 in total) were in Glasgow that August night to see the amateurs of Queen's Park win 5-3 on penalties after 120 minutes of football. The Aberdonians would have preferred Mick Jagger to that, and Jimmy Calderwood's side left the field to the boos of their small band of travelling fans after a performance which might have enjoyed a little more luck in terms of close misses becoming goals but was nevertheless described in a devastating piece of candour by an Aberdeen website as 'rank'.

So, when the big boys appeared in mid-September, there was no Aberdeen. The third round produced a couple of exciting ties at Kilmarnock and Inverness. Kilmarnock beat Livingston 2-1 after extra time and Anthony Stokes scored the only goal of the game for Falkirk at Inverness. The other results were predictable – Celtic beat St Mirren and Rangers beat Dunfermline, for example – but St Johnstone's 3-0 victory over Dundee United was particularly emphatic. Motherwell beat Queen's Park 3-0 at Hampden and both Edinburgh teams won with little bother: Hearts at Alloa, and Hibs beating last year's Scottish Cup Finalists Gretna 6-0 at Easter Road.

The quarter-finals on 7/8 November were particularly interesting. A five-goal thriller at Rugby Park, an Edinburgh derby and both members of the Old Firm losing at home is more than the average excitement at this stage. Tuesday night saw Falkirk at Celtic Park and Motherwell at Rugby Park.

Falkirk held their own for 120 minutes, a Maciej Zurawski goal in extra time being immediately cancelled out by Anthony Stokes. Celtic seldom do well in penalty shoot-outs and this night was no exception, the little-known and grossly undervalued Dutchman Evander Sno being the villain who missed the key penalty for Celtic. At Kilmarnock, the game swung to and fro with Killie going ahead and Motherwell equalising twice, but Danny Invincibile scored the third goal for Killie in the 72nd minute and there was no third comeback for the Lanarkshire men. The game was feisty and included Motherwell's assistant manager Maurice Malpas being put to the stand for arguing with the referee. It was all the sweeter for Kilmarnock who had recently gone down 5-0 to Motherwell in the SPL.

The following night saw the Edinburgh derby at Easter Road on TV. Hibs had recently appointed John Collins as manager to succeed Tony Mowbray and the team, as often happens with a new manager, played with panache and elan to beat Hearts 1-0 with a first-half Rob Jones goal. It was generally agreed that Hibs should have won by a great deal more and Hearts were left to ponder over the folly of allowing manager George Burley to go last season.

But even the Edinburgh derby had to take second place to the news that First Division St Johnstone had beaten Rangers at Ibrox. Steven Milne scored two goals early in the second half to put Rangers out and silence the chortling about what had happened to Celtic the previous night. Owen Coyle, the manager of Saints, was delighted, but Rangers' manager, a hunted and beleaguered Frenchman called Paul Le Guen, was forced to apologise for a 'terrible' performance. Rangers had fallen into the trap of accepting the media's candidate for the job after McLeish had been sacked and, sadly, the Frenchman simply did not understand Scotland. He fell out spectacularly with Barry Ferguson and did not even see the season through, facing the bullet in early January, his cause not helped by his poor command of the English language.

In early February 2007, in the semi-finals, Kilmarnock faced Falkirk at Fir Park and Hibs took on St Johnstone at Tynecastle. The Fir Park game had to be delayed because of traffic congestion in the streets outside the ground (hardly a common occurrence in Motherwell!) but it turned out to be a surprisingly easy 3-0 victory for Jim Jefferies's Kilmarnock side with a hat-trick from Steven Naismith. It was one of those days in which a team, Falkirk in this case, simply failed to turn up (almost literally true in the context of the traffic congestion) but it was a great night for the Ayrshire side who had been suffering, not for the first or last time, from some well-documented financial problems.

The other semi, the following night at Tynecastle, was a far closer affair, although Hibs eventually proved to be too strong in extra time. Steven Fletcher opened the scoring in the early stages with a fine volley and Hibs held on to the lead until well into the second half before St Johnstone scored a deserved equaliser from a Jason Scotland header. In extra time, however, a goalkeeping error from a David Murphy free kick gave Hibs the lead, and Abdessalam Benjelloun added a third. It was a great boost for the Hibs supporters who had recently been betrayed yet again by their club. Hibs had unaccountably decided to sell Kevin Thomson to Rangers. Cant like 'a nice piece of business' and 'you have to take the money when offered' did not impress the supporters, but another Hampden appearance did.

Hibs' supporters were still haunted by the League Cup Final of three years ago when their team had blown up before Livingston, but there was a grim determination on the buses as they set out to Hampden on 18 March for another go. They need not have worried, for the final, like that of 2005 and 2006, turned out to be surprisingly one-sided and Hibs landed their third Scottish League Cup.

Hibs were 1-0 up at half-time with a goal from Rob Jones but the game was still fairly even. Then, in the second half in intermittent rain, the game simply ran away from Kilmarnock with Abdessalam Benjelloun and Steven Fletcher adding another two as distinct from one Kilmarnock goal from Gordon Greer. Greer's goal made it 3-1 with about quarter of an hour to go and it gave Kilmarnock some sort of a chance, but the two late goals for Hibs ensured that they won 5-1 and that the city of Edinburgh was about to experience one of its rare football triumphs.

The teams were:

Hibs: McNeil, Whittaker (Martis), Hogg (McCann), Jones, Murphy, Sproule (Zemmana), Brown, Beuzelin, Stevenson, Benjelloun, Fletcher

Kilmarnock: Combe, Wright, Greer, Ford, Hay, Di Giacomo (Locke), Johnston, Fowler, Leven (Wales), Nish, Naismith

Referee: D McDonald, Edinburgh

Kilmarnock continued their melancholy tradition of losing League Cup finals, something that they had done in 1952/53, 1959/60, 1962/63 and 2000/01. But it was a great day for Leith. We again witnessed the moving spectacle of the supporters singing their anthem. It was impressive and showed the world that Hibs do indeed have a large support, although they do not always turn out in as great numbers as their players would have liked. But this was their day. However, those who felt that this might be a permanent return to pre-eminence for Hibs in Scotland under John Collins would be sadly disappointed.

Season 2007/08 was another action-packed season for Scottish football. Rangers emulated the achievement of Celtic five years earlier in 2003 in reaching the final of the UEFA Cup but they lost 0-2 to Zenit St Petersburg, and the misery was compounded when their fans disgraced them. Scotland were in with a chance of qualification for the European Championships but sadly blew up in Georgia before losing, less surprisingly, to Italy at Hampden. In the domestic season, Gretna, who had been in the Scottish Cup Final less than two years previously, folded and disappeared almost as quickly as they had appeared following the illness and sudden death of their owner. It is a strange story awaiting its historian, but it allowed a place in the Scottish League for Annan Athletic the following season.

Four former winners took part in the first round for the Scottish League Cup and they all won – Dundee, East Fife, Partick Thistle and Livingston – Livingston impressing everyone by beating Ayr United 5-0. Two of the winners, Dundee and Livingston, then played each other in the second round and it turned out to be a great game, 2-2 after extra time with Dundee winning 6-5 on penalties. Partick Thistle also won on penalties after a goalless draw against St Johnstone. East Fife's 1-0 win over St Mirren meant they had reached further in the League Cup than they had done for some time, while Hearts, Hibs and Dundee United all won through to the third round, not without a struggle in some cases.

Hibs, the holders, were not far from being dumped out at the ground where they had won the cup just a few months earlier. They were drawn at Hampden to play Queen's Park, scored two goals early in the second half, but then Queen's Park pulled one back and gave them a rough ride for the rest of the game. Motherwell beat Raith Rovers 3-1 at Fir Park, Kilmarnock had a long trip to Balmoor to play and beat Peterhead, Falkirk won narrowly at Links Park, Montrose and, at Tannadice, Dundee United needed a late goal to beat Ross County, a team who would have a good season and would win the Second Division (the third tier of four) that year.

The third round in September produced some interesting ties. Last year's winners Hibs went down 2-4 to Motherwell at home, possibly the first in a dreadful series of results that would lead to the sacking of John Collins in midwinter and more trauma for their supporters. It was hard to believe that the impressive singing of 'Sunshine Over Leith' was only a few months ago – but then again the Hibs directorate never did seem to realise that if you are going to sell star players, in this case Scott Brown to Celtic, they must be replaced by players who are just as good.

Hibs' neighbours Hearts had better luck, beating Dunfermline 4-1, but Celtic struggled at Dens Park in a televised game, winning only 2-1. Dundee United beat Falkirk 1-0, their goal coming from Lee Wilkie who had once played for Dundee. Inverness beat Gretna 3-0, while Hamilton's two young starlets and near-namesakes McCarthy and McArthur scored as they beat Kilmarnock 2-0. East Fife were compelled to move their tie v Rangers to East End Park,

Dunfermline for logistic reasons involving their ground and duly lost 0-4, while Aberdeen gave a hint that there might, at last, be something of a revival in the offing with a 2-0 win over Partick Thistle.

More encouraging signs for the Pittodrie faithful came in the quarter-final played on Halloween when the Dons beat Inverness Caledonian Thistle 4-1. It put them through to their first semi-final in either cup competition since 2000, a long time for supporters of a proud team like Aberdeen to have to wait. Dundee United's Noel Hunt scored a hat-trick against Hamilton Academical at Tannadice as United won convincingly 3-1. Rangers beat Motherwell 2-1 at Fir Park after goals from Nacho Novo and Kris Boyd, while the big surprise of the round was Hearts' win over Celtic at Parkhead in the televised game. It is not a place that Hearts often do well, but this time they rose splendidly to the occasion, surviving loads of Celtic pressure and then scoring through Andrius Velicka in the 77th minute after Celtic had claimed unconvincingly that the ball had gone out of play on the stand-side touchline. The same player then scored at the death to silence the rather disappointing crowd of 21,492, something that perhaps tells us a little about TV coverage.

Aberdeen and Dundee United were scheduled to play at Tynecastle in the semi-final on Tuesday, 29 January 2008 but the game was postponed because of weather conditions until the following week. It was only a stay of execution for the Dons because 12,046 fans saw another Aberdeen horror show. And yet things had looked so good for them when Andrew Considine put them ahead. Sadly for them, Darren Dods equalised almost immediately for United and then, in the second half, their defence fell apart and United scored goals through Christian Kalvenes, Craig Conway and Morgaro Gomis. Dundee United played well and deserved their place in the League Cup Final but Aberdeen's cause was not helped by the sending off of Lee Miller for two yellow cards with one of them entirely self-inflicted for arguing. The hurling of missiles at Aberdeen's goalkeeper Jamie Langfield by some youths rather advertised the fact that the Scottish educational system was no great success in Dundee.

The other semi-final had taken place by then. Rangers won 2-0 at Hampden on a heavy pitch before a crowd of 31,989 fans and Hearts had cause to complain about Rangers' first goal. It was scored by Barry Ferguson but an arm seemed clearly to have been used, something noticed by everyone except referee Mike McCurry. Ferguson, to his credit, admitted it afterwards, but there was no doubt about Rangers' second goal, a fine strike from Jean-Claude Darcheville, and Rangers were worthy winners as they reached their 31st Scottish League Cup Final. Once again, however, it was a manifestation of Hearts blowing up when they had to face Rangers.

It was Dundee United's sixth Scottish League Cup Final but, as everyone pointed out to them, the final was to be held at Hampden where they had already lost to Rangers on two such occasions in the past, their only two successes in this tournament having happened at Dens Park, Dundee. But they were given at least a chance by the press and the TV, for Craig Levein had built up a good side at Tannadice and they had beaten Rangers in the league in October. Rangers, under Walter Smith and Ally McCoist, were looking consistent as they challenged for four trophies, and they would have the undoubted advantage of having the game at Hampden in front of their own fans.

There was also Dundee United's traditional psychological problems about Glasgow and Rangers. And the game on 16 March 2008 was yet another collector's item of the Dundee United death wish. It was a fine, pleasant spring Sunday, as usually happened for League Cup finals. United scored in the first half through Noel Hunt and were playing comfortably in the second half. They were well on top and anxiety and depression were beginning to manifest themselves at the Mount Florida end with time slipping away and some of their weaker brethren showing signs of preparing to depart.

But Rangers kept pressing and, with five minutes left and the ball bobbing about the edge of the penalty box, Mark Kerr made a hideous mistake with a pass back which allowed Kris Boyd to run in and equalise. The bells of Hell were already going ting-a-ling-a-ling for United. This break gave Rangers extra time which they hardly deserved, but even then Dundee United went ahead with a fine drive from Mark de Vries. Yet Rangers never gave up and halfway through the second period of extra time, Boyd scored again, this time with a header after Dundee United had failed to clear a Kirk Broadfoot throw-in.

All went down to a penalty shoot-out taken at the King's Park end of the ground in front of the Dundee United fans. To their anguish, they saw Craig Conway, Lee Wilkie and David Robertson all miss. It was somehow appropriate that it was Kris Boyd who scored the crucial penalty in this rather undistinguished penalty shoot-out in which the goalkeepers did rather better than the penalty takers. Three Dundee United men and two Rangers had missed the target but Rangers won 3-2 and Dundee United fans once again made the long trip back from Hampden trophyless.

The teams were:

Rangers: McGregor, Broadfoot, Cuellar, Weir, Papac (Boyd), Hemdani (Darcheville), Dailly, Burke (Whittaker), Ferguson, Davis, McCulloch

Dundee United: Zaluska, Kovacevic, Kenneth, Wilkie, Kalvenes, Buaben (Robertson), Flood, Kerr, Gomis, Hunt (Conway), De Vries

Referee: K Clark, Paisley

Rangers had won the Scottish League Cup 25 times and they would also win the Scottish Cup this year. They would, however, miss out on the two trophies that they really wanted: the SPL where Celtic beat Dundee United at Tannadice to do the trick on the late date of 22 May, and their trip to Manchester where they missed out on the UEFA Cup.

Season 2008/09 saw Annan Athletic play their first game in the Scottish League Cup on Tuesday, 5 August at Dumbarton. They had already defeated Cowdenbeath in the Scottish League on the Saturday and they played well enough in this game. It ended up in 1-1 after extra time but the Sons of the Rock won 5-4 on a penalty shoot-out. The best game of the round was at Firhill where Partick Thistle beat Forfar Athletic 4-3 after extra time, and after Forfar had twice gone ahead in the 90 minutes. Nine goals were scored in the 90 minutes at Stair Park, Stranraer before 317 spectators with Morton winning 6-3. Recent winners Livingston needed extra time to dispose of lowly East Stirlingshire.

Even more recent winners Hibs fell again at home in the second round, this time in a thrilling encounter against Morton which they were unlucky to lose. Hibs were 2-0 down after 66 minutes and looked out but scored twice in the last ten minutes to make it 2-2 after 90. Steve Pinau then scored for the Easter Road men but, with time running out, Ian Russell equalised for Morton with a penalty kick before Ryan Harding scored a dramatic late winner. The 14,874 crowd may have left feeling disappointed with the actual result, but no one could complain about the level of entertainment.

It was not a great week for Edinburgh because the following night at Tynecastle, Hearts went out on penalties to Airdrie United after a 0-0 draw in which Airdrie played for a long part of the game with only ten men. The standard of football was 'dire' and Hearts got what they deserved after failing to score.

You could not say that about St Mirren, who thumped Dumbarton 7-0, nor Dundee United, who beat Cowdenbeath 5-0, but the rest of the second-round encounters were quite tight, with Aberdeen's 1-0 win over Ayr United at Somerset Park being a rather painful experience for the few travelling Dons fans in the 2,979 crowd. Livingston won 2-1 over St Johnstone at Almondvale, Falkirk won 3-1 at Kirkcaldy and in the battle of the Athletics, Dunfermline beat Alloa 1-0.

The third round saw the demise of Aberdeen at Kilmarnock. It was a strange game in that Kilmarnock won 4-1 but all the goals came in the first 35 minutes. It seemed as if defending was going out of fashion for a while and a basketball score seemed possible, but the game settled down and Aberdeen were unable to get back into the game. Rangers were fortunate to get the better of Partick Thistle at Firhill, needing a Pedro Mendes goal in extra time to win 2-1, and there was a similar scoreline in the tousy Lanarkshire derby at Fir Park where Hamilton Accies emerged victorious in a game which saw two red cards and 12 yellow ones.

Celtic beat Livingston comfortably 4-0 at Celtic Park, and Dundee United, Dunfermline and Falkirk all made progress with home wins over Airdrie, St Mirren and Queen of the South, but Morton, the heroes of the last round, went out at home to Inverness Caledonian Thistle in a thrilling encounter in which the Highlanders made a late comeback and won in extra time.

The quarter-finals were played at the end of October, three on the Tuesday night and Celtic playing at Kilmarnock in the televised game on the Wednesday. Celtic won that game comfortably 3-1 with goals from Scott McDonald, Shunsuke Nakamura and Aiden McGeady as against one from Danny Invincibile . The other three games were tight and close affairs. A crowd of 5,350 were at Tannadice to see Dundee United beat Dunfermline. Scott Robertson scored the only goal in a tight 1-0 game in which United were indebted to goalkeeper Lukasz Zaluska for a late save to deny Stephen Glass at the very death. Neil McCann, now in the veteran stage of a lengthy career, scored the only goal of the game at the Falkirk Stadium to beat Inverness, who felt aggrieved at being denied what looked like a blatant penalty and which referee David Somers apparently subsequently admitted that he had got wrong. Rangers completed the semi-final quartet by beating Hamilton 2-0 at Ibrox before 32,083 in a routine victory with goals from Kris Boyd and Kyle Lafferty.

The Old Firm were kept apart in the semi-final draw. Rangers played Falkirk and Celtic took on Dundee United, both at Hampden in late January. The Rangers v Falkirk game passed without any great trauma for Rangers. Two goals from Nacho Novo and one from Kris Boyd saw Rangers through 3-0 in a depressing game before a half-filled national stadium (24,507) and a pitch which was, frankly, substandard. Rangers' financial problems were already beginning to manifest themselves, as they had failed once again to make any impact on Europe and a cup-final appearance was quite welcome to bring in a bob or two.

The other semi-final, a night later, was played before a smaller crowd and on a pitch which was even worse, having been chewed up badly the night before, but that was hardly the main topic of conversation. The standard of football was dreadful and could not be entirely explained away by the state of the pitch; 120 minutes came and went without a goal or very many close chances, but it was the penalty shoot-out that made wonderful viewing for the TV audience, some of whom asked the question if it wouldn't have been better just to have penalties in the first place!

Celtic won 11-10 and, for the first time in Scottish football with every single player having had a shot, they had had to start going round for the second time. Scott McDonald of Celtic and Willo Flood of Dundee United took two penalties and poor Willo Flood was the man who missed. Ironically, he was on the brink of what would turn out to be a disastrous transfer to Celtic and the conspiracy theorists had their own view about why he missed. But he scored the first time and would not have been eligible to play in the cup final anyway. The other players (with the exceptions of Glenn Loovens and Lee Wilkie) scored their penalties, some of them brilliantly, with both goalkeepers, Artur Boruc and Lukasz Zaluska, scoring theirs as well. After it all died down, we had Celtic through to the final to play Rangers in what would be the 13th Old Firm League Cup Final. Of the previous 12, Rangers had won eight and Celtic four.

It was difficult to call this final. Neither team had asserted any dominance over the other one in the Scottish Premier League and the game between them a month previously at Parkhead had been an uninspiring 0-0 draw. The week before, Celtic had gone out of the Scottish Cup to St Mirren, and this may have given Rangers some psychological advantage.

The game was played on the pleasant day of Sunday, 15 March, the Ides of March on which Julius Caesar had been assassinated in 44 BC. This was of little real concern to the fans of both sides, as they made their way to Hampden, where the pitch had seen major surgery in an attempt to get it up to scratch for cup finals and internationals. They would see a game which was far from a classic but provided the usual talking points and arguments.

Seven men were booked by the occasionally overzealous Dougie McDonald but no one could have said that it was a dirty game. It was described as 'meaty' and 'feisty', but it was after all an Old Firm game! Perhaps indicative of the poor season that both teams were having, no goals came in 90 minutes and although the atmosphere was relentlessly tense, there was little in the way of classic football, apart perhaps from the occasional foray of the hitherto disappointing Aiden McGeady.

In the first minute of extra time, Celtic went ahead in front of the Rangers supporters when Darren O'Dea scored one of his rare goals from a Shunsuke Nakamura free kick. That looked as if it was going to be enough to win the game for Celtic, for they were by now well on top. Celtic's victory was confirmed in the very last minute when Kirk Broadfoot brought down Aiden McGeady. Again, the referee was possibly a little overzealous in brandishing the red card, but

Aiden McGeady was immediately seen to call for the ball because he wanted to take the penalty kick himself. The game was probably over by that time anyway – at least the emptying Rangers terraces seemed to indicate that – but Aiden duly took the penalty to release delirium on the Celtic terraces behind the goal, for Celtic had now won the Scottish League Cup for the 14th time.

The teams were:

Celtic: Boruc, Hinkel, Loovens, McManus, O'Dea (Wilson), Caldwell, Nakamura, Brown, Hartley (Samaras, Vennegoor of Hesselink), McGeady, McDonald

Rangers: McGregor, Whittaker, Weir, Broadfoot, Papac, Davis, McCulloch (Dailly), Ferguson, Mendes, Miller (Novo), Lafferty (Boyd)

Referee: D McDonald, Edinburgh

There would be ample recompense for Rangers in that they won the other two trophies, edging past Celtic in the league and beating a gallant Falkirk side in the final of the Scottish Cup. Surprisingly, Gordon Strachan left Celtic at the end of the season, which had not been a total failure, but the storm clouds, financial not football ones, were already being seen to gather over Ibrox.

But Rangers did have a good season in 2010. They won the Scottish League again, the Scottish League Cup in a rather remarkable final, and only lost the Scottish Cup to Dundee United in a quarter-final replay. Celtic, on the other hand, had a poor season with the likeable Tony Mowbray, who had been a tolerable success with Hibs a few seasons earlier, clearly finding the job at Celtic too much for him.

The League Cup started on 1 August as normal. Some games were one-sided in the first round. Remarkably, there were four 5-0 scorelines: Dundee over Stranraer, Dunfermline Athletic over Dumbarton, St Johnstone over Stenhousemuir and Ross County over Montrose. In this context, Partick Thistle might have felt failures for allowing Berwick to score in their 5-1 beating, and Brechin, Inverness and Queen of the South could only put four past their opponents. There were some closer games as well, notably the exciting Fife derby at New Bayview where Raith Rovers were 0-2 down after 20 minutes but came back to pip East Fife at the very end 3-2. Ayr United needed extra time to beat Stirling Albion, and the only game that went to penalties was at Airdrie where Alloa beat the home side 4-3 from the spot after a goalless 120 minutes. The surprise of the round was Albion Rovers beating Livingston 3-0.

On the Sunday (East Stirlingshire now shared with Stenhousemuir at Ochilview and Stenny had been at home on the Saturday), St Mirren continued the high-scoring theme with a 6-3 win over the 'Shire with Billy Mehmet scoring five of them. The Buddies had never really sparkled in the Scottish League Cup. They had reached the final in 1955/56; this was to be a year in which they would come equally close.

The second round saw St Mirren beat Ayr United 2-0 at Somerset Park. The high scoring continued with St Johnstone putting six past Arbroath at Gayfield and Inverness beating Albion Rovers 4-0. Both Dundee teams advanced, Dundee United winning 2-0 at Alloa and Dundee beating Forfar 4-2 at Dens Park. Raith Rovers had a slightly tougher Fife derby this time and lost 1-3 at East End Park, Dunfermline. Queen of the South did well to beat Partick Thistle 2-1 at

Firhill and there were victories for Ross County, Kilmarnock and Hibs.

Aberdeen, Celtic, Rangers and Hearts joined in the third round and there were some very close games indeed, notably at Dens Park where Leigh Griffiths in extra time scored the goal for Dundee that edged out Aberdeen. Hearts had to come from behind at Tynecastle to beat Dunfermline Athletic, but Rangers' 2-1 win over Queen of the South at Ibrox was easier than it sounded because Queens' goal came in the 90th minute when the game was virtually over. Celtic beat Falkirk comfortably 4-0 at the Falkirk Stadium, but St Johnstone shocked Hibs by beating them 3-1 at Easter Road after Hibs had scored in the first minute. St Mirren beat Kilmarnock 2-1 at Rugby Park, Motherwell were taken to extra time by Inverness at Fir Park but won through 3-2, and Dundee United returned from the long trip to Dingwall with a 2-0 victory. Not many people would have predicted that it would be those two teams who would contest the Scottish Cup Final next May.

The quarter-finals were played on 27/28 October 2009. On the Tuesday night, Dundee put up a brave fight at Dens Park against Rangers but went down to a 3-1 scoreline even though they had been level for a long time and Dundee were denied two penalties 'that even a blind man could see' according to Dundee's manager Jocky Scott. This was a necessary win for Rangers who had been going through a bad spell both on and off the field. A few bad results and increasing newspaper revelations about their financial position were making life difficult for Walter Smith and his men, but they deserve credit for grinding out a result.

Dundee's neighbours Dundee United fared no better, losing 1-2 to St Johnstone in a Tayside derby at McDiarmid

Park, their cause not helped by a Darren Dods own goal. The most emphatic win of the night was St Mirren's 3-0 win over Motherwell at St Mirren Park, a game which deserved to be watched by a crowd of more than 4,325. As the teams had drawn 3-3 on Saturday in a close and exciting league game, this match was a disappointment to Motherwell fans, but showed that St Mirren were plucky cup fighters. Michael Higdon and Ross Jack scored for the Paisley men and then Stephen Craigan had the misfortune to concede an own goal.

But the most significant game was the one played on the Wednesday night and televised. For the second time in three years, Celtic went out of the League Cup to Hearts at Parkhead. Neither Celtic nor Hearts had impressed their supporters so far this season and this was probably reflected in the poor crowd of 18,675 who saw an equally poor game. The only goal came from the penalty spot and was scored by Michael Stewart of Hearts, currently in dispute with the club and celebrating only minimally. Celtic were booed off the park by their disgruntled support and the result was a nail in the coffin of manager Tony Mowbray, a man whose body language and public utterances were already beginning to indicate that he was not really cut out for this mammoth job.

Fir Park was the venue for the first of the two semi-finals in early February 2010 and it featured Hearts against St Mirren. It was a good, close game with Hearts unable to find a way to goal to counteract Billy Mehmet's lovely strike early in the second half. The small band of St Mirren supporters, who had suffered much of late, rejoiced in the prospect of a cup final, their first since they won the Scottish Cup in 1987.

The other semi-final was a curiously low-key affair watched by only 17,371 at Hampden. One might have thought that this was the other semi-final because St Johnstone were dressed like Hearts and Rangers were wearing all white. Snow fell heavily at times during the first half but fortunately the Hampden pitch stood up well. Rangers scored through Steven Davis and Lee McCulloch in the first half and, although Derek McInnes's St Johnstone upped their game in the second half as the snow turned to sleet and eventually abated, Rangers remained in control and everyone seemed quite happy to get away home on this terrible night. Scottish football is no place for softies.

The weather could hardly have shown more of a contrast than it did for the Scottish League Cup Final on the day of the spring equinox, 21 March. The weather was splendid and the crowd of 44,538 (a little short of Hampden's capacity) saw a remarkable game. The standard of football was by no means good, but nevertheless it must go down as one of the greatest triumphs of Rangers' rich League Cup history. Credit is due to Walter Smith and Ally McCoist when one considers that this game took place with rumours of player discontent and the now-acknowledged serious financial problems in the background.

The main achievement was that Rangers won this game with only nine men. No goals came in the first half. Early in the second half, in an all-Thomson incident, Kevin of Rangers was sent off by Craig the referee for a nasty foul on Steven of St Mirren! If this were not bad enough, Danny Wilson was then red-carded for a professional foul tackle. It looked harsh but that was the law, so it was 11 Buddies v nine Gers.

In the 84th minute, Steven Naismith crossed for Kenny Miller to head home what turned out to be the only goal of the game with St Mirren unable to take advantage of their numerical superiority. Little wonder that the Rangers fans sang 'We only need nine men'. It was one of their proudest moments and one had to give them credit, as well as the fact that they had now won the trophy 26 times.

By the same token, it was one of the worst experiences for St Mirren supporters, there in large numbers, although maybe a little short of what one would have expected for a national cup final. They would never have a better chance of beating Rangers to lift a trophy and they must have kicked themselves long and hard on the way home.

The teams were:

Rangers: Alexander, Whittaker, Wilson, Weir, Papac, Davis (Edu), Thomson, McCulloch, Novo (Smith), Miller, Boyd (Naismith)

St. Mirren: Gallacher, Barron, Potter, Mair, Ross, Thomson, Brady (O'Donnell), Murray (Dorman), Carey, Mehmet (Dargo), Higdon

Referee: C Thomson, Paisley

A few days later, on the Wednesday night, things were reversed. Rangers went out of the Scottish Cup at Dundee United's Tannadice (a bit of a bogey ground for them) and St Mirren suddenly turned it on and beat a poor Celtic team 4-0, the result which triggered the sacking of Tony Mowbray. It was a strange few days in the rich tapestry of Scottish football. Dundee United would go on and win the Scottish Cup and Rangers would triumph in the Scottish League despite the HMRC net visibly tightening.

The Scottish League Cup seemed to have hit on a successful formula. The crowds remained disappointingly low, particularly in the midweek games, but those who did go were seldom cheated. The idea of playing the final in March was a clear success and the occasion always seemed to be blessed with good weather. Now a slight change was made in that the semi-finals were to be played on a weekend at the end of January with the intention of attracting a bigger crowd. The games would both be televised.

It often seems a pity, as would happen in 2010/11, for example, that some of the smaller teams would be out of the tournament before we reached August. (Bitter humourists pointed out that it was a similar experience for our larger teams in Europe!) Cowdenbeath lost 0-2 to Clyde on 31 July before a crowd of 667. It was hardly a great earner for the men from Central Fife. Stranraer were also unlucky in that they lost 1-7 to Morton at Stair Park before 470. Raith Rovers won a Fife derby 4-1 against East Fife and Queen of the South beat Dumbarton 5-1. Livingston joined East Fife as a former winner who bit the dust at the first time of asking when they lost 2-1 to Ross County in Dingwall.

Two of the second-round games went to penalty shoot-outs. Brechin City had a rare moment of glory by beating Dundee 3-1 on penalties after a 2-2 draw at Glebe Park and, in Dingwall, Ross County beat last year's finalists St Mirren 4-3 on penalties after a thrilling 3-3 draw. Elsewhere everything went pretty much to plan: Aberdeen won 3-0 at Alloa, Hearts beat Elgin City 4-0, Kilmarnock beat Airdrie United 6-2 and Dunfermline Athletic had a good win at East End Park, coming from behind to win 3-2 over Clyde.

In the third round, both Edinburgh teams fell. Hearts and Falkirk seemed to play each other quite a lot in the League Cup and produced high-scoring, tough affairs. This one was no exception at Falkirk Stadium with Falkirk edging it at the very death with a goal from Mark Stewart after Hearts' Craig Thomson had been sent off after tangling with a Falkirk player. Another nine players were booked in what was a far from easy game for referee Mr Winter. Hibs were well beaten at Kilmarnock 3-1.

Aberdeen had a struggle to beat Raith Rovers 3-2 at Pittodrie but Celtic and Rangers won comfortably – Celtic beating Inverness 6-0 and Rangers beating Dunfermline 7-2 – but Dundee United needed a penalty kick, an own goal and extra time to get the better of Ross County in a thrilling affair in Dingwall. Elsewhere, there were comfortable victories for St Johnstone and Motherwell.

The quarter-finals at the end of October were all thrilling encounters as well. On Tuesday, 26 October Aberdeen left it very late to beat an unlucky Falkirk at Pittodrie. They were 0-1 down at half-time and left the field to a chorus of boos (sadly by no means an infrequent occurrence at Pittodrie) but rallied. Paul Hartley equalised and then scored a penalty at the death to cheer up the fans, some of whom were nevertheless seen to clap Falkirk off the park at the end. At Fir Park, Motherwell beat Dundee United 1-0 thanks to a late goal from Alan Gow after United had done at least as much of the pressing as Motherwell had done.

The following night saw the Old Firm in action. Rangers were always on top of Kilmarnock at Rugby Park with goals from Andrew Little and Steven Naismith (one in each half) giving them a 2-0 victory while Celtic had more problems (or, putting it more accurately, gave themselves more problems) in beating St Johnstone at McDiarmid Park. Celtic's paranoia complex about referees and officialdom was in full swing due to various incidents, but tonight they went three ahead in the first 15 minutes, Anthony Stokes scoring twice and Niall McGinn once. They then scored again through Joe Ledley, but it was ruled out for offside, something that did little to convince Celtic fans of any innate impartiality of Scottish officials. It would not have mattered if Celtic had defended a little better, but before half-time Sam Parkin scored for the Saints and then, in the second half, Murray Davidson made it 3-2. Saints were unlucky not to get an equaliser and Celtic were much indebted to Fraser Forster in goal for a few fine saves.

The semi-finals paired Aberdeen with Celtic and Rangers with Motherwell. Both games were to be played at Hampden on the weekend of 29/30 January. Aberdeen cannot have gone into their game against Celtic brimming with confidence for Celtic had already beaten them 9-0 at Celtic Park that season. Indeed, Celtic were 4-0 up shortly after half-time and it stayed that way in one of Hampden's poorest-ever semi-finals with Aberdeen happy to restrict it to four and Celtic not bothered about adding to the tally. For a proud club like Aberdeen, it was simply awful.

Rangers had more bother beating Motherwell the following day in a better match. The game was very close. Maurice Edu's first-half strike for Rangers was cancelled out by Keith Lasley's deserved equaliser, but Steven Naismith grabbed Rangers' winner, even though Motherwell tried hard to take the game to extra time.

For the third time in the 21st century (and it was only 11 years old) there was another Old Firm League Cup Final. It was also the fourth time they had met each other in recent weeks, the last one being a shocking Scottish Cup quarter-final replay at Celtic Park where three Rangers players had been red-carded and Celtic manager Neil Lennon and Rangers assistant manager Ally McCoist squared up to each other for a spot of handbags. Both teams were also going head to head in the Scottish League. It was one of those seasons when those who said piously that 'Scottish football is not all about the Old Firm' had little to back up their case.

The League Cup Final was played on Sunday, 20 March on a pleasant spring day. It was close-fought and went to extra time. Both teams had been visited by senior police officers and been asked to behave. To a large extent, they did. Emilio Izaguirre of Celtic was sent off and several others were booked but the behaviour was far better than on other occasions. Rangers prevailed but it was close and could well have gone the other way, particularly if, on two occasions, the ball had gone in another direction after it had hit the post.

Steven Davis opened the scoring for Rangers in the 24th minute, then Joe Ledley equalised with a header before half-time, but as the game wore on in the second half, it was beginning to look as if Rangers were the stronger team even if they could not yet convert their pressure into goals. On the other hand, Celtic's two forwards, Georgios Samaras and Gary Hooper, were always capable of scoring, even though they did flatter to deceive on occasion. Ninety minutes came and went with no further goals, but in the 95th minute Nikica Jelavic made the decisive strike which brought the Scottish League Cup to Ibrox for the 27th time.

The teams were:

Rangers: Alexander, Whittaker, Bougherra (Hutton), Weir, Papac, Lafferty (Weiss), Davis, Edu, Wylde, Naismith, Jelavic (Diouf)

Celtic: Forster, Wilson, Rogne (Loovens), Mulgrew, Izaguirre, Brown (Ki), Kayal, Ledley, Commons (McCourt), Hooper, Samaras

Referee: C Thomson, Paisley

It was a watershed Cup Final. Rangers never looked back and went on to win the league after Celtic unaccountably blew up one night in May against their bogey team, Inverness. There was some recompense for Celtic, however, when they lifted the Scottish Cup beating Motherwell 3-0 on a rainy day in the final.

It was a watershed in a different and more ominous sense, for it was becoming less and less possible to avoid hearing the banshee noises of Rangers' creditors, particularly HMRC. Rangers, apart from a few other financial irregularities (to put it mildly), had apparently been under the delusion that they did not have to pay income tax. They managed to stave it off for a while, but Nemesis, who always punishes the wicked, arrived in a big way next Valentine's Day.

CHAPTER THIRTEEN

THE CUP GOES ROUND
2011–2013

IN THE next two years, 2012 and 2013, and again three years after that in 2016, three new names appeared on the League Cup. This was good for the competition and the game in general in Scotland in that it gave more clubs and the communities that they represented the opportunity to feel good about themselves for a short time and, by the end of the 2015/16 season, there were 15 names on the League Cup. At the start of the 2011/12 season, the trophy had now been competed for 65 times. Had it been a human it would have retired, but it was clearly still going very strong indeed. And that was despite some deplorable attendances in the early rounds.

One of the reasons for the cup going round to more clubs was the financial collapse of Rangers. In February 2012 they went into administration, but that was only the start of the story. Effectively, for several years Rangers were out of the equation when potential League Cup winners were discussed. They would get back into the Premier League eventually but the next few years were grievous ones for the supporters, and all their sufferings were rendered more acute by the realisation that the serious and potentially fatal wounds were all self-inflicted. Yet it was still possible to feel sorry for their supporters.

It was a shame, one often felt, that the first-round games of the Scottish League Cup attracted so little attention. They were played at the wrong time of the year with people still on holiday or still playing cricket or golf and, as these ties did not involve the well-supported clubs, they were poorly attended and did not feature highly in the press or TV. The biggest crowd in the first-round in 2011/12 was the southern derby between Queen of the South and Stranraer with 1,511 (a hard-fought 2-1 win for the Doonhamers), and the only other game that reached four figures was Partick Thistle's surprise 1-3 defeat to Berwick Rangers at Firhill where 1,255 witnessed a rather feisty encounter which involved three red cards.

Elsewhere there were plenty of goals. Livingston put six past Arbroath, Airdrie United put five past Stirling Albion, Dundee won 4-0 at Dumbarton and Raith Rovers 4-1 at Montrose. Brechin City and Clyde served up a six-goal thriller at Glebe Park with four of the goals coming in extra time and the Bully Wee winning through 4-2. There was a similar scoreline at Albion Rovers where Falkirk triumphed and the only game of the 15 (only the top 12 of last year's league placings were exempt this year) was Cowdenbeath v Stenhousemuir where the visitors triumphed 4-1.

In the second round, some old friends met. Aberdeen's failure to make it to Europe meant they were playing at this early stage and they were drawn against Dundee at Pittodrie.

This fixture, which in another age might have seen long queues and closed turnstiles, drew only 5,722, who saw an insipid game in which the Dons triumphed 1-0. There was a thriller of a Renfrewshire derby where St Mirren triumphed 4-3 at Cappielow and a Fife derby where East Fife beat Dunfermline 2-1 – one wonders how many of the 1,262 crowd were aware that they were witnessing a rerun of the Scottish League Cup Final of 1949/50?

The other Fife team, Raith Rovers, lost 0-2 at Airdrie United. Hibs comfortably beat Berwick Rangers 5-0, Motherwell beat Clyde 4-0 at Broadwood and St Johnstone beat Livingston 3-0. Ayr United pulled off a mini giant-killing when they beat Inverness Caledonian Thistle (then in the Premier League) 1-0; the other Highlanders, Ross County, did better, winning 2-1 at Hamilton. Queen of the South beat Forfar 3-0 and, in the Central derby, Falkirk beat their neighbours Stenhousemuir 3-1.

It was the third round in mid-September which produced a great deal of action, surprise and drama. East Fife had their best result in many years when they travelled to Pittodrie and put Aberdeen out of the League Cup. Admittedly, it was on a penalty shoot-out, but Aberdeen had been lucky to get that far, needing a late goal from substitute Rory Fallon to keep them in the game after a performance which an Aberdeen supporters' website tactfully described as 'disjointed'. The fans at the game were rather more forthright. Falkirk added to the many woes of Rangers (now ceaselessly trumpeted with something approaching glee in newspapers which Rangers supporters used to consider to be their friends) by beating them at the Falkirk Stadium with a late goal from Mark Millar to make it 3-2 after Rangers had seemed to rescue themselves by pulling back a 0-2 deficit. A win for Rangers might just have allowed them to temporarily ward off the evil hour that was now approaching.

Hearts also bit the dust at this stage, losing to Ayr United at Somerset Park 4-1 on penalties after 120 minutes in which both teams might have added to the 1-1 scoreline. Hibs and Motherwell also served up a cracker at Fir Park with Hibs scoring first and last in a 2-2 draw before eventually winning 7-6 on penalties in which goalkeeper Mark Brown saved twice in the shoot-out. More mundanely and predictably, Celtic beat Ross County 2-0 in Dingwall and Dundee United beat Airdrie United by the same score, but the best performance of the round was Kilmarnock's 5-0 win over Queen of the South.

The quarter-finals saw two good results for Ayrshire, an area of Scotland where one often feels there is a degree of underperformance now and again. Not on 25 October 2011, however, where Kilmarnock, experiencing a not particularly impressive league season under Kenny Shields, beat East Fife 2-0 with two late goals from Mohamadu Sissoko and Gary Harkins, East Fife's cause not helped by the dismissal of Robert Ogleby who managed to pick up two yellow cards before half-time. The Honest Men of Ayr went to Paisley and won 1-0 thanks to a late header from Chris Smith after an intriguing battle between the two sides. It was Ayr's second giant-killing of the competition and eyebrows were duly raised, but their supporters looked in vain for a sustained improvement in their league form!

A thriller at Tannadice saw 1-1 at full time, 2-2 at extra time and a 5-4 win for Falkirk on penalties. These statistics did scant justice to a great game which was effectively another giant-killing for Falkirk. Dundee United were left kicking themselves for their profligacy of chances in the 90 minutes, and poor Willo Flood was the only man who missed out on the spot kicks. Poor Willo had been there before, of course, in the semi-final of 2009. On the following night, the game that was billed as the tie of the round turned out to be rather one-sided as Hibs, although leading 1-0 at half-time to an own goal, flopped badly in the second half in the face of a rampant Celtic attack who scored four times.

And so to the semi-finals after the New Year. Kilmarnock, Ayr United and Falkirk all wanted to avoid Celtic but Falkirk were the unlucky ones, meaning there would be an Ayrshire derby in the semi-final. Discussion took place about where the said Ayrshire derby would take place but Hampden, in this case, was as sensible a venue as any and 25,067 joined the Ayrshire exodus to Glasgow on Saturday, 28 January. They saw a frustrating game as Ayr set out to defend and to rely on a breakaway or to take their chances on penalties. It almost worked as well, for Ayr goalkeeper Kevin Cuthbert was in fine form and kept Killie at bay until the 109th minute when Dean Shields, son of manager Kenny Shields, put Kilmarnock into their sixth League Cup Final. They had lost all five previous ones to Dundee, Rangers, Hearts, Celtic and Hibs.

The other semi-final was more predictable, for although Falkirk's Jay Fulton equalised Scott Brown's penalty before half-time, Celtic stepped up a gear and Anthony Stokes, a Falkirk old boy but now playing for Celtic, scored twice to set up a repeat of the League Cup Final of 2001. On that occasion Celtic won 3-0 over Kilmarnock. Most people would have expected a similar result in 2012. They were wrong.

The final was played at Hampden on 18 March. The authorities seemed to think that there was a colour clash again so Celtic wore a variation of their normal green and white and Kilmarnock played in yellow.

The weather was good once again. Celtic's forward line misfired several times in the first half and were little better in the second half, having no success against the inspired Cammy Bell in the Killie goal. Kilmarnock fought hard but most of their supporters were reconciled to eventual defeat or extra time and nerve-wracking penalty kicks. But then an obscure character from Belgium, Dieter Van Tornhout, headed home a cross from Lee Johnson in the 84th minute to put Killie ahead. Celtic fought back and might have had a penalty, but referee Willie Collum decided that Anthony Stokes had dived. Soon afterwards he blew for time to signal the first triumph of Kilmarnock in the Scottish League Cup.

Few people could grudge Killie, that grossly under-supported team, their moment in the sun, but there was tragedy as well, particularly for Kilmarnock's Liam Kelly. His father, who was at Hampden that day, died immediately after the final whistle so celebrations were muted. Ironically, both father and son were both Celtic supporters and Celtic were not slow to offer their commiserations. But the League Cup went to Ayrshire for the first time in its 66-year existence.

The teams were:

Kilmarnock: Bell, Fowler, Sissoko (Kroca), Nelson, Gordon, Kelly, Buijs (Johnson), Harkins (Van Tornhout), Hay, Shiels, Heffernan

Celtic: Forster, Matthews, Rogne (Ki), Wilson, Mulgrew, Forrest, Wanyama, Brown, Ledley (Commons), Stokes, Hooper (Samaras)

Referee: W Collum, Glasgow

It was a blow for Celtic but they had ample recompense the next time they met Kilmarnock when they travelled to Rugby Park to win 6-0 and clinch the Scottish Premier League. The Scottish Cup that year would be an all-Edinburgh affair won 5-1 by Hearts; 2012 would also be the year in which Rangers disappeared in their current form.

The demise of Rangers, who went into administration on 14 February 2012, had all sorts of implications. Amidst all the gloating and tee-heeing that went on throughout Scottish football at the getting of their just desserts, there was the serious point that Rangers (or Sevco or Newco, call them what you will) would not be playing in the top tier of Scottish football. Cynics suspected that there would be a rallying round of old pals to save them, but Rangers had few pals. They had antagonised Motherwell, Dundee United, Hibs, Aberdeen to name but a few – Celtic remained aloof and lukewarm – and they were duly demoted to the bottom tier. Their humiliation was complete and, for the Scottish League Cup of 2012/13, Rangers would be playing in the first round.

It was, however, a very different Rangers. Many of their players, who used to make statements about loving the club, who kissed the jersey and celebrated so vociferously when things went well, disappeared with their agents like snow off a dyke when the money was no longer there. It was a new young team who took the field to play East Fife on Tuesday, 7 August

2012 and 38,160 saw them win 4-0, the size of the crowd at least saying something about their continuing support.

Most of the other games had been played a week earlier. Livingston beat Stranraer 8-0 at Stair Park and Ayr United beat Clyde 6-1. The best game was a thriller at Stark's Park won 4-3 by Raith Rovers over Berwick Rangers, but there was also a close game at Hampden Park where Queen's Park needed extra time to beat Airdrie United 3-2 and Dundee had a close call at Peterhead where they won 4-1 on penalties after a dire 0-0 draw over the 120 minutes.

Rangers made further progress in the second round when they dumped Falkirk 3-0. It would have been a particular source of satisfaction to manager Ally McCoist, one imagines, for it was Falkirk who beat them last year when a victory for Rangers might at least have led to a stay of execution. Aberdeen needed extra time to beat Morton 2-0 at Cappielow while Stenhousemuir, whose moments of glory have been few and far between, beat Kilmarnock 2-1 at Rugby Park. It was better than it sounded, for Killie's goal came in the 90th minute long after their fans had gone home. Thus Stenhousemuir put out the holders of the trophy – not a sentence that one is likely to write very often!

Giant-killing was a feature of the second round. Hibs broke the hearts of their supporters when they lost 0-2 to Queen of the South. Technically, Raith Rovers' 4-1 win over Ross County at Dingwall was an act of giant-killing because Ross County were in the Premier League. An even more stunning act of technical giant-killing occurred at Hampden Park where 707 people saw bottom-tier Queen's Park win 2-1 over Dundee, who had been promoted at the last minute to the SPL to take the place of Rangers. Inverness Caledonian

Thistle and St Mirren won, St Mirren being particularly impressive with a 5-1 win over Ayr United, a team who had done well in recent years. Dunfermline Athletic, Livingston and Hamilton Accies also reached the third round.

The third round saw fewer shocks, although several of the more-fancied teams had to work hard to get through. Once again, pride of place went to Stenhousemuir who held Inverness to a 1-1 draw at Ochilview before losing 6-5 on penalties. Dunfermline Athletic had hard luck against Aberdeen who were heavily indebted to goalkeeper Jamie Langfield for many great saves before Scott Vernon scored for the Dons at the very death. It was also a 90th-minute goal from Lee Mair that saw St Mirren through against Hamilton Accies and Dundee United's first-half goal from Johnnie Russell was enough to see them through a difficult game at Palmerston against Queen of the South. More predictably, Celtic beat Raith Rovers 4-1, St Johnstone beat Queen's Park 4-1 and Hearts beat Livingston 3-1, while Rangers' beating of Motherwell 2-0 was only an act of giant-killing in the most pedantic sense of the word. It was more like the wounded (but not yet dead) giant rousing himself for an act of revenge. Rangers supporters in the 29,413 crowd were particularly delighted to see their team beat Motherwell, for Motherwell had, perhaps surprisingly, been one of the clubs who had worked hard to see them demoted and humiliated.

Rangers fell in the quarter-final. The desertion by so many of their stars in pursuit of more money, plus the ongoing uncertainty of the future of the club, had its effect. Inverness came to town and were always on top, winning 3-0, with goals from Andrew Shinnie, Graeme Shinnie and Gary Warren being enough to beat a dispirited Ibrox side. At

Parkhead, Celtic beat St Johnstone in a surprisingly one-sided 5-0 hammering, but the other two game were exciting ones which went to penalties, the away side winning in each case, St Mirren at Pittodrie and Hearts at Tannadice. At Pittodrie, Aberdeen had scored in the 90th minute but their comeback was in vain, while the Tannadice game was not without its incidents with Darren Barr of Hearts earning a red card.

The first semi-final was played at Easter Road on Saturday, 26 January 2013 between Hearts and Inverness and the choice of Easter Road was a wise one, for although Hearts supporters quite clearly outnumbered Caley ones (as one would have expected in the city of Edinburgh) the atmosphere was good. The game was tough and quite even. Andrew Shinnie scored for the Highlanders just after half-time but Michael Ngoo equalised. Several chances were missed at both ends, Scott Robinson of Hearts was red-carded with several others of both teams lucky to avoid a similar fate, and the game went to extra time and penalties. Nine out of the ten were scored but, with the last of the statutory ten, poor Philip Roberts of Inverness blazed over the bar and Hearts were now in their seventh League Cup Final.

The following day saw a seismic shock as St Mirren eliminated Celtic 3-2 at Hampden. Both managers were called Lennon, but on this occasion Danny of St Mirren won over Neil of Celtic. New signing Esmael Goncalves from Portugal scored early for St Mirren, Celtic equalised through Gary Hooper just on half-time, then in the second half referee Willie Collum awarded a penalty for each side for handball in the box. Both decisions were debatable, but Charlie Mulgrew missed his penalty for Celtic whereas Paul McGowan scored his for St Mirren. Steven Thompson scored a great goal for

St Mirren to make it 3-1 and, although Celtic scored a late, irrelevant consolation goal at the end, the Buddies were through to what was (surprisingly for a team which had such a good record in the Scottish Cup) only their third League Cup Final.

Hearts had won the tournament four times and St Mirren not at all. There was not much to choose between the two of them on league form – they were both struggling – but St Mirren had beaten Hearts 2-0 in Paisley three weeks before and for this reason the Saints were the favourites. On the other hand, Hearts were still the holders of the Scottish Cup so they knew how to win at Hampden. The game, played on Sunday, 17 March 2013, turned out to be one of the better League Cup finals.

A feature of the play was the excellent goals scored. Ryan Stevenson scored first and last for Hearts but, unfortunately for the Edinburgh men, St Mirren scored three in between. They came from Esmael Concalves, Steven Thompson and another newcomer to the club, Conor Newton, on loan from Newcastle United, who scored arguably the best of the lot.

Hearts had a lot to be proud about. For a spell in the first half they were well on top and really should have scored more goals. Their late fightback, after they had been virtually outplayed for a spell in the second half, made for fascinating watching, but it was not to be for them. The day belonged to St Mirren, a team which existed on a slim financial budget (as witnessed by the number of players with them on loan) and whose average gate was less than 5,000. They had been unable to fill their end at Hampden but they still had more supporters than came to a home game. The club would have been entitled to ask the fans where they went to every

Saturday. All this made the achievement of Danny Lennon and his men all the more praiseworthy.

The teams were:

St Mirren: Samson, Van Zenten, McAusland, Goodwin, Dummett, Teale, McGowan, Newton, McGinn (Carey), Thompson (Parkin), Goncalves (Mair)

Hearts: MacDonald, McGowan, Webster, Wilson, McHattie, Stevenson, Barr (Holt), Taouil (Carrick), Walker (Novicovas), Ngoo, Sutton

Referee: C Thomson, Paisley

From Kilmarnock in 2012 to St Mirren in 2013, and in 2014 the League Cup was destined to go in a different direction altogether, one which it should have gone a lot more often than it did. The direction was north. In the meantime, there was a touch of the same old story when Celtic won both the Scottish League and the Scottish Cup in 2013.

The 2013/14 campaign opened with glory for Forfar Athletic. They achieved something they had long promised to do: namely, beat Rangers. Many times had the paths of these two teams crossed in the League Cup and the Scottish Cup and the Loons always had bad luck. However, on a bright sunny but windy day at Station Park, Gavin Swankie scored twice (once in extra time) to win the day for Forfar. So far had Rangers fallen that it didn't even rate headline news. Two teams hit six. Raith Rovers beat Queen's Park 6-0 and Morton won 6-2 at East Fife, while Cowdenbeath won 5-0 at Berwick. In a tight Angus derby, Montrose edged it past Arbroath at Gayfield 1-0, while there were two thrilling 4-3 games, Airdrie beating Stenhousemuir and Stranraer apparently coasting 4-0 over Brechin until Brechin fought back to score three times and almost take the game to extra time.

In the second round, Forfar's reward for their defeat of Rangers was a trip to near-neighbours Dundee at Dens Park. It looked as if they might triumph again when they were 1-0 up at half-time with a penalty scored by Iain Campbell (son of outspoken manager Dick Campbell) but Jim McAlister equalised in regulation time and then, heartbreakingly, Peter MacDonald scored for Dundee in the 120th minute. Aberdeen persisted in their habit of making life difficult for their fans. Derek McInnes was now in charge but the game against Alloa was an insipid one with, if anything, Alloa looking the more likely to score before the Dons edged it 6-5 on penalties. Another game that went to penalties was at Stark's Park, Kirkcaldy where Hearts beat Raith Rovers 5-4 after a 1-1 draw. Dundee United left it late at Dumbarton, while Partick Thistle needed extra time to beat Cowdenbeath.

St Mirren's tenure of the Scottish League Cup turned out to be a very short one as they went down to Queen of the South 2-1 at Palmerston Park after extra time. This was in no way surprising given their form in league games since they had won the League Cup. The Doonhamers were the better team throughout the 90 minutes but, when Steven Thompson put the Buddies ahead in the 95th minute (only two minutes after St Mirren had missed a penalty), it looked as if they would prevail until Stephen McKenna and Michael Paton scored two great goals to win the game for Queen of the South.

The cup winners of two years ago, Kilmarnock, also failed to progress, losing to Hamilton 0-1. Falkirk beat Dunfermline Athletic 2-1, Livingston beat Airdrie 2-0, Morton beat Montrose 4-0 and, in another technical giant-killing, Stranraer beat Ross County 3-2 at Stair Park. Even the hardest-hearted of supporters would have to sympathise with Ross County, who had to face that appallingly long journey home to Dingwall on a Tuesday night. One wonders what time they arrived back? How many supporters did they have with them?

The third round on 24 September contained one major shock when Morton came to Celtic Park and won 1-0. It was fairly inexplicable, for Celtic had started the league well, but it was a night that their foreign flops Derk Boerrigter and Teemu Pukki failed once again and their dysfunctional forwards simply could not score against a tight Morton defence. Then, in extra time, Dougie Imrie slotted home a penalty given for handball to prove yet again that the Scottish League Cup is Celtic's least-favourite domestic trophy. That night also saw wins for Inverness and St Johnstone while Hibs and Stranraer entertained the fans at Easter Road with eight goals, Hibs winning 5-3.

The following night at Falkirk, Aberdeen at last hit form. Possibly buoyed up by the news of Celtic's defeat and therefore sniffing silverware, they really turned it on by beating the home side 5-0, Scott Vernon hitting a hat-trick. Dundee United also showed a welcome return to form in the League Cup with a 4-1 win over Partick Thistle at Tannadice, David Goodwillie being the hat-trick hero there; Motherwell edged home against Livingston at Almondvale, while Hearts continued being experts on the penalty spot. Last round, they beat Raith Rovers by this method. This time, it was Queen of the South.

The game at Tynecastle attracted 8,381 spectators and was a cracker with Queen of the South distinctly unlucky not to win in the 90 minutes. It was 2-2 at that point, but one of Hearts' goals had been a dubious penalty. Both teams scored in extra time, the game went to what Queen of the South's manager Jim McIntyre called 'the lottery of penalties', and Hearts won 4-2.

Their reward was a quarter-final clash against Hibs at Easter Road. Such games are always good, even for neutrals, with the word 'feisty' predictably employed – sometimes ad nauseam – and this one was no exception. It was a remarkable game in many ways. Hearts were by some distance clear at the bottom of the league and in the throes of one of their sadly recurrent financial crises, but they won this game 1-0 despite constant Hibs pressure. Goalkeeper Jamie McDonald was in superb form and Ryan Stevenson scored a cracker from well outside the box. In the latter stages, what little chance Hibs had disappeared when captain James McPake saw red for a two-footed lunge. It was one of the many frustrating nights for a Hibs supporter. But it was indeed a 'feisty' encounter.

There was excitement elsewhere as well with late goals being a feature. It was the 120th minute before Inverness Caledonian Thistle got their winner over Dundee United at Tannadice, the 90th minute before St Johnstone scored to sink gallant Morton at Cappielow, and Aberdeen pulled off one of their best performances in recent years to beat Motherwell at Fir Park. They had lost Joe Shaughnessy to a red card in the first 15 minutes thanks to a silly but not vicious tackle and held out against some desperate Motherwell pressure for the rest of the game, but then scored twice in the last ten minutes through Andrew Considine and Jonny Hayes to put themselves into the semi-final.

The semi-final, played at Tynecastle, between Aberdeen and St Johnstone on 1 February 2014, was surprisingly one-sided as the Dons simply took charge from the start with Jonny Hayes scoring in the third minute and in the 79th, and Peter Pawlett and Adam Rooney also finding the net in what was a rout. Aberdeen's supporters, who had possibly suffered more than most in recent years, left Edinburgh that day in joyous mood looking forward to their first national cup final since 2000. Things were apparently reviving in the north-east.

Their opponents would be Inverness. The Easter Road semi-final between the Highlanders and Hearts must go down as one of the most entertaining games in the history of this tournament. Inverness, having gone ahead with a great goal from Greg Tansey, tried to commit suicide by having two men sent off, lost two goals to Jamie Hamill but then fought back to equalise at the death of 90 minutes. They then held out 9 v 11 for 30 minutes of extra time and Hearts, who had twice won games in this year's tournament on penalty shoot-outs, were less successful this time. Inverness were through to their first-ever national cup final but what a painful experience that must have been for the lovers of the Jambos. The Highland fans sang, 'Nine men beat the Hearts, na, na, nanana, na!'

The League Cup final was played at Celtic Park on Sunday, 16 March 2014 because Hampden was under reconstruction for the Commonwealth Games to be held that summer. Celtic Park, in some ways a better stadium than Hampden, did a perfect job for a final that excited and interested the nation in its build-up at least, if not the game itself. Inverness were impressive and, being new boys, were keen to lift their first trophy. Aberdeen, who had not exactly set the North Sea oil rigs on fire with their performances in the 21st century, were chasing their first trophy since they won the League Cup in 1995/96, some 19 years before. Aberdeen were able to sell an astonishing 43,000 tickets and might have taken more but their request was turned down on safety grounds because it would have involved them sitting in the tier above Inverness supporters where missiles might have been dropped. Sadly, the Aberdeen support, like every other team, did contain a few boneheads who could have done exactly that.

The teams were:

Aberdeen: Langfield, Logan, Anderson, Reynolds, Considine (Vernon), Robson, Flood, Jack, Hayes (Smith, Low), McGinn, Rooney

Inverness Caledonian Thistle: Brill, Raven, Meekings, Devine, Shinnie, Watkins (Ross), Draper, Foran (Christie), Tansey, Vincent (Doran), McKay

Referee: S McLean, Glasgow

To put it tactfully, one would have to say that the first 90 minutes and extra time were competitive but goalless. Less charitable observers (including the supporters of both teams) were less kind in their assessment with the occasion which clearly meant so much to both sides and got the better of quite a few of the players. Aberdeen possibly had the balance of chances over the 120 minutes, but one never got the impression that anyone was going to score.

And so to penalties. Inverness's first two from Billy McKay and Greg Tansey were shockers and all Aberdeen had to do was hold their nerve. It fell to Adam Rooney to sink the final one and give Aberdeen the Scottish League Cup for the sixth time and to get the ghost of Alex Ferguson and the great team of the 1980s off their shoulders at last. Yet they did not convince all their supporters – one of them loudly proclaiming, 'Aa' that proves it that they can tak penalties better than Inverness. It disnae mak them a guid team!'

Nevertheless, a new era seemed to beckon for Aberdeen. They were still in the Scottish Cup, but St Johnstone would end up winning that Scottish Cup, and Celtic won the Scottish League for the third year in a row.

CHAPTER FOURTEEN

CELTIC REASSERT
2014–2021

FOR REASONS never satisfactorily explained, Neil Lennon left Celtic for the first time in summer 2014 and was replaced by an unknown Norwegian called Ronnie Deila. Summer 2014 saw the very successful Commonwealth Games held in Glasgow and the Scottish League Cup began as usual and on time, but without any great fanfare. Most games were played on 2 August, but one game had to be delayed until 26 August, the same night some of the second-round games were being played. This was Queen's Park v Rangers, postponed because of the Commonwealth Games. Hampden was unavailable and the game was eventually played in an unreal atmosphere at the Shyberry Excelsior Stadium, Airdrie, and won 2-1 by Rangers.

Earlier, there had been few shocks, although Stenhousemuir had lived up to last season's reputation by beating Airdrie 3-1. The best game of the round was at Stark's Park, Kirkcaldy where Raith Rovers beat Forfar Athletic 4-2 after extra time.

Dunfermline Athletic beat Annan Athletic 5-2, Dundee beat Peterhead 4-0 and Queen of the South put five past Elgin City at Palmerston Park. Two former winners had varying fortunes. Livingston beat Albion Rovers on penalty kicks whereas East Fife returned from the long journey to Stranraer with a 1-0 defeat.

Both Edinburgh teams had narrow escapes in the second round. Neither side were doing well. They had both been relegated and there was a distinct lack of credibility about Edinburgh football, and yet it was only two years since they had contested the Scottish Cup Final. Football in Edinburgh can be strange sometimes! Dumbarton were 2-0 up at Easter Road and some of the weaker Hibs brethren were heading for the pub bemoaning life when El Alagui pulled one back. He scored again, and right on the final whistle Sam Stanton (no apparent relation to the illustrious Pat of bygone days) grabbed the winner. Hearts were not a great deal better at Stenhousemuir but managed to hold off the Warriors and win 2-1.

The second round was remarkable in that eight of the 11 ties were decided by the odd goal – the winners being Hearts, Hibs, Rangers (who beat Inverness 1-0), Ross County, St Mirren, Livingston, Kilmarnock (1-0 over Ayr in a thrilling Ayrshire derby) and Partick Thistle. More comfortable wins were recorded by Dundee, who beat Raith Rovers 4-0, and Hamilton, who beat Alloa 4-1. The game between Falkirk and Cowdenbeath, on the other hand, went to penalties after 120 minutes of a lacklustre 0-0 draw and Falkirk won 4-3 on penalty kicks.

The third round took place on the midweek of 23/24 September 2014. Five games were played on the Tuesday night. Holders Aberdeen, now playing with a great deal more confidence than in recent years, beat Livingston comfortably 4-0, and Rangers delighted their fans with a 3-1 win at Falkirk. St Johnstone won 1-0 at Kilmarnock and Partick Thistle beat St Mirren by the same score at Firhill although they needed extra time to do so, while Hibs travelled up to Ross County to win 2-0 in what was technically a giant-killing given the respective divisions in which the teams were currently playing. Hibs finished the game without the services of Dylan McGeouch who was sent off when the game was already more or less won thanks to two first-half goals from Dominique Malonga.

The highlights on the Wednesday night were two derbies, one in Dundee and one in Lanarkshire. On Tayside, United had won 4-1 over Dundee at the weekend in the league, but this was a different game in which Dundee, playing for most of the game without the red-carded Martin Boyle, worked hard, missed a penalty and could not score. A glorious header scored by Jaroslaw Fojut from a corner kick in the last minute won the game for Dundee United. Red cards were also in evidence at New Douglas Park, Hamilton in the feisty Lanarkshire derby but the Accies triumphed 6-5 on penalties. There was less drama at Celtic Park where Celtic beat a poor Hearts side 3-0 with a degree of ease.

The quarter-finals, played on the last midweek of October, saw an impressive 6-0 win for Celtic over Partick Thistle in which John Guidetti scored a hat-trick, but the other games were a great deal closer. Adam Rooney, with a diving header in the first half, scored the only goal of the game at Pittodrie where Aberdeen beat Hamilton Accies. At Ibrox, before a small crowd of 13,023 (many Rangers supporters were unhappy about the way their new club was being run), St Johnstone missed quite a few chances before Lewis MacLeod won the game for Rangers with a late header.

The best game for the spectators was at Easter Road. Three times a young Dundee United side went ahead and three times Hibs equalised. All this in the 90 minutes! Extra time was less enthralling because the two teams were exhausted. The penalty shoot-out was a real drama with Dundee United winning 7-6 on penalties after United's goalkeeping hero Radoslaw Cierzniak saved twice from Matthew Kennedy and David Gray. It was a great game of football and even the defeated Hibs fans clapped their men off the park, more proud of them in defeat than on many occasions when they had played worse and achieved a better result.

There was a large talking point about the semi-finals which were played on the last day of January and the first day of February 2015. The Hampden Park pitch, not for the first time in its history, was awful. It had never recovered from the Commonwealth Games and other events that took place there (the very least of which was Queen's Park's home games) and some players and commentators were quite happy to use words like 'dangerous' to describe it. Be that as it may, there was no change of venue for either semi-final.

The New Firm semi-final between Dundee United and Aberdeen went ahead on Saturday. Games between these two are seldom thrillers and this one certainly wasn't, but Dundee United reached the final with a late header from Nadir Ciftci. This followed a strange goal at the start of the second half from debutant Donervon Daniels of Aberdeen which one had to watch several times before realising that he had headed it on from Andrew Considine's long throw-in.

This goal brightened the game up and Callum Morris headed home a corner kick from Gary Mackay-Steven to level things before Ciftci put Dundee United into their seventh League Cup Final.

It was confidently expected that Celtic would win the other semi-final against the much-diminished Rangers and that was exactly what happened. It was the first Old Firm game for almost two years, although Celtic supporters were at pains to point out that this was not the real Rangers, who had died in 2012 and been replaced by 'Newco' or 'Sevco'. Leigh Griffiths and Kris Commons scored good goals in the first half and Celtic's 2-0 victory margin was a lot less than it should have been, for Celtic were on top throughout as they reached their 30th Scottish League Cup Final. The pitch was indeed dreadful, but did not really affect the result of either game, and it would be re-laid before the League Cup Final on 15 March, the Ides of March.

But before that happened, Dundee United committed a spectacular and barely believable act of suicide, selling their two best players – Stuart Armstrong and Gary Mackay-Steven – not to an English or European team (which would have been bad enough) but to their League Cup Final opponents Celtic! The two players could not play for Celtic in the final because they were cup-tied, but they might have made a difference had they still been with Dundee United. The sale could not be justified on any grounds other than naked money-grubbing and the wonder is that Dundee United's supporters stayed with them. Both the team and fans did suffer. When Dundee United were relegated in 2016, it was a self-inflicted blow.

The final was predictable. The pitch was a great deal better in comparison with the semi-finals but the day, although pleasant enough, lacked the sunshine that often graced the occasion. Kris Commons scored for Celtic in the first half. Dundee United might have had a penalty when Scott Brown barged Ryan Dow, but then Sean Dillon was sent off for a horrendous tackle on Emilio Izaguirre and, with time running out, James Forrest put Celtic two up. 'Jamesie' then made a bit of a fool of himself when Celtic were awarded a penalty kick. He demanded the ball, took the kick and fired it straight at the goalkeeper. Not that it really mattered, though, for Celtic had more or less already won their 15th Scottish League Cup. It was Ronnie Deila's first trophy for Celtic and it was believed that this was the first step towards an inevitable treble. Celtic did win the Scottish League a few weeks later but they lost the Scottish Cup to Inverness Caledonian Thistle in a semi-final which was controversial, to put it mildly.

The teams were:

Celtic: Gordon, Ambrose, Denayer, Van Dijk, Izaguirre, Bitton (Henderson), Brown, Commons (Forrest), Johansen, Stokes, Griffiths (Guidetti)

Dundee United: Cierzniak, Dillon, Morris, Fojut, Dixon, McGowan, Butcher, Paton (Erskine), Dow, Rankin, Bilate (Anier)

Referee: R Madden, Glasgow

It was odd to see the two Edinburgh giants in the first round of the 2015/16 League Cup. In an even odder turn of events, they found themselves playing the two Angus teams, Arbroath and Montrose, at home: Hearts winning 4-2 and Hibs 3-0. The other Angus teams had mixed fortunes, Brechin losing to Ayr United but Forfar winning 2-0 against Queen's Park at Hampden Park. The south of Scotland derby between Annan

Athletic and Queen of the South turned out to be a thrilling affair, finishing 3-3 at 90 minutes before Derek Lyle finished the job in extra time. Berwick also needed extra time before they could get the better of Alloa Athletic.

Three games were played in Fife. Dunfermline Athletic beat Cowdenbeath 5-1 and Raith Rovers beat the other Rovers, Albion Rovers 3-0, with a degree of comfort. East Fife needed penalties to beat Dumbarton. There were two 5-0 wins, Falkirk beating East Stirlingshire and Morton beating Elgin City. Rangers, who had lost a play-off last May and were still not back in the Premier League, beat Peterhead 3-0. There were also wins for Livingston, Airdrie and Stranraer.

The second round saw some very close calls with only Rangers, Motherwell, Dunfermline, Kilmarnock and Ross County winning by more than one goal. Forfar Athletic had bad luck against Hearts at Station Park. Veteran goalkeeper Rab Douglas was in inspired form and Forfar took the Edinburgh men to extra time before losing a late goal and finishing the game with nine men, having lost two to an overzealous referee. Hibs were similarly fortunate to beat Stranraer at home, needing an own goal to do so, before their own disgruntled fans. Both Partick Thistle and Queen of the South went down 0-1 at home, Thistle to Falkirk and Queens to Morton. The best game for the spectators was at St Mirren Park where Livingston edged home 3-2. At Stark's Park, Raith Rovers beat Hamilton Accies 2-1 in another tight match.

The high-fliers of the third round were Ross County, who delighted their fans and surprised the rest of Scotland by beating Falkirk 7-0 at Victoria Park, but the big shock (if it could be called that) was St Johnstone's 3-1 win over Rangers at Ibrox. In a televised game, St Johnstone scored their three goals before half-time and, although Rangers pulled one back, there was no sustained fightback and the Perth men earned a rare win at Ibrox. The other half of the Old Firm had fewer problems in beating Raith Rovers 2-0 in a rather mundane game (although it was late before Celtic got their second goal) and Inverness beat Livingston by a similar score.

The city of Edinburgh did well in this round, both teams leaving it late. Hibs v Aberdeen at Easter Road is usually an interesting clash, and this one was no exception with the game delicately balanced until the last ten minutes when Jason Cummings and Dominique Malonga scored for Hibs. Hearts were involved in a thriller at Rugby Park. Kilmarnock's 80th-minute goal from Josh Magennis looked enough to settle the tie, but then Hearts managed to score twice at the death, the first from Juanma Delgado on the 90th-minute mark, then Sam Nicholson scored another following a Delgado miskick. It was a shame that only 3,249 were there to watch it.

The other games, also watched by pitiful attendances, went to extra time. At Tannadice, Michael Paton of Dunfermline Athletic scored first but Dundee United, although equalising before half-time through Callum Morris, could not force a win until extra time when Scott Fraser and Blair Spittal did the job for them. And there was real drama at Morton as well. It was 1-1 at 90 minutes and all the action came in the second half of extra time, Alec Samuel and Michael Tidser scoring for the home side with Louis Moult's late goal not being enough for Motherwell. This game also saw an unwelcome throwback to less civilised times as some Motherwell fans saw fit to clash with the police for a reason not immediately apparent to anyone capable of rational thought.

A Highland derby was a feature of the quarter-final draw and it was a good one too, with Ross County just getting the better of Inverness Caledonian Thistle at Victoria Park in spite of a late Caley fightback. St Johnstone continued their winning ways with a 3-1 win at Morton even though Morton scored first. The biggest game of the round (even though it drew only a small crowd of 11,598 to Tynecastle) saw Celtic beat Hearts 2-1 with all the goals coming late and Hearts' goal scored by Arnaud Djoum on the final whistle after Leigh Griffiths and Tommy Rogic had scored for Celtic.

A week later (so as not to clash with the Hearts game) Hibs took on Dundee United. Dundee United, now clearly on the slide and suffering from their self-inflicted asset-stripping of last year, went down 0-3 to a slick and professional Hibs team who scored through David Gray, Jason Cummings (with a penalty) and Lewis Stevenson to put Hibs into the semi-finals. They would be paired with St Johnstone while Celtic faced Ross County.

Hibs took on St Johnstone at Tynecastle on 30 January, a bitterly cold day with snow in the air; 16,971 was more than they would have got at Hampden and they saw a hard-fought game, which was perhaps a little lacking in the niceties of football. Hibs went ahead through a debatable penalty where contact seemed minimal and accidental, but Mr McLean said it was a penalty and Jason Cummings did the needful. Hibs, however, did not stay long in the lead for Joe Shaughnessy headed an equaliser five minutes later. It stayed level until the 74th minute when the fast-developing and impressive John McGinn rifled home a fine winner. St Johnstone were unlucky to lose but Hibs were not lucky to win and their fans went home across the city from Tynecastle in rare fine fettle that cold January day.

The weather was still cold the following day at Hampden, but at least the rain and the sleet stayed away. Ross County had beaten Celtic before at a semi-final stage in the Scottish Cup of 2010, but hardly anyone expected them to win this time. Celtic scored in the first minute through Gary Mackay-Steven but referee Craig Thomson, in one of his less explicable decisions, awarded Ross County a penalty kick and sent Efe Ambrose off after what looked like accidental contact. Ross never looked back after scoring the penalty through Martin Woods and deservedly won the game, scoring twice in the second half through Paul Quinn and Alex Schalk, even though Mr Thomson, in what seemed like a balancing exercise, also awarded Celtic a soft penalty. Sadly for their fans, Leigh Griffiths missed it. It was a fine day for Jim McIntyre and his Highlanders, but more and more questions were now being asked about Celtic's manager Ronnie Deila. It was not Craig Thomson's finest hour either.

The League Cup Final played on Sunday, 13 March, turned out to be unlucky for Hibs. They were not in a rich vein of form as they tried to get themselves back into the Premier League and there often seemed to be a death wish hanging over them as far as Hampden cup finals and semi-finals were concerned. On the other hand, they had won the trophy three times as distinct from Ross County whose first League Cup Final this was.

There were still a few empty seats, but 38,796 turned up to watch. The game started brightly enough for Hibs but it was Michael Gardyne who put the Staggies on top when he was put through after Hibs had failed to clear the ball from the middle of the park. Just on half-time, Hibs equalised. It was Liam Fontaine who picked up a ball just inside the penalty box and was able to turn and fire home to make it all square.

It was the same Liam Fontaine who also felt responsible for Hibs losing the cup at the end of the second half. After 45 minutes where goals might have been scored at either end, Michael Gardyne made ground down the left and crossed. Poor Liam Fontaine couldn't get enough on it and ended up putting the ball right in front of Michael Schalk who could hardly miss. Even then Hibs had time to put a little pressure on the Ross defence and force their on-loan goalkeeper Gary Woods to tip the ball over the bar.

But the triumph went to Ross County. However much one felt sorry for Hibs, one had to admire the pluck of the men from Dingwall. The town must have been totally empty that day, and what a night it was when the Staggies came home with the League Cup! The triumph of the Staggies showed that there is no real excuse for the other clubs who have hidden behind concepts of being a small club for too long. Small clubs can win trophies too. All that is necessary is a little drive and determination, the ethos of working together and a willingness to resist the deleterious financial blandishments of selling their best players. Ross County became the 15th team to win the Scottish League Cup. Hibs would still have a moment of triumph when they won the Scottish Cup (after 114 years) at the end of the season.

The teams were:

Ross County: Woods, Fraser, Quinn, Davies, Foster (Franks), Gardyne, Irvine, Woods, McShane (Murdoch), Boyce (Graham), Schalk

Hibs: Oxley, Gray, McGregor, Fontaine, Stevenson, Henderson, Thomson (Keatings), Bartley (Boyle), McGinn, Stokes, Cummings

Referee: K Clancy (Glasgow)

The Scottish League Cup was extensively revamped for 2016/17. For one thing, the final was to be played at the end of November, the thinking being that although the weather was likely to be worse, the competition would be out of the way before Christmas. Nevertheless, most people seemed to be of the opinion that pleasant bright March days were better than dark November ones.

But the main difference was a return to sections. For some time it had been felt that for a small team to lose one game on the first Saturday in August (sometimes even in July) there was a heavy price to pay, namely exit from the League Cup and no chance of a game against a well-supported team to boost finances. Thus sections (which had last been deployed in the 1980s) were brought back for every team apart from the four who qualified for Europe – in the case of 2016/17, that was Celtic, Aberdeen, Hearts and Hibs.

The other 38 teams of the Scottish League plus a representative from the Highland League and the Lowland League (in this case, Cove Rangers and recently relegated East Stirlingshire) would go into eight sections of five teams. The winners would qualify, as would the four best second-place teams and they would join the four teams who had qualified for Europe. The European teams plus the four best winners would then be seeded for the round of the last 16.

Not everyone agreed with the structure. The advantage was that there was now a second chance, and the sections would be drawn geographically north and south so that we wouldn't have Stranraer v Peterhead on a Tuesday night, for example. The disadvantages were that, as the section contained five teams, there would be two home and two away ties. The season would have to start a great deal earlier, namely the middle of July. Contrary to some woolly, simplistic, naive thinking about the desirability of summer football, the crowds were not great. Sadly, supporters did not rush to abandon their summer holidays to get back to see Dumbarton v Peterhead.

There was one welcome innovation that seemed to work. In the sections, a win was still three points and a defeat no points. A draw gave both teams one point, but a penalty shoot-out was held immediately after the 90 minutes (no extra time) for an extra point. Thus, one team earned two points from a draw. This was joined-up thinking and made good television. The non-footballing fans of the family will always enjoy a penalty shoot-out!

Three teams finished their sections with maximum points – Rangers, Partick Thistle and Alloa – and the closest section was group G where Hamilton, St Mirren and Ayr United all finished on nine points, all having won three games and lost the other. Hamilton won the group on goal difference and Ayr came second. Inverness, St Johnstone, Morton and Peterhead were the other sectional winners, the three other best-placed seconds were Dundee United, Queen of the South and Motherwell.

The second round was played as early as 9/10 August. Celtic and Rangers both demolished their opposition, Celtic winning 5-0 over Motherwell and Rangers beating Peterhead by the same score. Last year's beaten finalists (and Scottish

Cup holders) Hibs showed that there was nothing permanent about their cup success by losing 3-1 to Queen of the South in front of 7,646 mystified fans at Easter Road. A miserable midweek was completed for Edinburgh when St Johnstone beat Hearts 3-2 at McDiarmid. Aberdeen had a tight game at Ayr, winning 2-1 with all the goals coming in the first half. Dundee United had a reasonably comfortable 3-1 win over Partick Thistle and Morton came from behind to beat Hamilton Accies 2-1. But the giant-killing of the round was Alloa's 1-0 win over Inverness, Jason Marr's solitary goal being enough to win the tie for Jack Ross's impressive First Division side.

Alloa's reward was a trip to Celtic Park. Never in the whole of Celtic's 'Invincible' season did they have a harder task than they did against Alloa. Alloa, playing sensible football, held Celtic until the 83rd minute until James Forrest and Moussa Dembele provided some relief for a nervous home support who kept remembering losing to Morton at a similar stage in 2013. Alloa were applauded off the park by a now-happy and chivalrous Celtic crowd. Rangers had no bother beating Queen of the South 5-0 but Aberdeen had a very close call, having to wait until the 90th minute before Adam Rooney did the job for them against St Johnstone. The heroes of the round were Morton in the all-Championship tie at Cappielow. They scored twice in the first half against Dundee United through Jai Quitongo and Thomas O'Ware and held off a spirited Dundee United fightback to win 2-1.

In this expedited Scottish League Cup, the semi-finals were now played on the third weekend in October and Aberdeen took on Morton on the Saturday before the Old Firm once again locked horns on the Sunday. There were

16,183 at Hampden to see the first semi-final and Morton did themselves proud, but Aberdeen were just too good. Their second-half goals from Adam Rooney and Steven McLean saw them into their 14th League Cup Final, of which they had won six. The crowd might have been better at a different venue because leaving Aberdeen for a lunchtime kick-off necessitated a start very early in the morning, but where else was there? An Edinburgh venue would have made it only marginally easier and nowhere else could have held the 16,183 who did turn up. On the other hand, there would have been a lot more atmosphere and no one would have missed out because the game would have been on TV in any case. Dens Park or McDiarmid Park might have been possibilities.

The Old Firm clash was less finely balanced than the 1-0 scoreline would suggest. Celtic played the better football throughout, although one could never discount the possibility of Rangers scoring, but the goal came for Celtic. It was a rabona (off his back foot) by Moussa Dembele from a Leigh Griffiths pass in the 87th minute to put Celtic into their 31st final. Still unbeaten in Scotland this season (although with one or two embarrassing moments in Europe), Celtic were the favourites on 27 November, although the team most likely to topple them were thought to be Aberdeen.

This League Cup Final, apart from a brief spell at the start of each half, turned out to be a damp squib. Celtic won easily and Aberdeen's performance turned out to be a huge disappointment to their large support who were given half the ticket allocation. Unlike some other clubs, they were able to use up all the tickets that they were given. Tommy Rogic scored first for Celtic with a fine drive, James Forrest did likewise a quarter of an hour later and one already knew who the winners were. In the second half, Aberdeen had their best spell of the game for a quarter of an hour but were unable to score. A Moussa Dembele penalty kick settled the issue and the game finished with Celtic triumphant and many Aberdonians already heading to their buses for the long journey home.

The teams were:

Celtic: Gordon, Lustig, Simunovic, Sviatchenko, Izaguirre, Brown, Armstrong, Rogic (McGregor), Roberts (Bitton), Forrest (Griffiths), Dembele

Aberdeen: Lewis, Logan, Considine, Taylor, O'Connor (Stockley), Shinnie, Jack, McLean, Hayes (McGinn), Maddison, Rooney (Burns)

Referee: J Beaton

It would be the first stage of a treble in a remarkable season for Celtic, emulating their achievements of 1967, 1969 and 2001. They won the league by some distance from Aberdeen and beat the Dons in the Scottish Cup Final. Aberdeen had the distinction of being the runners-up in all three competitions. Celtic had now won the Scottish League Cup for the 16th time and it was Brendan Rodgers' first trophy for Celtic. It was also the 100th trophy in their history, depending on whether one counted the European Cup of 1967, the Coronation Cup of 1953 and the Empire Exhibition Trophy of 1938.

Celtic repeated their success in the 72nd Scottish League Cup, beating Motherwell in the final on a cold day at the end of November. The format of the competition was as last year with a sectional format beginning in the middle of July. Four former winners of the League Cup failed to make it to the knockout stages – Hearts, East Fife, Raith Rovers and St Mirren – while the sections were won by Falkirk, Dunfermline Athletic, Dundee United (who just edged past Dundee), Hibs, Ayr United, Motherwell and Livingston. The four best seconds were Ross County, Partick Thistle, Dundee and Kilmarnock and they qualified for the draw which now included Scotland's four European teams: Celtic, Aberdeen, Rangers and St Johnstone. Ironically, by the time that the games took place on 8/9 August, only Celtic were still likely to be engaged in Europe.

The draw took place at Dens Park on 30 July after the end of the Dundee v Dundee United sectional match and one of the ties that the draw threw up was Dundee v Dundee United. Many people felt that this shouldn't be allowed as they had already played each other, but there was nothing in the regulations to prevent it, and it did the coffers of both clubs no harm at all. There were even those who claimed that it was all a set-up. In happier times the two Tayside teams had played in the final of the 1980/81 competition; this time it was Dundee who won the game in a tight 2-1 encounter, Paul McGowan's strike settling the matter for Dundee.

In the other games, Celtic, Rangers and Hibs all had comfortable wins over Kilmarnock, Dunfermline Athletic and Ayr United, but it took Aberdeen all their time to get the better of Hamilton Academical, while in a thrilling encounter in the Highlands, Motherwell won 3-2 against Ross County after extra time, even though Motherwell finished the game with only ten men. Extra time was also needed at Falkirk to get Livingston through, while at St Johnstone, Partick Thistle delighted their travelling fans and shocked their hosts by winning 3-0.

The quarter-finals took place over the midweek of 19 to 21 September. Three of the games were on television. Ironically, the game that wasn't on television, Hibs v Livingston, was probably the best of them all, ending up a tight 3-2 win for Hibs with Anthony Stokes scoring a penalty late in the game. In the televised game that night, Rangers looked to have won the game at Firhill against Partick Thistle but Kris Doolan scored in the 90th minute to take it to extra time. Sadly for Thistle, Rangers scored twice in the extra period. On the Wednesday, Dundee gave Celtic little bother at Dens Park as Celtic won 4-0, even though two of their goals came very late. The only surprise came on the Thursday night when Motherwell defeated last year's beaten finalists Aberdeen 3-0 at Fir Park, with star man Louis Moult scoring twice for 'Well.

The draw took place immediately after the end of that game. Celtic and Rangers were kept apart with Celtic playing Hibs at Hampden on Saturday, 21 October and Rangers playing Motherwell the following day, both to be televised. There was a certain amount of unhappiness on the Saturday when Hibs failed to sell all their tickets, thus leaving empty seats (always a dispiriting sight on TV screens) which could well have been filled by Celtic fans. It happened again, but to a lesser extent, in the other semi. Celtic played in lime green while Hibs played in black. It was an unnecessary piece of pedantry by the authorities, for the colours do not really clash, but that is the way things are. The game was a good one, but two early goals scored by Mikael Lustig (aided by some poor goalkeeping) saw Celtic on their way. Hibs fought back with the aid of a dubious penalty kick, but Moussa Dembele scored twice for Celtic to settle the issue.

The following day saw a more unpleasant and physical encounter, with managers Stephen Robertson of Motherwell and Pedro Caixinha of Rangers invited to watch the game from the stand after a rather unedifying bust-up on the touchline. If no one had heard of Louis Moult before the game, they did now, for it was he who put Motherwell into the final to meet Celtic; one from a scramble which the Rangers defence failed to clear, one from a sublime lob over the goalkeeper into an empty net. Motherwell fans were delighted and the result tightened the noose around the neck of Rangers manager Pedro Caixinha. He would not be Rangers manager for much longer.

The final of the 72nd Scottish League Cup took place at Hampden on a cold but dry Sunday at the end of November. Celtic were the favourites and they entered Hampden not having lost a game since defeat to St Johnstone in May 2016, a streak of 64 games. They had beaten their own record (set in the unusual circumstances of the First World War) a few weeks previously and people, even their own supporters, reckoned they had to get beat sometime. Motherwell looked as likely to defeat them as anyone else for they had defeated Rangers and Aberdeen with a degree of ease, and with Louis Moult around, who could tell? Celtic were going for their 17th Scottish League Cup and Motherwell their second. Sadly, Motherwell had few supporters who recalled their only previous triumph in October 1950.

Due tribute was paid to Phil O'Donnell who had played with distinction for both teams before his untimely death on the field in December 2007. The first half was dull with little happening and, if anything, Motherwell were marginally the better team. It was a different story in the second half, however, as Celtic upped a gear and soon went ahead with a fine curler from James Forrest. Immediately after, in the moment that maybe turned the game, Craig Gordon had a fine instinctive save from a Moult header. Celtic scored again but in circumstances that they would not have wished and which left a nasty taste in the mouths of Motherwell.

Scott Sinclair went down in the box. There was some contact from Cedric Kipre but whether there was enough to justify a penalty was debatable. But penalty it was, and Craig Thomson then felt obliged (in terms of the letter of the law) to show a red card to Kipre. Kipre was distraught, and widespread sympathy was expressed for him, even though it was diluted after his brutal hack on Dembele in the first half. The penalty was a judgement call by the referee (who may have got it wrong) but the red card surely warranted a change in the law.

Be that as it may, Moussa Dembele scored the penalty, firing straight down the middle after the goalkeeper had gone to one side, and with the score at 2-0, a man down, and Celtic in rampant form, there was no comeback for Motherwell. Celtic should really have scored an awful lot more. This was manager Brendan Rodgers' fourth trophy win out of four since he had arrived at the club in summer 2016.

The teams were:

Celtic: Gordon, Lustig, Simunovic, Boyata, Tierney, Brown, Armstrong, Forrest (Roberts), McGregor (Rogic), Sinclair, Dembele (Griffiths)

Motherwell: Carson, Tait, Hartley, Kipre, Dunne, Grimshaw (Tanner), McHugh, Rose (Frear), Cadden, Moult, Bowman (Campbell)

Referee: C Thomson

Celtic went on to win another treble – the double treble as it was called – but by summer 2018 things had changed. In what was generally seen as Rangers fighting back, Steven Gerrard was engaged as manager. It was certainly a high-profile appointment, but while Celtic websites tended to poke fun at the fact that he had Roman Catholic connections and indeed had said in the past that he was a Celtic supporter, more serious objections were raised when it was pointed out that he had never been a manager. The ploy did not work as far as the League Cup was concerned, for Rangers went out of the competition at the semi-final stage to their old enemies, Aberdeen.

In the qualifying stages, a dream came true for English commentators when a penalty shoot-out at New Bayview ended in the fabled Forfar 5 East Fife 4. Local supporters of each side were less impressed, for the sounds in both Fife and Angus are quite distinct, but it was much made of south of the border and gave the two teams some welcome publicity. Not that it did either of them much good, for neither qualified. Three teams who impressed at the qualifying stages were Ayr United, Dunfermline Athletic and Livingston, the first two of them winning all four games, but as usual in this format, the tournament was bereft of any real excitement and really failed to attract any great media or public attention, even though one or two games were shown live on TV.

It was only when the four teams who had qualified for Europe – Celtic, Rangers, Hibs and Aberdeen – entered the competition on 18 August that things became interesting. The draw was seeded but we had the strange phenomenon of Motherwell, last year's beaten finalists, being unseeded, as indeed were Hearts who had won the trophy four times.

Not that it mattered for they both won their games against Livingston and Dunfermline Athletic, and were joined by Celtic, Rangers, St Johnstone, Aberdeen, Hibs and First Division Ayr United who beat Dundee mercilessly 3-0 at Dens Park.

Of the four quarter-finals, by far the best game to watch was the televised one at Easter Road which went to penalty kicks after 120 minutes of tense but goalless football. Aberdeen triumphed 6-5 from the penalty spot. In the other three games, Rangers comfortably disposed of Ayr United, Celtic needed a late Leigh Griffiths goal to get the better of St Johnstone at McDiarmid Park, and in a repeat of the scoreline of the 1954/55 Scottish League Cup Final, Hearts beat Motherwell 4-2.

It was then the fun really started. The draw paired Celtic with Hearts and Rangers with Aberdeen for the weekend on 27/28 October. It so happened, however, that both Glasgow teams were involved in European action on the Thursday night and could not reasonably be expected to play on the Saturday, so Sunday it was for both games. There appeared to be a clause in some silly agreement that compelled Hampden to be the venue for both semi-finals and someone came up with the idea of Rangers v Aberdeen at noon, and Celtic v Hearts at night.

There were at least three arguments against this vacuous notion. Aberdeen fans could not get to Hampden on time unless their buses left at an absurdly early hour, Sunday night was a silly time for a football match and fans from Ireland could not get a ferry home, and the police were understandably worried about four sets of fans all congregating in the same area of Glasgow on the same day. There would be nothing, for example, to prevent Rangers fans hanging around Hampden for an hour or two to have a nice friendly chat with their Celtic counterparts when their buses arrived. Words like 'madness' were freely bandied about by managers and journalists, not to mention the supporters.

So think again, Scottish League! Each of the four sets of fans saw reason to see themselves as discriminated against and picked upon. Eventually the solution of Hearts v Celtic at Murrayfield at 1.30pm and Rangers v Aberdeen at Hampden at 4.30pm was agreed. There was still a great deal of moaning, but it was rightly called 'Super Sunday' and the game in Scotland enjoyed a great deal of publicity with the games both televised on BT Sport.

The football was the easiest and the most enjoyable part. Over 61,000 came to Murrayfield to see Celtic and Hearts, making it Scotland's best-attended football match for nearly 30 years. After an even first half, Celtic scored three times through a penalty from Scott Sinclair, a goal from James Forrest and a brilliant strike from Ryan Christie. At Hampden, Rangers could not capitalise on their outfield pressure and paid the penalty when Lewis Ferguson headed the only goal of the game to set up the fourth League Cup Final between Celtic and Aberdeen and the second in three years.

The final took part on Sunday, 2 December at Hampden. Celtic duly won it, but this time they had to dig deep, as Aberdeen fought well. But it was Celtic who got the only goal of the game through Ryan Christie in a rat-a-tat goal whereby the forward shoots, the goalkeeper saves but the ball rebounds to the striker to finish it off. It was a superb piece of football; Christie controlled a Boyata ball with his left foot, shot with his right and finished off the rebound with his left.

Joe Lewis was the unlucky goalkeeper, but the same keeper also did well to save a Scott Sinclair penalty wrongly awarded by referee Andrew Dallas for a handling offence which took place outside the box and looked unintentional in any case. That would have made it 2-0, but 1-0 the scoreline remained. Celtic won their 18th Scottish League Cup and their third in a row. More impressively, Celtic had now contested seven domestic trophies since Brendan Rodgers arrived and won them all.

The teams were:

Celtic: Gordon, Lustig, Benkovic, Boyata (Simunovic), Tierney, McGregor, Rogic (Brown), Forrest (Ntcham), Christie, Sinclair, Edouard

Aberdeen: Lewis, Logan, McKenna, Considine, Lowe, Ball, Shinnie, Mackay-Steven (McLennan), Ferguson, McGinn (Wilson), Cosgrove (Anderson)

Referee: A Dallas

Celtic went on to win the other two Scottish trophies as well, but not before Brendan Rodgers suddenly jumped ship at the end of February 2019 to go to Leicester City. It was a move which defied analysis, but Celtic turned to Neil Lennon again who moved in seamlessly as acting manager and was given the job on a permanent basis about an hour after Celtic had won the Scottish Cup in May. The campaign for the 2019/20 Scottish League Cup opened once again in mid-July, this time to the backdrop of constant rain. Some games were televised on BT Sport, and every one of them seemed to be accompanied by torrential rain. They were also, of course, accompanied by low attendances, and notable fallers at this stage were former winners Dundee United, St Mirren and Raith Rovers, and previous runners-up in St Johnstone and Inverness, whose game against Dundee in the final game of the section was televised live and proved to be embarrassingly bad.

The heroes of the sectional stage were possibly Forfar Athletic, whose victories included one over St Johnstone, but they went down to Livingston in the knockout round of the last 16. Curiously, five of the eight ties went to extra time, although none of them reached the penalty stage, and Celtic, Hibs, Aberdeen, Kilmarnock and Partick Thistle joined Hearts, Livingston and Rangers in the quarter-finals. Dunfermline Athletic, showing welcome signs of a revival, possibly came closest to a shock as they held Celtic for 113 minutes at a sullen and angry Parkhead where the crowd were showing their displeasure at the selling of Kieran Tierney and defeat in Europe to a team with the unlikely name of Cluj. East Fife had their biggest League Cup occasion for some time when Rangers came to town, but the result was predictable. Partick Thistle's defeat of Ross County was technically a giant-killing, because the Dingwall men were now back in the Premier League. It was goals galore at Easter Road before Hibs got the better of Morton, while Aberdeen, who, like Celtic, had collapsed pitifully in Europe in midweek, were lucky to beat Dundee in extra time at a sadly empty Dens Park, a ground that used to be filled to capacity when Aberdeen arrived.

The quarter-finals were played in late September and, most unusually, all four games were played on the same night and with the same kick-off time. Celtic beat Partick Thistle 5-0 with a degree of ease while Rangers were a little fortunate to win at Livingston 1-0 in the televised game. The other two games went to penalty shoot-outs with Edinburgh triumphant in each case, Hibs beating Kilmarnock after 120 minutes of unproductive football and Aberdeen having the most cause to kick themselves. They had been 2-1 up for a long time at Tynecastle (both goals coming from Sam Cosgrove penalties) but conceded a late equaliser as the game went to extra time and penalties. Aberdeen then blew up spectacularly by missing their first three penalties, including one by the same Sam Cosgrove who had scored two in regulation time.

It was Edinburgh v Glasgow in the semi-finals on the weekend of 2/3 November. It was hardly a fair contest. Celtic and Rangers were at the top of the league and both going well in Europe whereas Hearts and Hibs were near the bottom. In addition, Hearts had sacked their manager Craig Levein in midweek and the vultures moved on to circle Easter Road where Paul Heckingbottom would be sacked on the Monday. Hibs put up some sort of a fight as they lost 2-5 on the Saturday night, but Hearts collapsed without a whimper 0-3 to Rangers on the Sunday.

The 15th Old Firm League Cup Final occurred on 8 December 2019. Rangers had won nine and Celtic five and every final except two had been settled by the odd goal, the two exceptions being 2-0 for Celtic in 2009 and their famous 7-1 in 1957. This one was played with a general election campaign going on in the background. In spite of, or perhaps, because of incessant Hampden rain (who said that 8 December was a good day for a cup final?) the game was tight but it was Celtic who emerged triumphant with a 1-0 win thanks to a Christopher Jullien goal which Rangers tried in vain to claim was offside. Rangers got a penalty and Jeremie Frimpong was sent off by the draconian Willie Collum, but Alfredo Morelos shot straight at Fraser Forster in the Celtic goal. Celtic, now under Neil Lennon once again – Brendan Rodgers having departed in those bizarre circumstances the previous February – had now won four Scottish League Cups in a row and ten Scottish trophies in a row!

The teams were:

Celtic: Forster, Frimpong, Ajer, Jullien, Hayes, Brown, McGregor, Forrest (Bitton), Christie, Elyounoussi (Johnston), Morgan (Edouard)

Rangers: McGregor, Tavernier, Goldson, Helander (Katic), Barisic, Kamara (Defoe), Jack, Aribo (Barker), Arfield, Morelos, Kent

Referee: W Collum

The Scottish League Cup of 2020/21 was the strangest of them all with the world in the grip of a pandemic caused by a coronavirus. This necessitated a later start to the season and games being played behind closed doors. The TV rights had been meretriciously sold to a subscription TV channel called Premier Sports and they, to their credit, did try to whip up some kind of atmosphere for the TV viewers. The sectional games were played on international weekends – possibly a good idea for international football can be sterile and disappointing – but at the end of it all in mid-November, it was noticed that former winners Raith Rovers, East Fife, Partick Thistle and Dundee United had not made the cut for the second round to be played on the weekend of 28/29 November.

The second round saw three major shocks as Hearts, Aberdeen and Celtic all went down to opposition that they would normally have been expected to beat: Hearts to Alloa,

Aberdeen to St Mirren and Celtic to Ross County in a dismal performance which had major implications for the club. Elsewhere, St Johnstone won at Motherwell, Dunfermline at Arbroath, and Livingston, who had just parted company with manager Gary Holt a few days previously, beat Ayr United 4-0. Hibs beat Dundee and, without the slightest bother, Rangers disposed of Falkirk.

The shocks continued in the quarter-finals, played in the middle of December, particularly at New St Mirren Park, where the Saints defeated Rangers in the last minute after Rangers had equalised the minute before that. Rangers had apparently been invincible up to that point. The other Saints, the ones from Perth, defeated Dunfermline in a penalty shoot-out. Hibs beat Alloa, although hardly convincingly, and the best win of the round was that of Livingston who beat Ross County, the conquerors of Celtic, 2-0.

The semi-finals took place on the weekend of 23/24 January, both cold days, at an empty Hampden Park with St Johnstone and Livingston emerging as winners. Hibs really should have disposed of St Johnstone well before half-time but it was the Perth Saints who scored good goals at the right time. The Paisley Saints were less lucky, going down 0-1 to Livingston in a tight game which might have gone in the opposite direction.

So, to the final of two teams, with one success in the Scottish League Cup between them. The game had to be played before an empty stadium on Sunday, 28 February 2021, but this did not in any way lessen the joy of St Johnstone and their fans who were watching the game on television in Perth. It was a hard-fought final but St Johnstone always remained on top, scoring through Shaun Rooney from a corner kick in the 30th minute. It was a fine triumph for manager Callum Davidson and his men.

The teams were:

St Johnstone: Clark, Kerr, Gordon, McCart, Rooney, McCann, Craig, Booth, Conway (May), Wotherspoon, Kane

Livingston: McCrorie, Devlin, Ambrose, Guthrie, Serrano, Lawson (Sibbald), Holt (Emmanuel-Thomas), Mullin (Forrest), Pittman (Reilly), Bartley, Robinson

Referee: D Robertson

Thus ended the 75th Scottish League Cup. It was now a venerable old trophy and very much a part of the Scottish football scene. It had done well, in spite of a few doubts at the start and from its own legislators who made awful changes to its format, often at the behest of unscrupulous sponsors. But football won out and the tournament has provided some marvellous entertainment for fans since 1946. We trust that this can continue.

The winners have been Rangers on 27 occasions, Celtic 20, Aberdeen six, Hearts four, Dundee three, East Fife three, Hibs three, Dundee United two, Kilmarnock one, Livingston one, Motherwell one, Partick Thistle one, Raith Rovers one, Ross County one, St Johnstone one, St Mirren one.

POSTSCRIPT

WHEN THE Scottish League Cup resumed again in July 2021, Covid-19 was still extending its ugly tentacles into all aspects of society, and several games did not take place. The policy was that a 0-3 victory was awarded to the opposing team when a club was unable to fulfil a fixture. Thus former winners Ross County and former finalists Falkirk were effectively eliminated for having Covid! Kilmarnock were also awarded a 3-0 defeat to East Kilbride, but this was for fielding an ineligible player. This did not prevent Kilmarnock from winning their section and the other section winners were Hearts, both Dundee teams, Raith Rovers, Ayr United, Motherwell and St Mirren, while Dunfermline, Arbroath and Livingston were the best-placed second teams.

The last-16 ties were played on the weekend of 13–15 August. The best performance of the round was Raith Rovers' home defeat of Aberdeen, for whom new manager Stephen Glass was clearly struggling. Three games went to penalties, the winners being Dundee United, Livingston and last year's winners St Johnstone. Celtic won the best-attended game of the round against Hearts, while Hibs, Dundee and Rangers all won at home.

Raith Rovers' reward for beating Aberdeen was a trip to Celtic Park towards the end of September where they lost 0-3, to no one's great surprise. Rangers accounted for Livingston, and the Dundee teams went down to St Johnstone and Hibs. The semi-final draw on the weekend of 20 and 21 November avoided a Celtic–Rangers clash, and pitted Celtic against the holders St Johnstone, and Rangers against Hibs, both games to be played at Hampden.

Celtic's 1-0 victory over St Johnstone was brought about by a goal from James Forrest, but the game was possibly more one-sided than the scoreline would have suggested. A major surprise came in the Sunday game. Rangers were 'between managers'. Steve Gerrard had jumped ship to Aston Villa in a move that brought him no credit in the eyes of Rangers supporters, and Giovanni Van Bronckhorst was at Hampden that day, but not yet in command of the team. The disorientated Rangers defence lost three goals to Martin Boyle in the first half, and although Scott Arfield pulled one back, Hibs remained in control throughout the second half.

The 76th League Cup Final was thus played at Hampden on Sunday, 19 December 2021. It was a strange occasion in many respects. December is never the best time for cup finals, especially a week before Christmas in the middle of a Covid outbreak! In the same way as Rangers were 'between managers' in the semi-final against Hibs, so too, incredibly, were Hibs in the final! Jack Ross had been sacked ten days previously in a move which defied belief in the context of a team which had reached a cup final. David Gray was in temporary charge against Celtic's Australian boss Ange Postecoglou.

It was an exciting game of football. The first half saw Celtic on top territorially but unable to force a goal, then early in the second half Hibs scored first through Paul Hanlon from a corner kick. Within half a minute of the restart Kyogu had equalised for Celtic, and the same player scored again when Hibs were debating the award of a free kick to Celtic on the halfway line. Hibs tried hard and had tough luck near the end, but it was Celtic's 20th Scottish League Cup.

The teams were:

Celtic: Hart, Juranovic, Carter-Vickers, Starfeld, Taylor (Ralston), McGregor, Turnbull (Bitton), Abada, Rogic, Johnston (Scales), Kyogu (Moffat)

Hibs: Macey, McGinn, Porteous, Hanlon, Stevenson (Doig), Newell, Doyle-Hayes, Boyle, Campbell (Allan), Murphy (Doidge), Nisbet

Referee: J Beaton